The Shift to Modernity

THE SHIFT TO
MODERNITY

Christ and the Doctrine of Creation
in the Theologies of
Schleiermacher and Barth

ROBERT SHERMAN

t&t clark

NEW YORK • LONDON

T & T Clark International, Madison Square Park, 15 East 26th Street, New York, NY 10010
T & T Clark International, The Tower Building, 11 York Road, London SE1 7NX
T & T Clark International is a Continuum imprint.

Cover design: Ralph M. Chisholm

Library of Congress Cataloging-in-Publication Data

Sherman, Robert (Robert J.)
   The shift to modernity : Christ and the doctrine of creation in the theologies of Schleiermacher and Barth / Robert Sherman.
      p. cm.
   Includes bibliographical references and index.
   ISBN 0-567-02860-7 (pbk.) — ISBN 0-567-02870-4
   1. Jesus Christ—History of doctrines. 2. Creation—History of doctrines. 3. Schleiermacher, Friedrich, 1768-1834. 4. Barth, Karl, 1886–1968. I. Title.
   BT198.S534 2005
   231.7'65'0922—dc22

                              2004025304

Printed in the United States of America

05 06 07 08 09 10   10 9 8 7 6 5 4 3 2 1

In memory of
Edith D. Sherman

CONTENTS

CHAPTER 1

Introduction

This book seeks to add one more voice to the still minority view that the theologies of Friedrich Schleiermacher and Karl Barth may have more in common than the many insistent assertions of the latter, or the partisans of either, would lead one to believe. While there is no easy reconciliation of the differences that do in fact exist between these two figures, I will argue that these differences do not always stem from irreconcilable starting points. Schleiermacher was the first theologian to take seriously the fact that the Western world had passed into "modernity," and to deal with that change systematically and comprehensively in his work. Barth was the first theologian of the twentieth century to mount a major challenge to the course plotted by Schleiermacher. Yet in developing his system he did not simply return to the age that Schleiermacher had left. Schleiermacher and Barth both stand on this side of the watershed between the premodern and modern eras, and this location suggests that there may be certain presuppositions, assumptions, or "moves" they share in doing their respective theologies. These common features may be only negative—that is, both figures may reject certain possibilities or claims for theology— but these common features may also be positive, in that both men may actually approach or explain certain matters in a similar fashion. In

1

either case, even where Barth does obviously differ with Schleiermacher, it appears that many of these differences might be explained better as modifications within a continuity than as fundamentally opposed positions. I would agree with David Tracy's general observation "that neo-orthodoxy is not really a radical new alternative model for theology, but rather is a moment—to be sure, a critical one—in the larger liberal theological tradition."[1]

To make my task a manageable one, this study will investigate one aspect of the theologies of Schleiermacher and Barth, namely, their doctrines of creation. Its thesis asserts that their respective systems each employ a christological orientation for what is said regarding creation. Moreover, it asserts that this approach allows them to solve the problem of maintaining dogmatic coherence and a continuity with the church's historic confessions while also meeting, either implicitly or explicitly, certain modern, external intellectual demands confronting those systems. To put it more sharply, it claims that each employs Christ as the hermeneutical key for interpreting creation, and that each does so in an effort to remain true to the faith handed down from the past while also maintaining intellectual integrity in the present. This underlying connection perceptible in both Schleiermacher's and Barth's work forges one continuity between them, and suggests that there may be certain fundamental similarities in their respective theologies in spite of other well-known differences.

Defining Terms and the Task

At the beginning, some clarification of various key concepts is necessary. Such phrases as "christological orientation," "doctrine of creation," "dogmatic coherence," and the suggested tension between "the church's historic confessions" and inherited faith on the one hand and "external intellectual demands" or "intellectual integrity in a modern age" on the other are all rather general. As such, they carry a host of meanings and associations not all of which are explored in this book.

---

1. David Tracy, *Blessed Rage for Order* (New York: Seabury Press, 1975), 27. The quote is Tracy's summary of the judgment of Wilhelm Pauck.

"Christological orientation" plays a crucial role in this discussion. It points to several distinct but interrelated aspects of the doctrines under consideration. To begin with, when this book describes the approach of Schleiermacher and Barth to creation as "Christological," I have in mind first of all the *method* of their respective expositions. That is, in developing and presenting their understandings of creation, I claim that both are influenced or directed in some manner by what they assume or develop with regard to Christ. They do not construct their doctrines of creation "in isolation," but in implicit or explicit reference to their christological presuppositions. Yet in certain instances I will refer to the *content* of those expositions also, indicating that christological influence is not merely extrinsic or "after the fact," but rather intrinsic and presupposed. Furthermore, "christological orientation" does not mean simply that a particular matter has to do immediately with the person and/or work of the "historical Jesus" or Christ understood narrowly. It may also indicate that a given doctrinal topic is only first fully explained and understood dogmatically in conjunction with some other, specifically Christian element. This means, with regard to method, that Schleiermacher's and Barth's doctrines of creation display, in one manner or another, certain christological presuppositions and influences well before they reach those doctrines dealing explicitly with Christ. With regard to content, this means I am claiming that the respective doctrines of creation of Schleiermacher and Barth contain elements that make them intrinsically Christian expositions, rather than fundamentally neutral and independent treatments that happen to lend themselves to christological supplements. While both men follow the traditional, "chronological" order of considering creation prior to Christ in their theological systems, it should become clear that the inner logic of these systems actually presupposes, and speaks through, their doctrines of Christ.

Stated somewhat differently, many of the fundamental assertions made in their doctrines of creation have their goal in and are completed by Christology; as such, Christology influences the way the doctrine of creation is expounded from the very outset. In Barth's case, this influence is pervasive and explicit. Indeed, he openly asserts that Christology is the actual and exclusive source of his doctrine of creation. In Schleiermacher's case, however, this influence is not as explicit.

In any case, this difference in emphasis should not obscure the observation that the primary object under consideration by Schleiermacher and Barth in their doctrines of creation is not the natural world per se, but *one's understanding of and relation to that natural world as a follower of Christ.* That is, Schleiermacher and Barth are not making dogmatic statements about the world so much as they are about the Christian community's *interpretation* of that world *as creation.* Indeed, it may not be too far-fetched to say that they are extending the Reformation axiom that theology can present no knowledge of God *a se*, but only God *pro me* or *quoad nos* to apply to the world as well. Hence, just as Luther and Calvin held that one could know truly neither God nor humanity in isolation, but only in a correlation viewed through the eyes of faith, Schleiermacher and Barth add the assertion that one can have no meaningful understanding of the world in isolation, but only as it is explained in conjunction with one's understanding of God and humanity.

Thus, their dogmatic theology presents no objective or discrete knowledge of the world, but rather an understanding of that world as interpreted by a faithful Christian community.[2] As such, this understanding will be compatible with whatever objective knowledge of the world one may gain from elsewhere. That is, Schleiermacher and Barth will not, on the one hand, attempt to prejudice or counter that objective knowledge through the assertion of either additional or contradictory "facts." They will, on the other hand, attempt to place such objective knowledge into the more comprehensive—that is, existential, moral, and even aesthetic—interpretive context offered by, and arising within, the community of faith. Stated in more detail, there are

---

2. See, e.g., Schleiermacher's opening sentence of §75, in Friedrich Schleiermacher, *Der christliche Glaube nach dem Grundsätzen der evangelischen Kirche im Zusammenhange dargestellt*, ed. Martin Redeker, 7th ed., based on the 2nd, 2 vols. (Berlin: Walter de Gruyter, 1960). Because Schleiermacher himself commonly referred to this work as his *Glaubenslehre*, I will cite it hereafter as *Gl*, with references made to the appropriate section (e.g., §75) and, where pertinent, subsection (e.g., §75.1). See also Niebuhr's comments on this topic in Richard R. Niebuhr, "Christ, Nature, and Consciousness: Reflections on Schleiermacher in the Light of Barth's Early Criticisms," in *Barth and Schleiermacher: Beyond the Impasse?*, ed. James O. Duke and Robert F. Streetman (Philadelphia: Fortress Press, 1988), 32.

certain differences between Schleiermacher's and Barth's respective notions of what constitutes "compatibility" (e.g., Barth's willingness to assert that "objective" knowledge may not be as objective as it claims). Such differences are really only minor ones, and for all practical purposes Schleiermacher and Barth take essentially the same approach in relating their dogmatic assertions to the knowledge of the world gained by other means and disciplines.

The "doctrine of creation" also requires some definition. A cursory reading of what each theologian writes under this heading leads one to think that comparing these thinkers' views is unnecessary. One could argue that Schleiermacher assigns only minor significance to the doctrine in his overall system; indeed, had he been able to absorb it into his doctrine of preservation, in effect dismissing it from his system, he would have. And if this is the case, how could Schleiermacher's treatment of the doctrine bear the weight of a comparison with Barth's, whose treatment spans four massive volumes? The sheer disproportion of pages spent on the doctrine by these two would appear to make a comparison a fruitless task.

This disproportion, however, is more apparent than real. The brevity of Schleiermacher's two propositions regarding creation do not indicate that he ignores completely other matters often considered in a doctrine of creation. He actually does address such matters, but under other headings than his explicit doctrine of creation. For this doctrine, he reserves a very limited and negative task, namely, the "warding off" of any "alien element" that could "creep into" the question of origins (*Entstehen*), the "whence" of the created order. For him, the doctrine of creation has to do only with the Beginning, understood in the strictest terms, and not with the created order commencing from that beginning, analogous to a mathematical point commencing a line but not being part of the length of that line. In his introductory propositions, (§§36, 38, and 39) Schleiermacher argues that the religious self-consciousness regarding the relation between the world and God is in itself one, even though church doctrine has traditionally considered it under two headings, creation and providence, so as to clarify the belief that God both creates and sustains the world. In other words, the division is a practical, dogmatic one, and should not be construed as suggesting any actual segmentation of our "fundamental feeling" or God's activity. Indeed, as Schleiermacher makes clear in §38, one could subsume either doctrine entirely into the other without losing anything. Nevertheless, the distinction can serve a useful purpose, helping to separate the necessary "negative" task described in his explicit doctrine of creation from the bulk of his constructive assertions about the world, which he locates in his doctrine of preservation.

Moreover, what Schleiermacher writes in §§30–31 suggests that an even greater amount of material might be available for comparison with Barth. He there describes the three basic forms that dogmatic utterances may take. The first form comprises those propositions that describe human "states of mind" or "spiritual conditions" (*Lebenszustände* or *Gemütszustände*), while the second and third forms are those that offer, respectively, conceptions of divine attributes and modes of action and expressions regarding the character or constitution of the world (*Beschaffenheit der Welt*). Schleiermacher maintains that these three forms do not possess equal dogmatic status; rather, the first is in fact the fundamental form, so that propositions of the second and third form can be judged admissible "only insofar as they can be *developed out of* propositions of the first form."[3] In other words, Schleiermacher gives his system as a whole a "three-tiered" pattern and a regulatory principle for maintaining the proper relation between those tiers as they extend through the three subdivisions of his system. The three subdivisions are, of course, the First Part of his system, which describes the Christian religious self-consciousness apart from the antithesis of sin and grace, and the Second Part, which is divided into two "aspects": the explication of the consciousness of sin and the explication of the consciousness of grace. Hence, his system overall is composed of nine distinguishable "sections," but the doctrines contained in each are not to be understood in isolation. Indeed, one can comprehend them fully only in their interconnection with each other and in their "movement" through his system as a whole.

So how does all of this relate to Schleiermacher's doctrine of creation? What he writes in §31.2, where he explains the implications of

---

3. *Gl*, §30.2; all translations from *Der christliche Glaube* are mine. Emphasis mine.

his approach with specific reference to his doctrine of God, suggests an answer. On the basis of his three subdivisions, he describes some divine attributes first as they are presupposed by the antithesis of sin and grace, second as they relate to the consciousness of sin, and third as they relate to the grace of redemption. In other words, his doctrine of God, "inasmuch as it is presented in the totality of the divine attributes, will be completed no sooner than the same moment the whole system is, whereas it is usually expounded uninterrupted and before all other points of doctrine."[4] The problem with the usual approach is that it fails to make clear the correlation between the doctrine of God and the other, more explicitly Christian doctrines contained in the system. Indeed, it can imply that the doctrine of God actually stems from a different source than these other doctrines, that is, from a source other than the *Christian* religious affections. Schleiermacher's approach eliminates these two shortcomings—a fundamental improvement, he maintains, even if it scatters his doctrine of God throughout his system. And it leads us to suppose, on the basis of the observation made above, that he took this approach as a means to reflect even in his method the Reformation axiom concerning our "knowledge" of God.

The same holds true for his doctrine of Creation. This means it is appropriate to say that Schleiermacher's "broader" doctrine of Creation actually comprises all those propositions of the third form regarding the character or constitution of the world, so that this doctrine too is only completed with the completion of the whole system. Richard Niebuhr recognizes this point as well: "Schleiermacher presents dogmatic statements concerning God and the World, that is, God and nature or the natural, throughout the entire body of [*The Christian Faith*]."[5] However, why does he expound his explicit doctrine of creation under the rubric of his first form rather than the third, and in what way might that explicit doctrine establish and influence everything else he says regarding the Christian's understanding of, and relation to, the surrounding world?

---

4. *Gl*, §31.2.
5. Niebuhr, "Christ, Nature, and Consciousness," 28.

The preceding observations suggest that the Schleiermacher material available for a comparison with Barth will expand beyond the few pages of his explicit doctrine of creation—which further suggests that the task of this examination is at least possible. In comparing Schleiermacher and Barth on the doctrine of Creation, we will be examining their respective understandings of the Christian's relation to and understanding of the natural world, in its origin, continuity, and consummation, in light of Christianity's traditional faith in God's creative, providential, and redemptive power. To distinguish an examination that considers only the beginning of the world from a broader one that examines the whole created order, I will label the former "doctrine of creation" and the latter "doctrine of Creation." Hence, Schleiermacher's doctrine of creation is, in fact, confined to §§40–41, but his doctrine of Creation extends far beyond those propositions.

The final set of phrases mentioned above emphasizing the need for, on the one hand, "dogmatic coherence," adherence to "the church's historic confessions" and maintaining an essential "faith" while, on the other, meeting certain "external intellectual demands" and maintaining "intellectual integrity in a modern age" also require definition. In general, they will be employed to point out the distinction discussed by several contemporary theologians. Schubert Ogden's comments are representative: "[T]o be assessed as adequate, a theological statement must meet the two criteria of appropriateness and understandability."[6] Explaining the first of these two criteria, he states that "a theological statement may be said to be appropriate only insofar as the understanding expressed by its concepts is that also expressed by the primary symbols of the witness of faith."[7] Explaining the second, he states that "it requires that no theological statement be assessed as adequate which is not also *understandable*, in that it meets the relevant conditions of meaning and truth universally established with human existence."[8] In short, dogmatic statements must be "true" to the faith, but

6. Schubert M. Ogden, "What Is Theology?" *Journal of Religion* 52 (January 1972), quoted in *Readings in Theology*, ed. Peter C. Hodgson and Robert H. King (Philadelphia: Fortress Press, 1985), 18.
7. Ibid., 19.
8. Ibid.

they must also be logically plausible according to intellectual standards (or at least one such standard!) available apart from that faith, which is to say, they may not be utterly nonsensical.

In a somewhat similar vein, B. A. Gerrish, in his work *Tradition and the Modern World*, suggests that in "liberal" (i.e., modern) theology there is an "inner" and an "outer" critical norm.[9] The inner norm refers to the determinative influence of Scripture and the Christian theological heritage upon any given system of theology, while the outer norm refers to the restraining or modifying influence of current, nonreligious intellectual assumptions and scientific knowledge upon any of those systems attempting to be "modern." In these terms, Schleiermacher and Barth are both "traditional" and "modern."

Calling them "traditional" means that both figures display, to a greater or lesser degree, the four following attitudes or guiding assumptions. First, in the doing of theology, there is an express desire to *maintain continuity* with the heritage of the past. Of course, the most immediate heritage for Schleiermacher and Barth is Protestant, if not Reformed, theology, and both display ample evidence of working in self-conscious continuity with that heritage. But they also both hearken back to the ancient church at crucial junctures, even though their grounding in Protestant tradition means they always reserve the right to criticize this older, as well as their more recent, tradition.[10] Second, in the doing of theology, there is an express desire to *protect the crucial elements* of that heritage. That is, in maintaining continuity with the past, it is not enough merely to avoid disjunctions or gaps in the conveyance or "development" of tradition; one must also ensure that the essence or identity of the faith is not mutated into something else.[11] Therefore, third, in the doing of theology, one will affirm that the essential elements of that heritage *have been defined already*, for example, in its catechisms, in its credal formulations, in well-remembered battles with "heretics," and in its Scripture. In other

---

9. B. A. Gerrish, *Tradition and the Modern World: Reformed Theology in the Modern World* (Chicago: University of Chicago Press, 1978), 7–10.

10. Ibid., 5–6, 47–48.

11. Needless to say, in actual practice, one theologian's "essence" may be another's "mutation." For a useful and extensive discussion of the issue, see Stephen Sykes, *The Identity of Christianity* (Philadelphia: Fortress Press, 1984).

words, the definition of an "essence" will not be a self-conscious attempt to place the old faith on a new foundation or even start a new faith, but will be instead simply the sincere attempt to bring the old and selfsame faith to new expression. And fourth, in the doing of theology, one will affirm it is done ultimately *in service to the church and the church's Lord*, and not some other lord, such as the state or the academy or the "marketplace of ideas."

Langdon Gilkey's observations in *Naming the Whirlwind* provide some guidance for speaking about "modern" or "outer norms." He describes four "accommodations" made by theological liberalism with the modern world, "none of which has been repudiated in subsequent movements in theology"[12]—including, as he later points out, neo-orthodoxy. Thus, these accommodations provide characteristics not just of liberalism but of all "modern" theology. First, influenced by the results and assumptions of the natural sciences, modern theology no longer asserted that it deals with divine and infallible propositions defining and describing the natural and historical world, but with human symbol systems attempting to clarify the meaning of existence. Second, made conscious of historical and cultural relativism, modern theology now recognized that Christian doctrine could not be done "once and for all"; rather, Christians of each new generation—and perhaps each different cultural context—had to work out their own dogmatic theology. Third, (evidently in keeping with the general shift away from supernaturalistic and eternal assumptions to the naturalistic and temporal ones of our first and second points) "modern" theology now defined the Christian life not in terms of a spiritual, primarily individualistic and "other-worldly" goal of salvation, but in terms of a concrete, social "this-worldly" goal of human justice and peace. And fourth, "Love of the dissenting neighbor rather than defense of the doctrines of the faith became the main Christian obligation, and tolerance became widespread among the churches."[13] As

---

12. Langdon Gilkey, *Naming the Whirlwind: The Renewal of God-Language* (Indianapolis: Bobbs-Merrill, 1969), 76. I have modified and paraphrased Gilkey's language here.

13. Ibid., 77. I will not discuss this last "accommodation" much in this book because it is not a topic of much concern in either Schleiermacher's or Barth's doctrine of Creation. However, Schleiermacher's description of what it means for Christianity to be a "teleological" religion—with its focus on "practical" contributions to the building of the kingdom of God (*Gl*, §9.1)—and Barth's early involvement in social-ist politics could both be taken as indications that they did indeed display this "liberal" characteristic.

with the preceding point, this one also arises almost inevitably from the first two: Once one accepts the narrowing and relativizing of theology's subject matter, the literal attack of one's opponents becomes unjustifiable. Thus, if one is a "modern" theologian and perceives some position or theology as undermining the faith, persuasion replaces persecution as the only viable recourse. In effect, one must add yet another theology or dogmatic to the historical list.

As one might expect, the amount and the means of influence exercised by these "inner" and "outer" norms in the work of our two theologians will vary considerably. In one instance, the heritage will predominate, while in another, the external assumptions will; in another instance, the influence of either may be explicit or implicit, while in yet another instance, the influence may affect the content of what is written, the structure into which that content is fitted, or both. As a result of this variety, there can be no simple equation of how Schleiermacher and Barth are themselves influenced by these two norms, but a demonstration that each is in fact responsive to the demands of theological tradition *and* the assumptions of the modern age in and of itself speaks in support of the second half of my thesis. It also offers clues as to how they use Christology to make this shift to modernity.

CHAPTER 2

The Character of Schleiermacher's Christologically Oriented Doctrine of Creation

On What Does One Ground a Doctrine of Creation?

A doctrine of Creation does far more than offer a set of assertions about the world's origin. It certainly does this. But it also offers an understanding or interpretation of the world as it continues to be, that is, in its ongoing and essential nature and/or in its immediate relation to persons perceiving it. Obviously, the two are related, but which has primacy? And how do we discern their relation? From one perspective, dogmatic priority seems obvious: Chronologically speaking, the Beginning came first, so it should be the first and fundamental topic of exposition. Hence, a doctrine of creation will describe how our cosmos was created in a particular way, with particular characteristics and particular characters. And the general assumption of most Christian tradition is that the doctrine learns of these particularities from the descriptions found in the Genesis creation narratives, which are usually understood as offering through revelation some sort of reliable, even factual, witness to the world's actual Beginning. Then, on the basis of these initial descriptions, a doctrine of creation goes on to explain how these original characters and events have determined our present creaturely nature and relations. The Beginning is foundational, and everything that follows is in some sense derivative—that is, what one "knows" from the past informs how one is to understand the present.

Yet from another perspective, one could argue that a doctrine of Creation should not begin with the Beginning, since it is by definition receding ever further into the past (and from which modern sensibilities assume no eyewitness or direct report ever came). Experientially, intellectually, and practically speaking, our present and immediate understanding of and interrelation with Creation has priority. We live in, influence, and are influenced by the surrounding world in certain ways, and it is in this manner that we discern its particular characteristics. Then on the basis of this present experience and knowledge, we make the plausible assumption that its character today was its character yesterday, and, extending this assumption back to a supposed starting point, that its character was in fact established in "the Beginning." Hence, what one knows about the present informs how one interprets the past. In other words, the Beginning is still understood as a crucial event, but it is asserted to be such not because we have an actual account of what happened but because our present experience retrospectively posits it as having defined all subsequent reality—including our present and future reality—in one manner and not another. Yet in that sense, any report of the details of the Beginning can be understood as secondary, even dispensable, because we still have immediately present to us its product, that is, "Creation." If we want to know what was begun in the Beginning, we need not look to the past but to the characteristics and processes currently surrounding us in the world. This approach has also had its Christian proponents, primarily those who have sought to establish a doctrine of Creation on a natural theology.

If these are the two alternatives, which best fits the approach taken by Schleiermacher and Barth? Given that they both deny the Genesis creation narratives as offering any historical information about the Beginning, and that Schleiermacher in particular only briefly concerns himself with the Beginning at all, it would appear they must reject the first approach. Yet they also both disparage attempts to establish a doctrine of Creation on a natural theology, which suggests they must reject the second approach as well. However, with certain qualifications, they do both take a variation of the second approach. Schleiermacher and Barth each begin their treatments of Creation *in the present*, by founding it upon an immediate and living "experience" rather than on some external vestige or even scriptural account from the past. In Schleiermacher's case, the immediate "experience" is the particular consciousness of sin and grace brought about by the Redeemer along with its modification of the general feeling of absolute dependence. On the basis of this present experience or feeling, the Christian understands the surrounding world in a particular way, and on the basis of this understanding, feels justified in abstracting certain limited claims about the world's origin and consummation. In Barth's case, the immediate experience is the revelatory encounter with Christ in the church's proclamation. On the basis of this present experience or event, the Christian is given to understand the world in a particular way, and to understand that all the other, "secondary" revelations given in Scripture regarding the origin, nature, and end of Creation are to be interpreted through Christ.[1]

In other words, both Schleiermacher and Barth posit a specifically religious, indeed, *christological* experience in the present—either an "internal" feeling or an "external" event—as the prerequisite necessary for dogmatics to expound a doctrine of Creation. This experience colors the Christian's understanding of and interrelation with the surrounding world. This experience, standing as it were *between* the Christian and Creation, prevents any resultant theology from being merely a natural theology. And in Barth's case, this experience, standing between the Christian and the Genesis narratives, allows those passages to be understood in other than literal or historical-critical terms. Hence, according to both theologians, a Christian dogmatic does not, indeed cannot, interpret the world from a neutral or

---

1. I am aware that in using the term "experience" to claim a common starting point for Schleiermacher and Barth, I am sidestepping the significant differences that exist between the former's presupposition of the subjective "fundamental feeling" and the latter's presupposition of the objective revelatory "encounter" or "event." Describing these differences could fill another book entirely. Nevertheless, the "feeling" that Schleiermacher posits is not merely subjective or psychological, but prompted by an awareness of the whole of reality, while the "revelatory event" that Barth posits is not objectively self-evident, but requires the response of faith before it becomes meaningful. In this sense, I believe I may (for purposes of this book) appropriately use the term "experience" for both theologians to label that combination of external orientation and internal significance discernible in each.

detached perspective, but only from a committed one. On the one hand, the fundamental religious experience is such that it necessarily modifies and in a certain sense encompasses all other concerns and ways of seeing them. It "particularizes" even the general, so that, in reference to Creation, the world is no longer understood simply on its own, but always in conjunction with God's activity in Christ. From this position, on the other hand, one comes to recognize that the world on its own is actually far too ambiguous to lend itself to only one complete and "objective" interpretation—which is perhaps the main reason why natural theologies, no matter how scrupulous their logic, can never finally produce irresistibly convincing and adequate "natural religions."[2] Both Schleiermacher and Barth affirm that the Christian's understanding of Creation and redemption must be thought of, and dogmatically expounded, as parts of a whole. They also both affirm that this is necessitated not by some arbitrary decision, but as a result of the one cardinal experience that each in his own way presupposes.[3] Given this starting point, one cannot help but understand Creation in a particularly Christian or christological way.

Schleiermacher's Christological Orientation

What would constitute a proof that Schleiermacher's doctrine of Creation has a christological orientation? Such an orientation could appear

---

2. See Andrew Louth, "Barth and the Problem of Natural Theology," *Downside Review* 87 (July 1969): 268–77. Louth makes some useful comments on the distinction between natural theology and natural religion, and in so doing speaks to that which both Schleiermacher and Barth rejected. On p. 270, Louth says that "natural theology may be understood as asserting that man by virtue of his natural reason has the capacity to know God. And it is perfectly consonant with recognition of the claims of natural theology to hold that unless he is helped by revelation man always uses his capacity wrongly and falls into idolatry."

This understanding, Louth suggests, is the one with the longest history in Christian thinking (e.g., one can certainly hear echoes of it in Book 1 of Calvin's *Institutes*). It is not, however, the only understanding available to us; according to Louth, in the seventeenth and eighteenth centuries some thinkers came to suppose "that by the light of natural reason they could know enough about God to be able to worship him adequately and save their souls" (p. 270). This supposition is what Louth calls "natural religion"—and *this* in particular is what Schleiermacher and Barth reject, although I would argue that they do so on different grounds. For Schleiermacher, the problem lies in the assumption of what "natural reason" can accomplish. Living in a post-Kantian age, he no longer supposes that reason has the capacity to establish such a natural religion. For Barth, the problem lies not just in the inadequacy of human reason but also in its inevitable presumptuousness; regardless of whether its insights might be correct, human reason will always try to exercise its control. Hence, natural religion will always be idolatry.

3. Support for this understanding may be found in the work of Stephen Sykes, who describes both Schleiermacher and Barth as major representatives of the "inwardness" tradition. See Sykes, *The Identity of Christianity* (Philadelphia: Fortress Press, 1984), chs. 4 and 8.

in a variety of ways with a lesser or greater degree of christological coloring; it could refer to Schleiermacher's method, in that his doctrine of Creation is derived from the consciousness of Christians. Needless to say, this would seem to be christological only in the most nominal sense, since the doctrine itself could still be essentially generic. Or it could be that Christ is in some sense the goal or consummation of Schleiermacher's doctrine of Creation. This possibility could produce one of several scenarios. It could be that Christ is such a goal only incidentally, tacked on to an explicit or narrower doctrine of creation only after the fact, without influencing the form or content of that doctrine. Or this goal might in some way determine the form of that narrower doctrine without affecting its content. Or, finally, this particular consummation could affect both the form and the content of that doctrine, but perhaps only implicitly and not explicitly. In other words, there is a wide range of ways in which Schleiermacher's doctrine of Creation could be inclined toward or by Christ. In this chapter I will try to discern which of these possible approaches best describes his position, and thus the manner in which his doctrine can be labeled "christologically oriented."

The crucial first step in completing this task is to recognize that Schleiermacher expounds his understanding of Creation in a system, and that we should have some sense of the assumptions driving that system before we examine any particular doctrines or propositions contained in it. (That examination will occupy us in chapters 5 through 7.) *The Christian Faith* is not merely a collection of discrete doctrines, but a true system—indeed, it is one of the greatest works of dogmatic systematizing in Christian history. And it is a work made all the more noteworthy by the fact that Schleiermacher conceived it as an integral part of the even larger theological system described in his *Brief Outline on the Study of Theology.*[4] All of its parts cohere in virtually seamless interrelation. This means one must consider the whole of it in order to understand fully its various parts, as well as vice versa.

---

4. See Friedrich Schleiermacher, *Brief Outline on the Study of Theology*, trans. Terrence N. Tice (Atlanta: John Knox Press, 1966), §§16, 18, 24–31, 69–102, 195–202. Martin Redeker also offers a good introduction to Schleiermacher's systematizing; in fact, he uses the term to characterize a whole period of Schleiermacher's life and work. See Martin Redeker, *Schleiermacher: Life and Thought*, trans. John Wallhausser (Philadelphia: Fortress Press, 1973), 73–180, with the pages most pertinent to my discussion of system being 100–113.

Thus, the overall framework of his work may tell us as much as any given passage.

More specifically, this suggests that while Schleiermacher expounds his explicit doctrine of creation in the first main division of his system (under the heading "The Development of That Religious Self-Consciousness Which Is Always Both Presupposed by and Contained in Every Christian Religious Affection"), we must recognize that his full understanding of the created realm may not be completed under that doctrine or even that division. This division connects and interacts with the other main divisions of his system, and it also depends upon them. We should not make the same mistake made by some of the early readers of Schleiermacher's work, who viewed the First Part of *The Christian Faith* as presenting the essential theological constant from which all else was then derived. This misplaces the heart of Schleiermacher's dogmatic and misunderstands its dynamism. But if we recognize that the work as a whole was indeed meant to operate as a system, with each of its various parts interacting with its other parts, then what Schleiermacher writes in its latter divisions must influence what he includes in its initial portions. We would certainly not suppose that Schleiermacher wrote the First Part without the Second Part already in mind, yet this is, in effect, the assumption made by those who view his work as a drawn-out series of deductions from the "first principle" of absolute dependence. Instead, we must recognize that the progression from general to particular evident in his work also contains influences flowing the other direction. That is, the heading of his First Part and the doctrines contained under it delineate in some manner how the "question" must be formulated in order to fit the "answer" already present in the religious consciousness of the Christian community. After all, the First Part's presuppositional character does not necessarily mean it *had* to be expounded first in Schleiermacher's system; he could have placed it just as legitimately in the second position, because it is an *abstraction from* an actual and particular Christian feeling. That there is such an interchangeability available to his dogmatics derives from the underlying interconnectedness and unity of the various feelings in Christian consciousness. Schleiermacher himself describes the unity of this connection rather extensively in the second of his *Two Letters* to Lücke and in a more abbreviated fashion at the outset of the "First Part of the System of Doctrine" in *The Christian Faith*. Each offers important evidence for confirming my thesis.

Looking to the first of these two sources, Schleiermacher indicates that he could have organized his work in two different ways, namely, with the two parts in the sequence he actually employed or in a reversal of that sequence. I will label the former sequence the "customary order" and the latter the "experiential." In its customary order, *The Christian Faith* would follow the traditional sequence, evident as early as the Apostles' Creed, of starting with the most universal or "chronologically first" doctrines of God and creation, and building upon them the more particular or "chronologically later" doctrines—Christ, redemption, the church. But in its experiential order, this sequence would run the opposite direction: Those elements of first importance to the specifically Christian religious consciousness would likewise be prior in dogmatic expression, with the more general elements abstracted from that consciousness in a secondary position. Schleiermacher tells Lücke that he could have opted for this experiential order instead of the more customary order and been justified in doing so: "Surely, it would have been natural and proper for a theologian who comes from the reformed tradition and who does not believe this tradition should be put aside even in the present state of church union to have followed much more closely the outline of the Heidelberg Catechism."[5]

The point is obvious. Nearly the first two dozen questions and answers in that catechism are formulated with reference to redemption. First it speaks of the "comfort" made available to believers in Christ through his sacrifice and salvation, then of the human sinfulness that made such redemption necessary, and then of the divine righteousness that both demanded and provided such a sacrifice and redemption. Only with question 22 does the Heidelberg Catechism begin to address the specific articles of the Apostles' Creed, and only in questions 26–28 does it first present an explicit consideration of God's

---

5. Friedrich Schleiermacher, *On the "Glaubenslehre": Two Letters to Dr. Lücke*, trans. James Duke and Francis Fiorenza, American Academy of Religion Texts and Translations Series 3 (Chico, Calif.: Scholars Press, 1981), 337.

creation and providence. It takes this approach presumably in order to maintain redemption as the central fact of Christian life, and as the lens or framework through which Christians view and interpret all other facets of existence—even if these facets logically or chronologically precede the historical appearance of Christ and his initiation of redemption. This is the approach Schleiermacher suggests he could have taken as a theologian in the Reformed tradition.

But Schleiermacher does not, in fact, reverse the order of his First and Second Parts, exchanging the tradition of the Apostles' Creed for that of the Heidelberg Catechism. He recognizes that were he to do so, that is,

> if the propositions now in the first part, which in their present form serve only as an external work, were to follow the Christology, the doctrine of the church, and the exposition of the divine love and wisdom, they would certainly take on a warmer tone and likewise appear *in their specifically Christian perspective*.[6]

This result certainly would have had its benefits. Yet after weighing these and other advantages, Schleiermacher enumerates why he decided to retain his original order. First, he states his dislike for anticlimax. Specifically, he observes that he would have had to reverse his exposition of the divine attributes, considering last God's "original" or "natural" attributes and first what he elsewhere calls God's "derived" attributes,[7] that is, the divine wisdom and love. He implies that such a move might satisfy his critics, but that for him it would mean presenting his "best" at the start of his work.[8] His explanation is rather convoluted on this matter, but it does seem justifiable to say that he wants to maintain his doctrine of the divine wisdom and love as some sort of culmination, and not just of his doctrine of God but of his entire system. This desire may not seem immediately relevant to our consideration of his doctrine of Creation—indeed, it could be taken as an implicit diminution of that doctrine, in that his explicit treatment of it is located in his less than "best" part. Far from being irrelevant or

---

6. Ibid., 58; emphasis mine.
7. *Gl*, §50.4.
8. Schleiermacher, *On the "Glaubenslehre,"* 59–60.

denigrating, however, the divine love and wisdom actually clarify and help complete his doctrine of Creation. In any event, this first reason is based on what could be called a pious concern: He wants to present his system in the most effective order possible.

Reconciling Faith and Science

Second, Schleiermacher claims to be unable to offer a dogmatic system capable of reconciling Christian faith and free scientific inquiry in any other order than the one he actually employs. The problem, evidently, would have been an unavoidable curtailing of his more general doctrines: "After a complete discussion of the doctrines of redemption and the kingdom of God, there would have been scarcely any other option than to deal as briefly as possible with all those doctrines now contained in the first part."[9] Why he sees this as his only real option is not readily apparent, although the danger he sees in an abbreviated treatment is suggested in a rather drawn-out explanation. Schleiermacher holds that the increasing knowledge of science and the comprehensive nature of its explanations would soon leave no room for certain beliefs long held to be an essential part of Christianity. In particular, he cites the traditional understanding of creation, indicating that the church might have to "do without" not only its belief in the six-day creation, but "the concept of creation itself, as it is usually understood."[10] One could, of course, adopt a siege mentality, withdrawing into a bastioned church and fighting off all inroads and insights of science. But for Schleiermacher this was neither a viable nor a desirable alternative. He refused to be forced into choosing only faith or science, and sought instead a way of reconciling these two realms.[11] Indeed, Schleiermacher

---

9. Ibid., 60.
10. Ibid., 60–61.
11. Martin Redeker summarizes Schleiermacher's situation and attitude with great lucidity: He experienced the shock to Christian proclamation and certainty of faith resulting from the collapse of traditional notions of God and of the biblical mythology, and the erosion of traditional biblical and dogmatic authority. He was particularly concerned with the changes brought on by the devastation of supernaturalistic metaphysics in the wake of modern science and Kant's critical philosophy. Even so, he did not join the chorus of those who complained about the collapse of the older dogmatic, biblical-mythological outlook with its values and ideals. He was confident that the gospel would be rediscovered and authenticated in a new way. (Redeker, *Schleiermacher: Life and Thought*, 2.)

maintained that the evangelical church must endeavor "to establish an eternal covenant between the living Christian faith and completely free, independent scientific inquiry, so that faith does not hinder science and science does not exclude faith."[12] He goes so far as to say that if the present church cannot find the resources for such a covenant in its Reformation origins, then that Reformation "fails to meet adequately the needs of our time and we need another one, no matter what it takes to establish it."[13] Of course, he immediately points out his conviction that the Reformation can indeed supply such resources.[14] Yet they must be culled and re-presented in order to meet the needs of the modern church in founding this covenant, and this task cannot be accomplished in a cursory or abbreviated fashion. Consequently, the First Part of his system had to be as extensive and involved as it in fact was. Moreover, it appears that it was most useful coming first, in order to serve as a circumscribing and reorienting prologue to the more central Christian doctrines expounded in the Second Part.

In other words, the First Part has as one of its tasks the dissecting, purging, and rejoining of certain traditional and general doctrines so that the more specific doctrines of the Second Part may be, on the one hand, rooted in assumptions not antithetical to science and, on the other, able to complete those initial ones in a characteristically Christian manner. The distinction cannot be applied absolutely, of course, but in reference to the two subthemes of my thesis there is a sense in which the First Part appears to expound traditional doctrines with a definite eye toward the "outer norm" or the "external intellectual demand,"[15] while the Second Part appears to expound them primarily with an eye toward Christ, the essential focus of the "inner norm."[16] If this is in fact the case, then it does not seem illogical to conclude that his second reason for maintaining the present sequence of the First and Second Parts is also an aspect of his first reason: It would

---

12. Schleiermacher, On the "Glaubenslehre," 64.

13. Ibid.

14. Based on the comment of B. A. Gerrish in another context, the primary location of such resources would be the various Reformation confessions. See Gerrish, "Nature and the Theater of Redemption: Schleiermacher on Christian Dogmatics and the Creation Story," Ex Auditu 3 (1987): 122.

15. Recall Schleiermacher's characterization of it as an "external work."

16. Recall my distinction between external and internal norms, pp. 8–9.

be an anticlimax for his system to end with the part displaying apologetic overtones. As a Christian dogmatic, it is much more powerful to end with the exposition of how the general presuppositions of the faith are filled out and completed by its christological essence and orientation. Yet even if this is the case, the fact that he could have reversed the order, thereby showing the propositions of the First Part "in their specifically Christian perspective," suggests that those propositions do indeed possess that specificity, whether or not it is actually highlighted.

The Method of the *Glaubenslehre*

The second source available to us in explaining the nature of the connection between *The Christian Faith*'s First and Second Parts is, as one might expect, the opening of that work itself. There we find yet more evidence of how the doctrine of creation must be fitted into a christological framework or orientation in order to be complete. To be sure, it sounds initially as if Schleiermacher is divorcing his statements concerning creation in this First Part, based as they are on "God-consciousness," from the christologically determined doctrines in the Second Part, based on the consciousness of sin and grace. In the lead sentence of the First Part, he expresses his intent to "leave out of account completely the particular content of every distinct stimulation of Christian affection and recognize our statement as in no way determined by these variations."[17] Yet he immediately adds to this position the observation that "if one wanted to assert that there could be Christian pious moments in which the Being of God simply is not involved in this way, that is, in which God-consciousness simply is not included in self-consciousness, our proposition would exclude that person from the sphere of Christian belief."[18]

How does Schleiermacher keep these statements together? And why? The first suggests that the doctrines derived from the consciousness of absolute dependence upon God have no necessary link to those derived from a particularly Christian consciousness, and yet the

---

17. *Gl*, §32.1.
18. Ibid.

second insists that no Christian can be without them. Does this not stand the thesis of this book on its head, by suggesting that the God-consciousness "completes" the Christ-consciousness?

Schleiermacher answers these questions with the following: "It must also be stated that this God-consciousness, as it is here described, constitutes an actual pious moment *not by itself alone, but always only in connection with other particular determinations.*"[19] To explain this distinction, he offers an analogy, in which he says "that this God-consciousness keeps its identity as it simply relates to the individual moments of all manifestations of Christian piety, just as in life generally the self-positing [*Ichsetzen*] of each person relates to the individual moments of his existence."[20]

In other words, this more "general" God-consciousness and the doctrines elucidated from it are abstractions from the "particular" consciousness of the Christian believer. Logically, they have a certain priority, in the sense of being a constant presupposed by and contained in every moment of Christian pious self-consciousness; but in actual experience, this particular consciousness of the Christian has priority, because it is the *source* from which the general consciousness is abstracted. Thus, dogmatic exposition may begin with the doctrine of creation and then move on to deal with Christology, but this does not mean the more general doctrine of creation is the foundation or basis for the more particularly Christian doctrines that follow it. Rather, the more particular religious experiences act as the source or basis for the more general religious experiences, including those bearing upon our relationship with creation. B. A. Gerrish makes much the same point:

> The idea of absolute dependence, articulated in the doctrines of creation and preservation, cannot *ground* or *justify* Christian faith. . . . If one is to speak of "foundations" or "grounding" at all in Schleiermacher's theology, then it is the particular that grounds the universal, not the other way around. The actual foundation of the Christian's confidence in the divinely governed world-order is faith in Christ.[21]

---

19. Ibid.; emphasis mine.
20. Ibid.
21. Gerrish, "Nature and the Theater of Redemption," 132.

Schleiermacher's whole theological system reinforces this point by claiming to be nothing more or less than a description of the *Christian's* religious self-consciousness. The First Part is not to be construed as being derived from some "generic" religious self-consciousness. Hence, at the very least, one may call his doctrine of creation "christological" simply because the source for this doctrine is not a neutral considera-tion of the natural world (the approach taken by Deists) nor specula-tion upon an assumed universal religious knowledge (the approach taken by Rationalists) but is instead the particular religious conscious-ness of the *Christian* in that world. This coincides with one of the pos-sible ways of defining christological orientation outlined above.[22]

Yet matters are still not as clear as they might be. No doubt Schleiermacher did intend to abstract his doctrine of creation from a specifically Christian self-consciousness. But does that mean his actual exposition of the doctrine is inherently Christian? As a doc-trine intent on avoiding any account of the influences of the charac-teristically Christian, does it then become so neutral that it might have been abstracted just as easily from another specific religious self-consciousness? Based on what he writes in §§4, 8, and 9 of *The Christian Faith*, one might argue that either of the other two monotheistic faiths—Judaism or Islam—could have been used to abstract a doctrine of creation identical to the one expounded here in a Christian dogmatic. If that were the case, then it would be impossible to maintain the claim that Schleiermacher's doctrine of creation is intrinsically christological. The determining factor would not be the particular influence of Christology, but only the particu-lar influence of monotheism.

Schleiermacher indicates how we should address these questions in §29. He makes it clear that the doctrine of creation, as well as the other doctrines of his First Part, should indeed be considered "Christian" and not merely generically monotheistic. At issue is the manner in which the various elements of Christian consciousness are categorized and given expression in a dogmatic system. In actual Christian experi-ence, the pious elements produced by the antithesis of sin and grace are always bound together with the pious elements not produced by

---

22. See pp. 16–17.

that antithesis, with the former influencing the perception of the latter in any given moment. Yet analysis of such moments should lead one to recognize that these latter elements must precede—logically, if not experientially—the specifically Christian elements, and Schleiermacher employs this distinction to organize the expression of Christian consciousness in his *Glaubenslehre*. He explains that he will relate the two sets of elements

> in such a way that the First Part will contain such doctrines (the possibility of which has already been granted in general) *in which the characteristically Christian stands out less strongly*, whose expression therefore may also coincide most easily with those of other faiths. Yet they are, for all that, by no means constituent parts of a general or so-called natural theology. They are, rather not only in every case statements about the pious self-consciousness, and thus truly dogmatic propositions, but they are also distinctly Christian, by means of the relation [*Beziehung*], *residing in the design [Anordnung] of the whole and thus repeatable with each proposition, to the characteristically Christian.*[23]

This passage offers two critical pieces of information for addressing the questions we have raised. First, it indicates that the doctrines of the First Part can be considered neutral only in an artificial, and not essential, sense. In its effort to expound Christian consciousness clearly, dogmatics finds it useful to organize an exposition which fragments that which in itself is undivided. As a result, certain elements of that consciousness may appear more generic than they actually are, because of the categorization imposed upon them by the needs of systematic dogmatic expression. Within the bounds of category and place, these elements may indeed lend themselves to comparison with their doctrinal equivalents in the other monotheisms. But such a comparison is feasible only because the specifically Christian source and orientation of these elements has been downplayed by their location in the dogmatic system. They are not the product of a detached, generic consideration of the external, natural

---

23. *Gl*, §29.2; emphasis mine.

world, but of a specific, historically grounded and living faith—which points to the second piece of information offered in the passage just cited.

Schleiermacher states that these apparently neutral expressions derived from Christian consciousness do indeed maintain a distinctly Christian character, by means of the overall design of his dogmatic system. Taken individually and statically, the various doctrines of the First Part may seem essentially generic, but taken within the context of the system as a whole, their Christian character becomes obvious once again. The doctrines of the First Part describe the basic structure of the relation between God and the world and *some* of the content of that relation—but not *all* of that content. Describing the full content of the relation between God and the world is the task of the Second Part. In other words, the fragmentation of the Christian consciousness necessary for the step-by-step expression of that consciousness in a dogmatic system is overcome only with the *completion* of that expression, for only then does dogmatics attain an integrity and comprehensiveness equivalent to that of the original consciousness from which it is derived. As such a whole, the dogmatic system "reminds" us that its First Part does not stand on its own, but is oriented to and in need of the Second Part for its completion and full expression. This reminder appears in Schleiermacher's statement that the reference to the characteristically Christian, which exists in the overall "arrangement," "design," "disposition," or "direction" (*Anordnung*) of the system, could be made explicit in each individual doctrine of the First Part. To be sure, Schleiermacher does not carry through on this possibility; it would have added, after all, a great deal of repetitive clutter to his system.[24] Yet the very acknowledgment of such a possibility by Schleiermacher ought to make us wonder what such an explicit connection would look like. We have affirmed that his *Glaubenslehre* is not simply a collection of discrete doctrines, but a true system. What this term *Anordnung* suggests is

---

24. By contrast, Barth *does* in his own way carry out such a possibility. He makes explicit a whole host of various cross-references and connections between his doctrines of Creation and Christ, which is one reason his treatment is so long. Indeed, if one were to throw academic caution to the wind, one might be tempted to conclude that the key difference between them really only boils down to this *procedural* variation.)

that it displays not only an overall unity and cohesiveness but also a movement or "growth," which begins in the First Part and culminates in the Second Part.

Schleiermacher's "Organic" Method

Perhaps the best way to illustrate Schleiermacher's approach, and his understanding of the relation between the doctrines of the First and Second Parts of his system, is through a comparison of two alternate analogies. In the first, an architectural image prevails. This image maintains that Christianity and the other two monotheisms have very similar or even identical foundations, and perhaps even comparable framing, but that they are then clad in differing facades and equipped with dissimilar fixtures. As a result, when one considers each building in its finished form, it would be easy to assume that each is different from the others. However, if one were to look at the blueprints for each, it would become clear that they are fundamentally the same. Therefore—to return the analogy to its dogmatic implications—in structuring one's account of a given monotheistic faith, one's initial propositions would reflect this underlying or structural identity, perhaps by taking the form of "a general or so-called natural theology." The more particular aspects of that faith would be considered, but only in propositions added on later. To be sure, such additions can dramatically influence the overall impression and final effect of a dogmatic system as a whole. But they do not negate or even influence the generic character of the foundation upon which they rest.

As one might expect, the analogy appropriate to Schleiermacher's approach is far different. Instead of architectural imagery, biological or organic imagery seems to underlie his exposition. Consider the fact that he himself proposes in §§7–10 a taxonomous classification of the various religions which, with certain qualifications, is not unlike that used to describe the biological realm. He might say that each of the three monotheisms is a different plant, and that this is most obvious when one considers them in their fully grown forms. One may, of course, prune them back to bare branches and stalk so that the individual features of each are temporarily less evident. Such an exercise might serve to highlight certain similarities among them, as members of the same genus. But similarity must not be mistaken for identity. After all, one should not forget during the imposition of pruning that the plant will return eventually to its characteristic and full form. Clipping off its extremities does not alter its genetic predisposition to develop according to one, and only one, specific pattern. While the previous analogy suggests that upon a given foundation various kinds of buildings could be constructed, this analogy suggests that from a given stalk only one kind of plant will grow. Therefore—to return once again to the dogmatic sphere—in structuring one's account of a particular monotheistic faith, one's initial propositions may display a superficial generality, but they will also reflect, in one way or another, the inner uniqueness of that faith. This Schleiermacher does, primarily through the *orientation* of these propositions within the system as a whole, but also in certain instances through the particular assertions made in those propositions. They do indeed appear more neutral than his later propositions, but the nature of his system reminds us that they are also destined to "grow into" these later propositions. The latter are not simply a collection of interchangeable additions built on top of the former; rather, the former, in spite of any neutral appearance, are "genetically predisposed" to produce the latter. In other words, in the realm of religion as in the realm of nature, ontogeny may indeed recapitulate phylogeny on an embryonic level, but in its adult form the organism will be specific and distinct. Thus, if we once again think of the various manners of "christological orientation" defined at the outset of this chapter, we see that we have progressed even further. Schleiermacher's doctrine of Creation is christological not merely because it is derived from the consciousness of Christians and not merely because its goal is understood incidentally to be Christ. Instead, it appears to be guided toward Christ from the very outset, and it seems that its content must in some manner be influenced by Christ as well, because of its "genetic predisposition."

The distinction made by this analogy should be clear. But one may still ask: Does it accurately reflect Schleiermacher's method? Are there any other passages in *The Christian Faith* that support it? The answer appears to be yes. If we turn back to §10, we may find a number of

statements relevant to this interpretation of Schleiermacher's innovative approach. Having posited and partially explained his assumption
of the universality of human piety in his opening propositions,
Schleiermacher also suggests that in its actual manifestation this piety
takes a number of distinct forms. By so doing, one might imagine he
is negating the basic tenet of his whole theological enterprise, that is,
undermining his assertion of a universal faith with his recognition of
the uniqueness of particular historical faiths. But, of course, such a view
misunderstands Schleiermacher. He does not assert that all humans
share a certain set of fundamental *beliefs*, but rather that all share a natural *capacity* for belief, or more accurately, a capacity for piety. How
that capacity is actualized into a particular set of beliefs depends upon
historical factors separate from that capacity in and of itself.

The nature of these factors and how they contribute to the
uniqueness and coherence of a particular religious communion is
Schleiermacher's topic for §10. The proposition for this segment of
The Christian Faith states:

> Each particular configuration of communal piety is *one*, in part exter-
> nally, as an historical continuity proceeding *from a definite starting
> point*, and in part internally, as *a peculiar modification of all that* which
> may also be found in each developed manner of faith of the same type
> and level; and from both taken together, one may learn the peculiar
> essence of each configuration.[25]

This formula does indeed suggest that there are certain elements common to various religions. But it should be obvious as well that its
emphasis tends more toward the particular than the universal. On the
one hand, each religious communion is unique because it originates in
a particular set of historical circumstances. On the other hand, each one
is unique because it has an orientation or insight that shapes its "common" basic assumptions in a particular way. To be sure, Schleiermacher
suggests that there are degrees of uniqueness: The less a communion's
particular orientation is the product of its particular historical origin,

---

25. *Gl*, §10; latter emphases mine.

the less distinctiveness or integrity will that communion display. Conversely, the more a communion's orientation stems from a particular time and place, or more especially from the particular "impulse" of one founder, the more distinct and theologically integrated will that communion be.[26] Accordingly, one may indeed affirm that certain general assumptions and even beliefs may be in a restricted sense "shared" by more than one communion, and to this extent Schleiermacher still displays a certain willingness to recognize what some might (mistakenly) call "universal doctrines." But he also makes clear that such correspondences are more characteristic among the lesser developed religious communions, because their essential natures are not as well defined, and therefore lend themselves to such academic comparisons. The more highly developed religions—namely, Islam, Judaism, and "the most perfect form" Christianity[27]—are, however, *very* distinctly defined, and thus, it would seem, *least* open to the assertion that they share a number of identical or common beliefs. In reference to these monotheisms, Schleiermacher describes his proposition as asserting "that the same indeed is present in all, but that in each one everything is present *in a different manner.*"[28] He acknowledges that this is not the common assumption:

> The prevailing view, on the contrary, is that the greater part is the same in all communions of the highest stage, and that to this element common to all there is *simply added in each something particular* so that, for instance, to present only a rough illustration, the belief in one God, with all that pertains thereto, is common to them all, but in one is added the obedience to the commandment, in the other instead of this the belief in Christ, and in the third the belief in the prophets.[29]

This is the mentality that underlies the thinking of proponents of natural theology and makes the notion of a universal natural religion so appealing. It assumes that the more general doctrines are in fact

---

26. *Gl*, §10.1.
27. Ibid.
28. *Gl*, §10.2; emphasis mine.
29. Ibid.; emphasis mine.

historically universal, that they therefore have a certain foundational character, and that this character remains essentially unchanged by the more particular doctrines that follow, built, as it were, on top of these initial doctrines. As I have asserted, however, Schleiermacher rejects this architectural imagery. With reference to the "common emphasis" described above, Schleiermacher argues that the combination of a belief in one God and in Christ can be explained further only by supposing that the belief in Christ either is "*without* influence upon that selfsame and already present God-consciousness, and upon the way in which that consciousness unites with the sensible affections [*Erregungen*]" or that it *does* have an influence "but only upon *some* pious affections, while the bulk of them would be formed entirely the same way in Christianity as in other monotheistic faiths."[30] In other words, belief in Christ would no longer be a *religious* belief, properly speaking, or it would no longer have the capacity to form a *distinct* religious faith and communion.[31] Schleiermacher holds that his formulation avoids these two pitfalls precisely because it recognizes that the "specific element"—in this case, Christ—can and does modify *everything* in Christianity that it has in common with the other monotheistic faiths.[32] Indeed, even to speak of commonalities between monotheistic religions would appear to be possible only as that mode of speaking is borrowed from the philosophy of religion, as the heading under which he groups §§7–10 indicates. When one moves to the dogmatic system proper, however, it appears that the "peculiar modification" takes control, so that discussion of commonalities is, strictly speaking, inappropriate.

Yet is Schleiermacher boxing himself into a corner with this line of reasoning? Does the manner in which he defines the particularity of religious communions, especially those on the monotheistic level, actually negate his ability to assert a similarity as well? How can a given communion be truly *individual* and still belong to a general *kind* of piety? At first glance, Schleiermacher seems to offer answers that only beg the question. Recall the wording of proposition §10: Each

30. Ibid.; emphasis mine.
31. Ibid.
32. Cf. Niebuhr's analysis on this point in Richard R. Niebuhr, *Schleiermacher on Christ and Religion* (New York: Charles Scribner's Sons, 1964), 228–37, and my discussion of Niebuhr in appendix A.

communion is "one" in part through "a peculiar modification of all that which may also be found in each developed manner of faith of the same type and level."[33] Elsewhere, a paraphrase of this formula asserts "that the same indeed is present in all, but that in each one everything is present in a different manner."[34] What, precisely, do these statements mean? Are they not presenting a formula which cancels itself out, in effect saying that religions of one type and level are "the same, only different"? In what sense are these religions the same? In what sense different? And how is the "similar element" of a given religion related to its "peculiar element"? Schleiermacher rejects a simple "substructure: same / superstructure: different" construal of the situation, but what is he himself proposing?

The Particularity of Christianity

Schleiermacher offers some clues in §10.3, where he considers the concepts of "individual" and "kind." At first, it appears that Schleiermacher actually only restates the obvious: An individual is such inasmuch as it is different from other individuals, while a kind (or species, or type) is such inasmuch as its various members are the same. As a result, the two concepts seem to be simply the product of two alternating perspectives. A given object will stand as either an individual or a member of a kind, depending upon whether one considers its peculiarities or commonalities. Yet such an understanding keeps that which makes an object individual always distinct from that which makes it also a member of a species. One set of characteristics is simply added on to another set of characteristics, with no integration of the two. This is simply the architectural model reappearing, the one Schleiermacher rejects. Its flaw is that it is too static, too inanimate. It assumes that the factors which make an object both individual and a member of a kind are simply inert characteristics, which do not interact with or affect one another. Schleiermacher, however, perceives them to be very dynamic and interrelated. Indeed, the "individualizing" characteristics of a particular object exhibit their individuality in part precisely in the

---

33. *Gl*, §10.
34. *Gl*, §10.2.

way in which they influence or determine the existence and activity of
the universal characteristics of that object. The God-consciousness
that is a *natural* attribute of the human makeup is always only realized
in the *historical*; the "essential capacity" only comes into being in a
"temporal actuality." This reminds us of a point made earlier, namely,
that neither the particular nor the general ever exist in "pure" form,
but only in symbiotic relation. Reiterating Schleiermacher's basic formula, the former always presupposes the latter, while the latter only
exists as an abstraction from the former.

How then does all of this shape the way in which Schleiermacher
will compare and contrast various religious communions, or, more to
the point, how will it allow him to expound Christianity as both one
of several monotheisms and also unique? What conception of the
general and particular will he offer so as to avoid the implication of a
"natural religion" and a "natural theology"? One passage seems especially pertinent:

> Should the attempt be made to state something general, in order that
> the apologist of any particular manner of faith be less likely mistaken,
> then we would simply abide by the following: that in every peculiar
> manner of faith, the God-consciousness (in and of itself the same
> everywhere on the same level) adheres in such a pre-eminent manner
> to some relation of the self-consciousness, that it can unite itself with
> all other determinations of the self-consciousness only by means of
> that [i.e., the relation to which it first adheres], so that to this relation
> all others are subordinated, and to all others it imparts its color and
> tone. Should it appear that hereby we are expressing more just a differ-
> ing rule for the connecting [*Verknüpfung*] of pious moments than a
> difference of form or content, then we have only to notice that each
> moment is itself a connection, namely, as a transition from the preced-
> ing moment to the following one, and thus must become a different
> moment as well, if the pious self-consciousness is placed under a dif-
> ferent manner of connection.[35]

---

35. *Gl*, §10.3.

This passage is important for two reasons. On the one hand, it suggests again *that* the belief in Christ influences everything Christianity has in common with the other monotheistic faiths. On the other, it also indicates more fully *how* that belief exercises its influence, namely, in a manner that is much more "organic" than "architectural." As a result, it offers support to my contention that the First Part of Schleiermacher's system is intrinsically Christian, although perhaps only implicitly rather than explicitly. Recall the citation from §29.2 that we have already considered,[36] which recognizes the doctrines of the First Part as "distinctly Christian, due to the reference, residing in the design (*Anordnung*) of the whole and thus repeatable with each proposition, to the characteristically Christian"[37]—which is to say, the Second Part. On its own, this citation could be taken to mean that the First Part is Christian only by association and not intrinsically—that in itself it is neutral, but due to its *connection* with the Second Part it "ends up" Christian. However, when this citation is understood in light of the above passage from §10, we see that such an interpretation is too simplistic.

Insofar as particular doctrines are meant to correspond to and elucidate the variety in pious experience overall, we are justified, for the purpose of dogmatic clarity, in separating and organizing these doctrines in whatever way best expresses the logic or structure of that experience as a whole. But we should not thereby conclude that each particular doctrine corresponds to a discrete pious moment, and that the series of doctrines from the more general First Part to the characteristically Christian Second Part corresponds in any way to an equivalent series of feeling in actual Christian experience. Such a conclusion can only lead to the error seen by Schleiermacher in the "prevailing view," namely, that in Judaism, Christianity, and Islam the majority of beliefs are the same while only a few are different, "added on" as it were to the generic ones. The problem with this view lies in its failure to recognize that the feeling of absolute dependence—which, of course, Schleiermacher views as common to not only these three but to all religions—never exists in isolation, but always in conjunction with

---

36. See p. 26.
37. *Gl*, §29.2.

something else. That is, the God-consciousness actually manifests itself only insofar as it "adheres" in a certain "preeminent manner to some relation [*irgendeiner Beziehung*] of the self-consciousness."[38] What is this "relation" or "reference"? It is the historical element, the particular conduit or lens through which the God-consciousness passes to become actual, and it is different in each religious communion.[39] What is the particular relation in Christianity that plays this primary role, and how, precisely, does it determine the God-consciousness?

In the passage from §10, Schleiermacher does not immediately indicate the individual relations that could be inserted into the formula he is developing. He states only that the God-consciousness is combined with "some relation." This lack of specificity must not be construed as a flaw, of course, because his express purpose in §§7–10 is to describe how the various pious communions differ in general, in a fashion borrowed from the philosophy of religion. Nevertheless, the ramifications of this passage will be obscure until it becomes more specifically Christian. This Schleiermacher himself does with his next proposition, which begins his presentation of Christianity according to its peculiar essence, in a fashion borrowed from apologetics. Recall that he advanced the formula with the apologist in mind. §11 states that Christianity is essentially distinguished from other faiths "because everything in it is related to the redemption accomplished through Jesus of Nazareth."[40] *This* is the historically given and inwardly unique element that modifies the God-consciousness of Christians in a peculiarly Christian way; *this* is the specific referent of the self-consciousness that, conjoined with an otherwise indeterminate God-consciousness, produces an actual, complete faith.

Yet how does this peculiar relation or reference accomplish its particular determination of the God-consciousness, and as a corollary, how does it extend its influence to all other determinations and relations of the self-consciousness? I have already suggested that it acts as a conduit or lens, due to the primacy of its connection with the

38. *Gl*, §10.3.
39. Stephen Sykes detects this same assertion being made already in Schleiermacher's speeches in *On Religion*. See Sykes, *Identity of Christianity*, 84.
40. *Gl*, §11.

God-consciousness and the mediating task it performs between that consciousness and all other forms of the self-conscious. To cite Schleiermacher, the connection of the God-consciousness to this relation is preeminent or superior (*vorzüglich*); all other relations are subordinated to it (*untergeordnet*). Moreover, these latter relations are not only ranked below, but also are affected by that initial relation, for it imparts to them "its color and tone." In other words, it is not just that different religious communions each have a unique primary relation in that preeminent position, ranking differently relations that are otherwise the same among communions of the same level and type. Rather, that primary relation actually *modifies* everything subordinated to it. Put together in a particular way, the parts themselves are transformed in the process.

Schleiermacher evidently recognizes that this latter point can be easily missed or misconstrued, so he explains it more fully. In so doing, he gives us further indication of just how dynamic and truly systematic his approach is, in contrast to the "prevailing view." I will summarize it thus: Various pious moments—and by extension, the doctrines derived therefrom—should not be viewed as individual beads to be placed in some order on a string or, to stay more in keeping with our earlier analogy, as individual building blocks with a set form and content that remains unaffected by the manner in which they are placed one on top of the other. Such a conception is too atomistic or architectural, and does not recognize the effect the building (as an *activity* directed toward a specific end) has upon the building (as a *construct* made of various parts). Instead, Schleiermacher suggests, the various pious moments should be viewed as just that, namely, moments or instances of a continuum or tendency. As a result, the form and content of any given moment cannot be fully comprehended or described without taking into account the fact that it is *tending*, and tending in a *particular* direction—that is, in Schleiermacher's terms, that it is linked to all other moments with a *particular* "manner of connection." Indeed, one cannot even experience the moment, let alone describe it, without acknowledging that it has no discrete and definitive form and content at all apart from that tendency. Hence, as the overall tendency is set, so are the individual moments. In other words, for individual moments to be complete and fully formed, they must have been given an initial impetus and a specific method or pattern of continuity. This pattern is their particular "manner of connection," and it serves as a sort of genetic code guiding and informing the replication of the original moment or impulse over time.[41]

Of course, the preceding does not mean that the piety and doctrine of each religious communion is so fully particular that there can be no point of contact or comparison between communions. One can discern similarities, certainly among religions sharing the same level, and even more among religions sharing the same level and type. In so doing, the observer of religions simply accomplishes in the sociological realm what the taxonomic organization of nature does in the life sciences: It divides its objects into hierarchical categories such as class, order, family, genus, and species. But such similarities do remain at most just that: similarities. This is why Schleiermacher qualifies his statement regarding the generality of the doctrines in his First Part: Their Christian element stands out less strongly, therefore their dogmatic expression lends itself most easily to comparison with equivalent doctrines in other faiths.[42] He does *not* say the Christian element disappears altogether, and he *does* take pains to speak of a coincidence between faiths as a matter of *doctrinal expression*, which implies a certain limitation as to how far any coincidence may be pushed. The doctrines themselves never become identical, because they arise from different religious experiences. To be sure, the less a doctrine or moment of piety bears the imprint of its specific source, or the less obvious its purpose and direction in the whole, the more generic will

---

41. Niebuhr describes it thus in *Schleiermacher on Christ and Religion*, 248:

> The doctrines of creation and redemption stand in a peculiar tension. Each possesses its own integrity; neither finds its justification entirely in the other. Each expresses a distinguishable content of the Christian religious consciousness. But inasmuch as everything in Christian faith "is related to the redemption accomplished by Jesus of Nazareth," the consciousness of creation is informed and reformed by the relation to Christ, and from the perspective of this relation to Christ the awareness of utter dependence is in itself incomplete apart from the life and presence of the second Adam. This is the sense in which the doctrine of creation is Christomorphic.

While these comments are helpful, I believe they are not as accurate as they could be. I discuss my reservations regarding Niebuhr's position more fully in appendix A.

42. *Gl*, §29.2.

it appear and the more easily may it be perceived as similar to comparable moments or doctrines in other communions. Yet the perception and description of such similarities remains always a matter of degree and a somewhat artificial exercise. To Schleiermacher, there is never an immediate self-consciousness of "similarity" or of "generic" piety—just as in the natural realm there are, for example, no actual mammals "in general." What similarity there may be is really only discernible at the level of objective consciousness or at the level of dogmatic expression itself. And even then, similar moments of piety or similar doctrines are never so construed as to be thought of as interchangeable between religions of the same level, or even level and type. The particular element always retains its preeminence. Logically, it presupposes a general element; in actuality, the general only exists in particular ways, always displaying a unique "color and tone."

Why is all this relevant to the thesis of this book? Because it suggests how we are to understand the relation between the First and Second Parts of *The Christian Faith*—or more specifically, the relation between the doctrines in the First Part concerning creation and the doctrines in the Second Part toward which they are oriented and that fulfill them. We have learned that actual pious moments are never generic, but always particular. Certain general elements may be abstracted from them as logical presuppositions, but this is always only a secondary, after-the-fact exercise. Such general elements never exist on their own as an actual moment of pious experience. Moreover, we have also learned that actual pious moments are never discrete or static, but are always "in motion," and that the agent which gives them their dynamic character is also the impulse which gives them their particular character. As a result, the particularity displayed by an actual kind of piety resides not only in a certain part of its experience in any given moment (e.g., in the "characteristically Christian" form and content of such a moment) but also in the overall orientation or direction of its several parts. From what Schleiermacher says at the conclusion of §10.3, this orientation or "manner of connecting" the various relations within a moment of piety imparts to all those relations "its color and tone." In other words, the primacy of the particular element in pious experience not only orients the general element in a specific direction, but it also *influences in some manner its form, and thus ulti-mately its content, in each given moment.*

Thus, when it comes time to express the actual experience of Christian piety in a dogmatic system, such a work ought to reflect both the generic and unique qualities of that experience, and the ultimate and intrinsic coherence of that experience overall. It must present the distinction discernible within individual moments between the general and the particular elements of piety, but it must also take into account the orientation inherent to all these moments and the manner in which this orientation enables the general elements to be completed by the particular ones. Schleiermacher's *Glaubenslehre* certainly meets these two needs. Regarding the first, one may envision, as it were, a "vertical" line dividing those doctrines that are less prominently Christian from those that are more prominently so. This represents Schleiermacher's explicit distinction between his First and Second Parts. But superior to this distinction, one ought also to envision a second line, "horizontal" and dynamic, representing the unique and uni-fying impulse of Christianity, that binds together the two parts of *The Christian Faith* and makes it a true system. Schleiermacher does not himself designate such a unifying line, but it is what he means when he speaks of the "design" or "orientation [*Anordnung*] of the whole" in §29.2. Without this orientation, his Second Part would be nothing more than a Christian addition to a natural theology.

By now, Schleiermacher's approach should be clear. The next step examines some of his specific doctrines themselves, to see if they do, in fact, conform to this christological formulation. In addition, does his actual presentation of those doctrines allow him to meet his other concerns, that is, the maintenance of the essence of Christian tradition and the establishment of "an eternal covenant between the living Christian faith and completely free, independent scientific inquiry"?[43]

Before I turn to those tasks, however, I will consider in chapters 3 to 5 Barth's christologically oriented doctrine of Creation, and clarify the manner in which it is compatible with the interests of both the "inner" and "outer" norms.

43. Schleiermacher, *On the "Glaubenslehre,"* 64.

CHAPTER 3

The Character of Barth's Christologically Oriented Doctrine of Creation

Neo-*orthodox* and *Neo*-orthodox

In contrast to Schleiermacher's christological orientation, Barth's is much more straightforward. Schleiermacher uses his introduction to establish the ground rules for his dogmatic exposition, and once established, he seldom reiterates them. Instead, he leaves it to his readers to draw the necessary and full connections when considering later, specific doctrines and his system as a whole. Barth, however, is never so terse. On the contrary, both his long-windedness and repetitiveness are legendary. (Indeed, for all his love and praise of Mozart, it seems ironic that his writing comes across more as the theological equivalent of Wagner.) Yet his expansiveness makes it easier to recognize and trace the christological orientation of his doctrine of Creation. Indeed, from the very outset of his treatment, and throughout in its structure and content, Barth's doctrine of Creation is not only christological, but explicitly christocentric. One of the tasks of this chapter will be to present the logic of Barth's position, largely through a consideration of the first segment of his doctrine of Creation §40.[1]

---

1. Karl Barth, *Kirchliche Dogmatik* III:1, *Die Lehre von der Schöpfung* (Zollikon-Zurich: Evangelischer Verlag, 1957). Hereafter, I will refer to Barth's magnum opus in the shortened form *KD*,

However, not only does Barth take a christological approach, but he takes this approach as a way to reclaim and restate for his own age what he views as essential in the Christian faith,[2] while also producing a dogmatic compatible with certain "external intellectual demands" of that age. That Barth viewed this faith as having been either sidetracked or neglected by the liberal theologians of the nineteenth century goes almost without saying. He viewed their approach as a dead end, with its shortcomings epitomized in two rather selectively interpreted occurrences of 1914: Troeltsch's giving up of his chair of theology for one in philosophy, and the support that most of Barth's former theology teachers expressed for the Kaiser's war policy.[3] Barth's reaction, as he later describes it, was unequivocal:

> In despair over what this indicated about the signs of the time I suddenly realized that I could no longer follow either their ethics and dogmatics or their understanding of the Bible and of history. For me at least, 19th-century theology no longer held any future.[4]

If the Christian faith was to be maintained and continued, another approach would have to be worked out—or perhaps more accurately to Barth's way of thinking, "rediscovered" and "reappropriated."

To get a sense of this "new yet old" approach, I need simply mention two of the characteristics displayed throughout much of Barth's work. On the one hand, he radically downplayed the historical-critical method, beginning with his monumental *Epistle to the Romans*, in favor of an approach that sought to rekindle the immediacy of the divine-human encounter through the words of Holy Scripture. On the

---

with reference made to the appropriate volume (e.g., *KD* III), part (e.g., *KD* III:1), section (e.g., *KD* III:1, §40), and, where pertinent, to the appropriate subsection (e.g., *KD* III:1, §40.1). Full bibliographic information on these volumes is given in the bibliography. All translations are mine.

2. I recognize that speaking here in terms of an "essence of Christianity" could be deemed inappropriate, since Barth himself was suspicious of the motives behind such efforts at distillation. But because he does speak of a "center of theology," as Stephen Sykes points out, I assert that such terms are not entirely unjustified in relation to Barth. See Sykes, *The Identity of Christianity* (Philadelphia: Fortress Press, 1984), 176, 193.

3. In fairness to Troeltsch, it should be noted that, with regard to his move to a chair in philosophy, certain academic factions were working against him and, with regard to the support for the Kaiser, he was not among those academics who signed.

4. Karl Barth, *The Humanity of God*, trans. John Newton Thomas and Thomas Weiser (Richmond, Va.: John Knox Press, 1960), 14.

other, he often presented his theology not by inventing new forms, but by adopting the credal and catechetical formulations of the past and using them as the springboard for his own comments, as he did, for example, in his *Credo*, his lectures on the Heidelberg Catechism and on Calvin's Catechism, and his *Dogmatics in Outline*.[5] Not surprisingly, both tendencies show up throughout his doctrine of Creation, where Barth appeals to the formulations established by the Apostles' Creed—formulations that appear again and again over the course of his exposition. Likewise, to give the most obvious example, the bulk of *Church Dogmatics*. III:1 consists simply of Barth's exposition of the Genesis creation narratives. As he observes in the preface to that volume, he came to see "the appropriate dogmatic task here to be nothing other than the repetition of the 'saga'" contained in those narratives.[6]

Quite simply, Barth rejected any modern skepticism or condescension toward Scripture or the theological legacy of the past. Instead, he pursued a course based on Scripture and descended from, in conversation with, and, in many respects, guided by that theological legacy. To shift the image somewhat, he argued that modern theologians must have the same loyalty to the Bible as their forebears, while serving their apprenticeship under the tutelage of the old masters. If they appreciate the truth and insights to be garnered from that instruction, they will maintain their allegiance to Scripture and continue to respect their teachers even when they have set up shop on their own.

Yet Barth was certainly not enslaved to the past. He makes this quite clear in some cautionary remarks aimed at one of the two theological trends evident to him in 1951:

> The other path, which *rebus sic stantibus* I also provisionally regard as a dead end, is that which today is chiefly taken by many (luckily not by all) Lutherans, namely, the path of a modernizing restoration of the Protestant dogma of the sixteenth century and its presuppositions from the early church. Against the reproach that I have disregarded the theological Fathers, I need make no protest in view of the content of the

---

5. For a slightly different construal of this "new yet old" approach, see Sykes, *Identity of Christianity*, 200.

6. *KD* III:1.

hitherto appearing volumes of this dogmatic and my other writings. But it is one thing to orient oneself to the Fathers, to learn from them, actually to take up their unforgettable [*unverlierbaren*] perceptions—if that's what's meant, I will henceforth gladly let my neighbors on the left chide me as "orthodox"—but it is quite another thing to wish to think and speak on principle from out of their perceptions and confessions, or from out of any one church order [*Kirchentum*]. Nobody should claim to have learned that from me (seeing how some have already made me responsible for encouraging this undertaking!). "Confessions" exist so that one may work through them (not once, but ever anew), but not so that one returns to them to settle down domestically in them, in order then to do one's further thinking out of them and bound to them. It never served the church well to pin itself stubbornly to *one* man— whether he was named Thomas (let us be glad that we neither have nor need a Thomas!) or Luther or Calvin—and in his school to pin itself to *one* form of its doctrine. And it absolutely never served the church well to look, as a matter of principle, backward rather than forward, as if it actually wanted to agree to a "realized eschatology," as if it actually did not believe in the coming Lord![7]

These comments suggest why Barth felt no qualms about introducing certain major innovations into his own theology. He was not bound to one heritage, but felt free to draw on many; he did not look solely to the past, but felt free to gaze at the present and future. After all, to use the image mentioned above, he has set up shop on his own. As a result, if he chooses to engage the Christian faith in conversations with the modern mind, he may freely do so.

Moreover, Barth implies that the justification for such conversations stems from one's obligations as a theologian, rather than from any obligation imposed by outside standards. Paraphrasing parts of the above quotation, one is to look forward rather than backward, and to speak out of one's own perceptions of faith and not merely to repeat those of the past. Yet if one actually follows these guidelines, it becomes virtually inevitable that one's theological constructions will be determined at least in part by the needs and concerns of one's

---

7. *KD* III:4, foreword.

contemporaries. Once this happens, the door is open to the influence of the assumptions underlying those needs and concerns. In fact, far from being merely a theological throwback, Barth took seriously the insights and challenges of contemporary science, history, and philosophy.[8] Indeed, to the dismay of some of his readers, there are certain traditional assumptions that Barth simply discarded.[9] But he also insisted that dogmatics would meet these challenges of modernity on its own terms, while also engaging them with its own insights and challenges. In other words, he envisioned a relation between equals engaged in both give and take.

Barth's Response to Modernity

To begin with, then, seeking such a relation between a long-established Christianity and his own age hardly means Barth proposed a new form of assimilation or accommodation of an "ancient" Christian faith to a modern ethos. He did not view himself as "bringing up to date" an otherwise obsolete faith. One need only cite the precedent he established in *The Epistle to the Romans* to be disabused of this interpretation. Barth wrote this revolutionary work quite aware that it simply ignores concerns produced by the historical distance separating Christianity's original age and his own:

> My whole energy of interpreting has been expended in an endeavour to
> see through and beyond history into the spirit of the Bible, which is
> the Eternal Spirit. What was once of grave importance, is so still. What is
> to-day of grave importance—and not merely crotchety and incidental—
> stands in direct connexion with that ancient gravity.[10]

Clearly, Barth did not view the issue of historical relativism as presenting any insurmountable, or even real, problems for Christianity.[11] The

---

8. See Langdon Gilkey, *Naming the Whirlwind: The Renewal of God-Language* (Indianapolis: Bobbs-Merrill, 1969), 82–83.

9. See Gregory G. Bolich, *Karl Barth and Evangelicalism* (Downers Grove, Ill.: InterVarsity Press, 1980). Bolich does a good job summarizing, among other things, the critical observations of American evangelicals such as Cornelius van Til.

10. Karl Barth, Preface to the first edition of *The Epistle to the Romans*, trans. Edwyn C. Hoskyns from the 6th ed. (London: Oxford University Press, 1968), 1.

11. Other theologians, however, are not so sanguine. See Sykes, *Identity of Christianity*, 195.

theologian could remain unconcerned with "modernizing" or "demythologizing" (consider, e.g., his long-running disagreement with Rudolf Bultmann), because in Barth's view the problems posed by the modern era are essentially no greater than those of past eras. What he writes concerning certain justifications for dogmatic prolegomena would seem to apply here: "The assumed difference of our age in comparison to earlier ones cannot be substantiated theologically. Has there ever been an age in which theology has not fundamentally confronted some all-out negation of the revelation believed in the Church?"[12]

Having to face the challenges of rationalists, atheists, secularists, competing religions, and different cultural assumptions is something the church has had to do from the very beginning, and thus it has always tailored its dogmatics at least in part according to those challenges. "The situation of the church that forms the space of dogmatic work is not always the same, but time and again imposes special conditions on this work."[13]

In other words, while Barth did not view historical relativism as posing any insurmountable problems to theology, he did in fact accept the notion of historical relativism itself. As a result, he readily acknowledged that dogmatics is a "historical exercise," that is, it is not a *repository* of eternal truths formulated in one way once and for all, but a *task* that must be done anew in each age.[14] To view it otherwise is to make the mistaken assumption that the divine address in revelation is equivalent to the human appropriation contained in dogmas.[15] Barth firmly rejects any such equation:

> Revelatory truth is the freely acting God on his own and all alone. The dogmas set forth in the creeds, which are venerable because they are the earned results of dogmatic labor in the common knowledge of the church at a distinct time, can and should *guide* our own dogmatic labor, but at no point take the place of that labor by virtue of their authority. Furthermore, dogmatics *cannot* be engaged in the mere compilation, repetition, and definition of biblical teaching. . . . That is

---

12. *KD* I:1, §2.1.
13. Ibid.
14. See *KD* I:1, §1.2.
15. Ibid.

why dogmatics as such does not ask what the apostles and prophets have said, but rather what we ourselves should say "on the basis of the apostles and prophets."[16]

That is, God's revelatory truth *updates itself* in the ever new and self-consistent divine act. As a result, it neither needs nor is open to human adjustment or revision. However, the human explanations and formulations of that truth have *always* required periodic renewal, because only in this manner can each successive generation own up to its responsibilities before God's revelation. Moreover, if each generation takes this responsibility seriously, seeing itself as simply doing what each previous age has done and each future age will do, then the all-too-human tendency of presuming to possess and control the *final* truth will have a harder time arising.

Indeed, according to Stephen Sykes, it is precisely this issue of control that leads Barth to distinguish between "systematic" theology and the more "appropriate" approach. Paraphrasing and summarizing Barth's position as expressed in *Church Dogmatics* I:2, §24.2, Sykes suggests that Barth rejected systematic theology "because system tends to mean the presupposition of 'a concretely formulated first principle or a whole series of principles,' followed by a development consisting of an analysis of it or them. But how can such a procedure allow for obedience to the Word of God?"[17]

The implication is that "man-made" concepts now direct one's theology, rather than the freely acting God just described, which means it cannot avoid becoming an idolatrous exercise, rather than a properly pious and obedient one. To counter this tendency, says Sykes,

> Barth points us, in general illustration of correct dogmatic method in operation, to the example of Calvin. Specifically, against the more scholarly method of fundamental articles, Barth sets Melancthon's and Calvin's method of *Loci*, or topics "which did not pretend . . . to be rooted and held together in any higher system than that of the Word of God". . . What [Calvin] did was to gather in a certain arrangement the

---

16. *KD* I:1, §1.2.
17. Sykes, *Identity of Christianity*, 189.

topics which the faith itself seems to require, adequately interrelated inasmuch as all refer to the confession of Jesus Christ, but not systematically deduced from one basic principle.[18]

In other words, one's exposition will display a certain orderliness, but the substance of that exposition will be in no way determined by, or subordinated to, one's systematic "principle." Instead, it will be determined by, and subordinated to, the Word.

This issue of control also gives Barth's understanding and acceptance of historical relativism its distinct twist, and makes him reject such moves as demythologization. In relativizing the past, according to Barth's critique, such approaches also implicitly absolutize the present, by means of the assumption that only in the modern era has human knowledge really "come of age." By claiming such a distinction for modernity, we actually vest our own perspectives and assumptions with final say over all the insights and claims handed down to us from the past. Hence, the danger of approaches such as demythologization is that in modifying the form in which revelatory truth is conveyed, they may also alter, corrupt, or even eliminate its content. In response, Barth sought to turn the notion of historical relativism back on its most insistent promoters in order to reduce the likelihood of such conscious or unconscious usurpations of power. He did this with his implication, however historically anachronistic it might in fact be, that past generations, too, have always had to confront challenges akin to those posed by modernity, and thus have always had some sense that their theological formulations were relative to their particular situation. If this is the case, then no special claims can be made for modernity.

Barth uses much the same logic in his comments about the relationship between theology and science. Consider what he writes in the first volume, indeed the first subsection of the first proposition, of his *Church Dogmatics*. He offers three "practical" reasons for designating theology as a "science," and in so doing he also describes its relation to the other sciences. His points are worth quoting in full:

---

18. Ibid., 197, citing Barth from *KD* 1:2, 870.

By designating theology as "science," it brings itself into line; it recognizes itself as a human striving for truth in solidarity with other such endeavors of this sort now assembled under this term; it actually protests against the idea of its ontological elevation above these others (an idea that could easily creep in by using the distinction-asserting designations of the ancients, i.e., *doctrina* or even *sapientia*); it remembers that it is indeed *only* "science," and thus it remembers the "secularity" in which it works, even in its own relatively special way, even in the highest realms.[19]

In other words, one of the reasons for designating theology as a science is to maintain its *own* humility. It is not the "queen" of the sciences, and thus may not lord it over them or claim any special prerogatives. It must forsake the grandiosity that too often characterized it in the past, and recognize that it is a human effort just as they are. Out of this recognition, however, arises the next point:

By not simply relinquishing the term "science" to the others, it furthermore registers (with all due respect to the classical tradition) the necessary protest against any general and admittedly "heathen" concept of science. It can really do no harm to its most stalwart representatives or to the university to be reminded by the proximity of the theologian under the same roof that the quasi-religious absolutism of their interpretation of the concept is not in fact undisputed, and that the tradition commencing with the name of Aristotle is in any case only one among others and that in any case the Christian church certainly does *not* count Aristotle as an ancestor.[20]

That is, as a "science" itself, theology is not only "humbled," but it may also challenge the other sciences to humility. Barth argues that no single science has a right to monopolize that title, and neither is there any one theory of science that can qualify or disqualify the individual sciences. As he wrote earlier in §1.1: "The decision, whether someone or something is what he or it claims to be, is always decided

---

19. *KD* I:1, §1.1.
20. Ibid.

by an *event* proving or not proving this claim, and not by ever-so-weighty stipulations concerning the legitimacy or nonlegitimacy of the claim."[21]

For Barth, the "event" that legitimates the science of theology occurs in the encounter with Christ. In fact, the encounter with Christ and the message it communicates determine Barth's last point:

> Finally, by actually including itself under the same name with the other "sciences" (despite the fundamentally irreconcilable difference in the understanding of the term), theology demonstrates that it does not take their heathenism seriously enough to separate itself under another name exclusive of them; on the contrary, it counts them along with itself as part of the church, in spite of their failure vis-à-vis the theological task and in spite of a concept of science that is unacceptable to theology. It believes in the forgiveness of sins and not in the final reality of a heathen pantheon.[22]

In other words, theology places itself among and converses with the other sciences not as a concession or due to external compulsion, but in order to remain true to one of its own most fundamental principles. While there may be no final justification on the human level for such a universalist and inclusive attitude, in light of the "legitimating event" establishing theology, this would appear to be the only possible option. Of course, one can easily imagine at least some scientists in the other disciplines detecting and being put off by the condescension evident in this passage, but it is likely no worse than a similarly superior attitude displayed by some non-Christian scientists toward theology.

This is the way Barth describes the relation between the theological and other sciences in *Church Dogmatics* I:1; in writing his doctrine of Creation, the same assumptions are present. As a result, it is hardly surprising to find in Barth no explicit concern of the sort voiced by Schleiermacher to Lücke that the church might have to "do without" not only its belief in the six-day creation but "the concept of creation

---

21. Ibid.; emphasis mine. By stating it in these terms, Barth is obviously claiming that the sciences are all ultimately "grounded" in a similar manner, and are therefore in that respect "equal."
22. Ibid.

itself, as it is usually understood." Yet if Barth's theology is not merely atavistic, blithely ignoring such issues, why does he not suppose there might be such a "doing without"? Like Schleiermacher, Barth rejects a siege mentality for theology, asserting that its task is not to close its mental gates and fight off any and all encroachments of modern and scientific insight and discovery that might undermine a literal understanding of the creation story: "Retreats behind Chinese walls never served theology well."[23] But unlike Schleiermacher, he shows no preoccupation with establishing "an eternal covenant between the living Christian faith and completely free, independent scientific inquiry, so that faith does not hinder science and science does not exclude faith."[24] For one thing, Barth already takes for granted the distinct and independent status of the dogmatic and other scientific disciplines. In that sense, nothing needs to be "established."

But Barth also understands the relations between these disciplines in a significantly different way than Schleiermacher. For Schleiermacher, the science of dogmatics is certainly distinct from the other empirical sciences, because the former has as its object an "inward fact" or "feeling," while the latter have as their objects "outward facts." However, even given this difference, they also operate, as it were, on the same level. Thus, there can be no overlap or competition between them. Indeed, Schleiermacher clearly meant this precise apportioning of their respective tasks and spheres to promote the closest possible cooperation between them—and in an age that had not yet heard the challenges of Marx, Huxley, and Freud, this was not an unreasonable hope. Barth, by contrast, does not make a distinction between "inward facts" and "outward facts," or between "feeling" and "knowing;" rather, he distinguishes between what could be called "ordinary" knowledge and the "knowledge of faith." Were this a perfect world, with reciprocal respect shown by every science to each of the others, there would be no tension between these concepts. But this is not a perfect world, and he fully recognizes that there can be confusion, overlap, and competition between the various disciplines in defining and pursuing their

23. Barth, *Humanity of God*, 18.
24. Friedrich Schleiermacher, *On the "Glaubenslehre": Two Letters to Dr. Lücke*, trans. James Duke and Francis Fiorenza, American Academy of Religion Texts and Translations Series 3 (Chico, Calif.: Scholars Press, 1981), 64.

proper concerns. So while one is going about one's appropriate business, on occasion one may be required as well to guard one's discipline against improper encroachments and to exercise critiques of other disciplines—perhaps doing nothing more than challenging them to adhere to their own professed methods and ideals.[25] Consider, for example, comments made in Barth's preface to his *Church Dogmatics* III:1 on the doctrine of creation (some of which I have already cited):

> Someone will likely reproachfully inquire why I have not tackled the question of natural science, which is so obvious in this context. Originally, I reckoned I would have to do so, until it became clear to me that, in reference to that which the Holy Scripture and the Christian church mean by the divine work of creation, there can be absolutely no natural scientific questions, objections, or even supplementary assistance [*Hilfsstellungen*]. Hence, one will find in the heart of the present book a great deal about "naive" Hebrew "saga," but nothing at all about the apologetic and polemic that might have been expected here. In point of fact, I saw the appropriate dogmatic task here to be nothing other than the repetition of the "saga"; moreover, I found this task far more noble and more rewarding than the dilettante vexations to which I would have had to apply myself otherwise. *Natural science has free scope beyond that which theology has to describe as the work of the Creator. And theology may and must move freely where natural science—which is strictly that and not surreptitiously a pagan gnosis and doctrine—has its proper*

---

25. Cf. David Tracy, *Blessed Rage for Order* (New York: Seabury Press, 1975), 27–28. His observations reinforce and supplement this reading of Barth:

> Indeed, the neo-orthodox theologians can be interpreted as the theological expression of the same role of both acceptance and negation of liberal modernity which Marx, Freud, and Nietzsche played in the wider secular culture. . . . Not a lack of regard for the theological relevance of cultural analysis (as with the orthodox), but a different, a post-modern cultural analysis impelled the early Barth to challenge his liberal forebears. The fact is that the neo-orthodox theologians (here Barth joins Bultmann, Brunner, Tillich and the Niebuhrs) shared the repugnance of the postwar cultural period for the evolutionary optimism and for the now oppressive modernist model of autonomous man's possibilities widespread in the late nineteenth- and early twentieth-century liberal periods. On this interpretation, the criticism which neo-orthodoxy made against liberalism and modernism was not a simple rejection of the liberal enterprise. Rather, neo-orthodoxy was a continuation of that enterprise . . . [but with certain critiques. One was the insistence] . . . that the liberal analysis of the human situation was able to account at best for human finitude and possibility, but was utterly unable to account for those negative elements of tragedy, of terror, indeed, of sin in human existence.

boundary. It is also my opinion, however, that future expositors of the Christian doctrine of creation will still find worthwhile problems in determining the where and how of this mutual boundary.[26]

In other words, Barth does not undertake his dogmatic task with a view to establishing an "eternal covenant" between faith and science, and thus by extension, between dogmatics and the various specific sciences. Rather, he simply assumes their respective autonomy and self-determination. Ideally, each discipline will converse with and even learn from the other, but neither is subservient to, dependent upon, or answerable to the other. In a sense, the contrast with Schleiermacher is not so much one of substance as of "mood." Schleiermacher sought a spirit of peaceful coexistence and cooperation, although it must be acknowledged that certain comments throughout *The Christian Faith* do suggest his dogmatic work would not be compatible with a strictly materialistic or reductionistic science.[27] Barth, however, is consistently more wary, assuming the need to maintain a stance of "armed neutrality."[28]

Perhaps what Barth says about the role of the historical-critical method in biblical interpretation applies in this broader relation also: "It is concerned with the preparation of the intelligence."[29] What does this mean? It certainly implies in part that once one is so "prepared," the dogmatic task proper proceeds according to its own rules and purpose.[30] But what else does it imply? It is a rather loaded phrase, and Barth might be hiding some of his concessions behind it. For example, is it the historical-critical or scientific preparation of the intelligence that disallows any historical or literal understanding of the Genesis narratives? One can hardly imagine dogmatics foregoing historical or literal claims on this matter—even if they were not of central concern— had not the sciences in some manner compelled it. Thus, when Barth limits from the start the scope of traditional claims, he is simply making a virtue of necessity.

---

26. *KD* III:1, foreword; emphasis mine.
27. See, e.g., passages in *Gl* §§4.4, 34.2, 47.1, 49.1, 55.1, 59.1–3, and 158.1.
28. Perhaps the 1940 photograph of Barth as a member of the Swiss armed auxiliary best captures this attitude! See Eberhard Busch, *Karl Barth: His Life from Letters and Autobiographical Texts*, trans. John Bowden (Philadelphia: Fortress Press, 1976), 296.
29. Barth, *Epistle to the Romans*, 1.
30. Cf. Gilkey, *Naming the Whirlwind*, 87.

Nevertheless, such preparation can also be made to serve a more positive role for dogmatics by clarifying the boundaries between dogmatics and science. For example, when Barth describes the Genesis narratives as presenting "nonhistorical history" or "saga," he does so in part to assert the limitations of the social and even natural sciences, and to delineate the proper realm of dogmatics. Consider his efforts to discriminate in the following example between different kinds of history:

> The history of creation is unhistorical [*unhistorische*] or, more precisely stated, *pre*historical history [*prae historische Geschichte*]. We will therefore take good care not to fall back into the equally impossible exegetical and dogmatic proposition that it is *not* history, but the costume of an ahistorical [*geschichtslosen*] and timeless reality. Yet we will, on the other hand, declare on exegetical and dogmatic grounds that it is *not historical* history. Not all history is historical. We repeat: precisely in its immediacy to God, all history is in fact unhistorical, that is, it cannot be deduced and compared and for that reason it is undemonstrable, not perceptible, and not conceivable—it is all this without ceasing on that account to be genuine history. Precisely in its decisive components or dimension, precisely in that respect in which alone it is finally important and interesting, all history is unhistorical—just because it is genuine history. And this all the more, and more tangibly, the more this component predominates, the more this dimension—the immediacy of history to God—becomes manifest. The history of creation has *only* this component. In it, Creator and creature stand opposite one another *only* in immediacy. Precisely for this reason is it in a supreme sense genuine, but also in a supreme sense unhistorical, prehistorical history. And for precisely this reason, it can also only be the object of an unhistorical, prehistorical narrative *presentation* and narrative *account [unhistorischen, praehistorischen Geschichts darstellung und Geschichts schreibung].*[31]

This passage suggests that Barth was aware of some of the debates occurring in his age among historians over what constitutes legitimate

---

31. *KD* III:1, §41.1.

historical knowledge. The historiographical assumptions of the nine-teenth century no longer held complete sway in the academy, so there was room for concepts such as "nonhistorical history."[32]

If we ask what Schleiermacher might have thought about Barth's suggestion that the historical-critical method and the insights of the sciences (i.e., the nontheological ones) only "prepare" the intelligence for biblical exposition, we can well imagine that he would have agreed. Schleiermacher, too, held the various subdisciplines of theology to be distinct and autonomous from the nontheological historical and nat-ural sciences, even though the methods employed by each were often similar. Yet when one considers the wording of his comment to Lücke regarding the "eternal covenant" between science and faith, the rela-tion does not appear to be one between equals. In the relation of sci-ence and faith, the norms of science seem to be the given to which faith must adapt, so that the latter will neither hinder nor be excluded by the former. One detects in Schleiermacher's phrase no indication that faith might legitimately challenge or limit the claims of science. And if this is so, one cannot help but conclude that the same would hold true as well for the theological sciences, dogmatics included. This certainly marks a contrast with Barth.[33] This contrast could reflect nothing more than a certain theological reserve on Schleiermacher's part or bluster on Barth's. But it might also reflect a difference in circum-stances, and thus a difference in perceived needs and possibilities. The explosive expansion of the sciences in the nineteenth century was just beginning during Schleiermacher's life, but to someone of his insight their implicit and radical challenge to church tradition was clear. Indeed, their challenge was likely far more pressing and monolithic than it would be in a later era, when the limitations and drawbacks of the sciences had become more obvious. After all, Schleiermacher wrote at a time when the potential benefits of the scientific and industrial revolution appeared virtually limitless and the authority exercised by the mindset behind that revolution went almost unchallenged among "sophisticated" thinkers. Barth, however, began his doctrine of Creation with a clear memory of the First World War and under the

---

32. Cf. Van A. Harvey, *The Historian and the Believer* (Philadelphia: Westminster Press, 1966), ch. 3.
33. Cf. my consideration of Barth's attitude toward, and willingness to challenge, the other sciences, pp. 48–50.

shadow of the Second—cataclysms that demonstrated how some fruits of the tree of science, technology, and industry were far from beneficial. Moreover, it was clear that the tree which produced them could not, of itself, prevent them. As Barth later observed regarding the challenge facing nineteenth-century theologians and those of his own era: "We have lived through harder times, have endured worse things than they did, and we are thereby, strangely enough, made more free. . . . Modern man can no longer impress us, as he impressed them, in light of his performances in this century."[34] It may be more a matter of style than substance, but Barth comes across as far less on the defensive than his predecessor.

A further and more explicit statement of Barth's position vis-à-vis science and the doctrine of Creation appears in a letter written in 1965 to his grandniece, Christine Barth. He comments on a classroom situation about which she had written him, concerning biblical and scientific accounts of creation. His response again indicates his understanding of the role and relation of the two accounts, and it merits full quotation:

> Has no one explained to you in your seminar that one can as little compare the biblical creation story and a scientific theory like that of evolution as one can compare, shall we say, an organ and a vacuum-cleaner—that there can be as little question of harmony between them as of contradiction?
>
> The creation story is a witness to the beginning or becoming of all reality distinct from God in light of God's later acts and words relating to his people Israel—naturally in the form of a saga or poem. The theory of evolution is an attempt to explain the same reality in its inner nexus—naturally in the form of a scientific hypothesis.
>
> The creation story deals only with the becoming of all things, and therefore with the revelation of God, which is inaccessible to science as such. The theory of evolution deals with what has become, as it appears to human observation and research and as it invites human interpretation. Thus one's attitude to the creation story and the theory of evolution can take the form of an either/or only if one shuts oneself off

---

34. Barth, *Humanity of God*, 17.

completely either from faith in God's revelation or from the mind (or opportunity) for scientific understanding.

So tell the teacher concerned that she should distinguish what is to be distinguished and not shut herself off completely from either side.[35]

Barth's position holds that when the biblical and scientific accounts of "the Beginning" are properly understood, they are complementary rather than mutually exclusive. Each account has its own subject matter, method, and purpose—and thus its own proper boundaries. If each stays within its boundaries, it need be responsible only to its own norms. For the church, then, there is no reason to suppose that it might have to "do without" *parts* of the traditional story of creation, because its task is to understand or reinterpret the *whole* of that story in the appropriate manner. After all, if the witness to the becoming of all reality distinct from God "naturally" took the form of a saga or poem, then naturally it must be interpreted as such. This means that all the various details included in that witness ought to be given their due, although according to the norms implicit in the genre of "saga." Similarly, if science seeks to explain that same reality in its "inner nexus," then "naturally" it will employ a different genre of understanding and explanation, namely, scientific hypothesis.

To put it in the plainest terms, Barth simply assumes from the outset that the creation narratives do not present a literal, historical account of the world's origin. As a result, he stands under no obligation to excise any part of them that might conflict with current scientific theory, because the possibility of conflict has been ruled out by definition. In this regard, he simply concedes the field of natural or historical explanation to science, thereby showing himself to be firmly planted on the modern slope of the premodern/modern divide. But neither does he view the "objective" sciences, whether natural or social, as capable of demonstrating irrefutably that the cosmos in fact exists, that it in fact came to be, and that it is in fact a "creation," with all that that notion implies. Science can only *presuppose* these first two points—a move that is itself a form of faith—and only a specific faith

---

35. Karl Barth, *Letters, 1961–1968*, ed. Jürgen Fangmeier and Hinrich Stoevesandt, trans. and ed. Geoffrey W. Bromiley (Grand Rapids, Mich.: Wm. B. Eerdmans, 1981), 184.

can affirm the last point.[36] In this regard, Barth does not so much contradict scientific knowledge as suggest its limitations, and thus also the limitations of any dogmatic too much under the influence of the prevailing modern ethos. He will suggest that "objective" knowledge must be supplemented—indeed, undergirded—with a "knowledge of faith" received through revelation. Consider the following segment taken from an excursus found early on in Barth's doctrine:

> In the face of all ancient and modern science, one ought to have argued from the very outset as follows: If the world is not created by God, then it does not exist. If we do not recognize it as created by God, then we do not recognize that it exists. That it is created by God, however, we recognize only on the basis of God's self-witness and therefore in faith. Therefore, we recognize only in faith that the world exists. The pressure on theology coming from science would have been more tolerable later if theology had itself pressed more strongly and effectively its own (*in thesi* solemnly enough affirmed) divine science earlier, if it had been clear in recognizing that it is above all the creatures and not the Creator of which we are not certain, and that in order to be sure of it we need proof or revelation. If theology had said in this case and in this comprehensive sense that the creation of the world by God can be recognized only in faith, then as a result the pernicious appearance of a rearguard action would have also been avoided.[37]

Does this position differ with Schleiermacher's? The correct answer appears variously to be: probably not, no, and yes. First of all, insofar as Barth considers the whole of the creation story to be a saga, he may well be doing without that which Schleiermacher predicted the church would have to relinquish, namely, the belief in the six-day creation and the concept of creation "as it is usually understood." If that "usual" understanding is a *literal* understanding, then neither Schleiermacher nor Barth advocate it. Both understand the Genesis account as a "poetic" rather than historical, scientific description of the world's origin. If one has natural or historical questions to ask about creation,

---

36. See Barth's excursus in *KD* III:1, §40.
37. *KD* III:1, §40.1.

then one should turn to the sciences, which may or may not be able to answer, depending upon the current state of scientific knowledge. Thus, secondly, Schleiermacher and Barth concur in their understanding of the realm in which science operates and the "raw material" it considers. When Barth suggests that scientific hypotheses such as the theory of evolution seek to explain the reality of creation "in its inner nexus"—a realm that dogmatics does not properly consider—it evokes Schleiermacher's assertion that explaining the inner dynamics of the natural causal nexus is a task of the natural sciences alone, because dogmatics deals solely with God's relation to nature as a whole.

Yet ultimately, Schleiermacher also understands the Genesis account of creation to be *merely* poetic, the product of a primitive human imagination seeking to fill in the gaps in human knowledge by the only means open to it at the time. Thus, its various details are neither a proper object of dogmatic consideration nor a useful complement to science; indeed, the supposed "knowledge" it offers is to be *replaced* by that produced through scientific investigation, because the proper role and sole capacity of dogmatics is the explication of the pious feeling.[38] Barth would certainly agree that on this level, biblical "knowledge" is no longer valid. Nevertheless, he still views the Genesis accounts as a proper, indeed essential, object of dogmatic consideration for this doctrine. On the one hand, science has no access to the absolute beginning, while, on the other, even as poetry, that account may still act as a vehicle of God's revelation. In this capacity it may actually serve as an underpinning for science. Indeed, without such an underpinning, the knowledge gained through science would seem to lack any ultimate significance, and probably any conscience as well.

In other words, Schleiermacher meets the external intellectual demands confronting his doctrine of creation by paring away any and all mythological content evident in Scripture (including the Genesis creation accounts) to reach the still valid "existential" or "affective" core of biblical testimony, which he assumes may then be explained in a manner compatible with science. As a result, his doctrine of creation proper is itself quite brief. It simply specifies and explicates this core

---

38. Cf. *Gl*, §40.

feeling retroactively, in reference to an event from which no immediate experience has come but which is to be understood as both logically plausible and foundational. The further—and by far the most substantial—exposition of this feeling is then carried out in his doctrine of preservation and in those sections of the first and second parts of his system dealing with the constitution of the world, which is to say, in reference to conditions that are immediately felt. Barth, by contrast, meets these demands in his doctrine of creation by affirming that, yes, the content of the creation stories presents a "saga" rather than objective information, but that this is hardly a shortcoming, since the "historic [*geschichtliche*] reality" of the beginning of creation and time "eludes all historical [*historischen*] observation and reporting."[39] On this topic, even the historian or scientist cannot present "objective information." Consider Barth's statement in *Dogmatics in Outline*:

> If we take this concept [of creation] seriously, it must be at once clear that we are not confronted by a realm which in any sense may be accessible to human view or even to human thought. Natural science may be our occupation with its view of development; it may tell us the tale of the millions of years in which the cosmic process has gone on; but when could natural science have ever penetrated to the fact that there is one world which runs through this development? Continuation is quite a different thing from this sheer beginning, with which the concept of creation has to do.[40]

Of course, this does not mean the role of saga is to augment historical or scientific explanation with "objective" data or information otherwise unavailable. But this saga does offer both general affirmations and distinct interpretations that the social or natural sciences cannot. Hence, Barth sees it as the proper object of dogmatic exposition precisely because it is an original and authoritative source for the church's affirmations about (1) God's activity in relation to the *whole* of creation, and thus the *meaning* of creation in general and

---

39. KD III:1, §41.
40. Karl Barth, *Dogmatics in Outline*, trans. G. T. Thomson (1949; repr., New York: Harper & Row, 1959), 51.

(2) many of the essential—which is to say, *proper*—characteristics of creaturely existence. Without the concept of "creation," without the unity of purpose and meaning contained within that concept, the cosmos can be nothing more than brute process. Considered strictly on its own, it is not only mute but meaningless, an apparently endless succession of beings and events with no other "purpose" than the continuation of the process. If we are to find some significance beyond this perpetual motion, if we are to find some meaning for the individuals involved, we must look not to the sciences but elsewhere.

Barth's position is that the Christian tradition and modernity are independent yet complementary, and he does not so much argue this position as simply assert it. Nevertheless, his exposition does indeed reveal certain "concessions" to modernity while also suggesting some limitations to the methods and positions of science and historical criticism. Indeed, this pattern of "Yes, but . . ." is characteristic of Barth's approach, and it appears throughout his exposition: Yes, the church must surrender any assumption that the creation narratives give us a literal account of the world's beginning, and if it wants "objective" information about the inner workings of the cosmos, it should follow the instruction of the sciences. But the sciences cannot, if they are true to their professed techniques, offer answers to questions regarding the world's ultimate origin, meaning, value, or goal. Only faith can do this, and of course the "faith" Barth uses is the one handed down to us through Christian tradition.

Barth's Christological Orientation

Barth makes the christological orientation of his doctrine of Creation both clear and pervasive. In his first propositional heading, §40, Barth initiates the entirety of his doctrine. In it, Barth presents his most basic assertion about creation:

> The insight that humanity owes its being and character, together with all the reality distinct from God, to God's creation, is realized solely in the reception of, and in the reply to, the divine self-witness, that is, solely in faith in Jesus Christ: in the recognition of the unity of Creator and

creature actualized in him and in the life in the present mediated
through him, under the authority and in the experience of the goodness
of the Creator vis-à-vis his creature.[41]

In other words, to speak of the world around us as a "creation"—and
of its logical corollary, a "Creator"—requires a prior affirmation of the
divine self-witness in Jesus Christ. That is, one cannot develop even
the notion of the world and cosmos as creation, let alone a full-blown
doctrine of creation, without having first acknowledged God's revelation of the Creator-creature union in Christ. Without this divine confirmation, one cannot know that the world is, in fact, a creation. The
evidence available is ambiguous at best, and might even suggest the
world is an illusion or even a nightmare. But Christ makes it possible
to affirm—among other things—that the world is a creation, that
human life does have significance, and that existence is at root good.

In so doing, of course, one must also recognize that that affirmation will always have the character of an article of faith, in the same
way that one's affirmation of Christ is an article of faith. One ought
not suppose that once creation is affirmed, the doctrine itself is filled
in by means of a scientific consideration of the world around us.
Even though it has assertions to make about that world, these do not
derive from empirical observation and inductive reasoning. Nor is
the doctrine based on any sort of Cartesian deduction from one's own
existence—even one's existence as a Christian. It is rather the response
to, indeed the "reproduction" (*Wiedergabe*) of what one receives in
revelation. Barth explicitly states that the "perception" or "realization"
(*Erkenntnis*) reproduced in a doctrine of creation is in no way something one develops or procures independently. It is "neither innate nor
accessible by way of observation and attendant reasoning," nor do we
possess for it any "organ" or "capability." Rather, it is something
"effected" solely on the basis of faith, "that is, in the reception of and
in response to the divine self-witness," although on that basis it is
indeed effected.[42] This self-witness is, in the first instance, Christ himself, but in Christ one will also recognize an encounter with the Creator.

---

41. *KD* III:1, §40.
42. Ibid.

Does this approach differ from Schleiermacher's? If one describes Schleiermacher as grounding his doctrine on "feeling" rather than "revelation"—that is, on a strictly internal, affective, and preverbal "sense" present in an individual rather than on an external and explicit "message" presented to a community—then the difference between him and Barth is obvious. If one adds to this the observation that for Schleiermacher the "feeling of absolute dependence" is a universal characteristic of human nature, in contrast to Barth's claim that the perception of the world and ourselves as "creatures" is not innate or the product of some inherent capability but comes solely from receiving the divine self-witness, then the difference appears even greater.

Yet from another perspective, apparent differences begin to dissolve. To begin with, one must recognize that Schleiermacher does not ground dogmatics *directly* upon pious feeling, and especially not the pious feeling of a single individual. Rather, as he states clearly in §19 of *The Christian Faith*, it is based on the doctrines (i.e., the public and common beliefs) "prevalent in a Christian church community at a given time."[43] Hence, his immediate dogmatic ground is neither merely subjective nor preverbal. Moreover, even if one were to trace matters back to the original "feeling of absolute dependence" behind these beliefs, one would still encounter Schleiermacher's assertion that this feeling never exists in isolation and is never manifested in a generic or universal way. Instead, it always actually exists only as it is modified in some specific, historical manner. For Christians, of course, this modification is effected by the consciousness of the antithesis between sin and grace brought about by the Redeemer—a consciousness that is in no way viewed as self-generated, but as entirely dependent upon the Redeemer "and his self-proclamation."[44] Thus, like Barth, Schleiermacher seems to be saying that the actual *Christian* perception of the world and ourselves as creatures is not innate, nor something we procure independently, even though Schleiermacher's position does clearly assume we have a prior capability for receiving it. If one then recognizes that this modified consciousness, far from being merely an

---

43. *Gl*, §19. See particularly his description of what he means by "prevalent doctrine" in §19.3. Cf. *Gl*, §27.

44. This reference to the Redeemer's "self-proclamation," which sounds so Barthian, comes from *Gl*, §19, postscript. See *Gl*, §11 as well.

amorphous "sense," actually produces a very specific set of feelings that in turn can produce very specific doctrines, then the contrast between a preverbal, apparently ill-defined state and an external, explicit message also diminishes—particularly when that message of revelation is not to be equated simply with the words of Scripture or the preacher. In other words, Barth and Schleiermacher appear to come from different directions, only to end up at nearly the same place. That is, both of them argue for the objectivity of their respective approaches, even while those approaches ultimately trace back to a basal "experience," which Schleiermacher describes in terms of feeling and Barth describes in terms of encounter or event.[45]

This encounter between the Christian and Christ thus serves as the presupposition for all that Barth will write. While Barth's dogmatic may appear outwardly to follow the "customary" order of theological exposition, insofar as his doctrine of Creation precedes his doctrine of reconciliation, its inner logic actually follows the "experiential" order.[46] Christ becomes the "known quantity" enabling a full and detailed formulation of a doctrine of Creation. But can we be more precise about the character and implications of this presupposition for Barth's doctrine? Where and when does this faith-producing encounter occur? What exactly is the nature of the faith produced by this encounter? Why does Barth make it the exclusive starting point for his doctrine? And what will the answers to these questions suggest about the remainder of Barth's exposition?

To begin with, Barth does explicitly state that all of his dogmatic deliberations stand or fall on Christ being this known quantity. But he states just as clearly that

> Jesus Christ is a known quantity in the comprehensive sense presupposed there and only there where he has called persons to *faith* in him and where he has found *faith* among them, that is, through the work of the Holy Spirit of the Father and the Son in the living realm [*Lebensraum*] of his community. We have presupposed that for us as his own, as members of his Body, as adherents of his church, He is in fact this known

---

45. See pp. 15–16. Cf. Sykes, *Identity of Christianity*, 191.
46. See p. 15.

quantity. And then, in light of this known quantity, we have seen and understood that the proposition concerning the creation of heaven and earth by God is true and necessary.[47]

The answer to our first question is, then, that the encounter occurs within the church. On the basis of its *present* living relation to God, in Christ, through the Holy Spirit, the faithful community will know that it is justified in applying to the world a very particular understanding or interpretation of that world's ongoing nature and origin. On the basis of its own encounter with Christ, each generation of the faith must seek to make its own enunciation of this "known quantity" as it pertains to Creation.

Of course, this does not mean that each generation is simply abandoned to its own devices, as if there were no carry over from one age to the next. The resources bequeathed to the community—preeminently through Scripture, but also in the creeds derived therefrom—certainly enable and require continuity between each new expression of a doctrine of Creation.[48] But that continuity is not automatic. For it to occur, there must first be faith.[49] In other words, the Christian understanding of Creation is not objective, and its claims are not self-evident or even empirically obvious to those outside the community. Instead, its claims are based on the revelation of God—which is, according to Barth, actually the only source of certainty. Yet this should not be taken as suggesting that a well-constructed doctrine of Creation has only a limited and parochial reach and applicability. It will also attempt to comprehend all that exists, thereby being universal. Thus, the Christian understanding of Creation should not be viewed as arbitrarily imposed upon the world, nor as forcing that world into an interpretation that obviously does not fit it, but as reflecting its real and intrinsic character. Nevertheless, this affirmation can only be made from within the community.

Thus, Barth is simply exercising a necessary restraint in the face of modern hermeneutical norms, which would challenge any biblically

---

47. *KD* III:1, §40; emphasis his.
48. Ibid.
49. Cf. Sykes, *Identity of Christianity*, 200.

derived statements claiming to present an objective description of the cosmos or a historically accurate account of "the Beginning." He does indeed show such restraint. But given some of the passages already cited, one can also clearly see that his position represents a challenge to the basic assumptions of the natural and social sciences, insofar as those disciplines suppose they are in every respect more certain than theology and that they alone have the right and means to describe *in toto* the world's character, its origins, and its ultimate purpose. For example, given the unique nature of "the Beginning," the retrospective assertions of science about it may be no more than a "pagan *gnosis*" derived not through a legitimate application of the scientific method but from the naturalist presuppositions of a scientific "faith." To be sure, the scientific method does have a role to play, but it also has its limits, and these are not always recognized. To counter this tendency, Barth frequently challenges particular scientific assumptions that, to his mind, exceed what could be legitimately derived through application of that method. Consider some of his assertions about the Genesis narratives, and notice the polemic against an obvious, though unspecified, opposing viewpoint:

> The creature does not exist by chance. It does not merely exist; rather, it exists meaningfully. It actualizes, simply by the fact that it is, a purpose, a plan, an order. It exists not by accident but by necessity, and therefore not as an accident but as a sign and witness of this necessity. This is already given in the very fact that it is a creature, and therefore the work of the Creator, of God. As God himself does not exist by chance, but in the power of his own divine meaning and his own divine necessity, so does the creature exist through him and so is the creature a revelation of his glory. The act of creation is as such the revelation of the glory of God by which he gives the creature meaning and necessity. . . . God makes it, by giving it being and existence, the exponent of his purpose, his plan, his order. . . . In and with this creation, God grants that it be this exponent. That is the revelation of God's glory in the act of creation. The divine meaning and the divine necessity that the creature makes visible, which it as such signifies and bears witness to, is but the free love of God. . . . From this standpoint one must say that it simply was not

created to be anything other than the recipient of this gift, and thus that it simply does not exist otherwise than as the recipient of this gift.[50]

The natural and social sciences may indeed relate much about the internal characteristics and processes evident in the world and human history to the observant eye and critical mind. Here too Christianity may learn, submitting its own views on nature and history to cross-examination. But when the sciences step outside their appropriate arena to make claims about the ultimate cause (e.g., evolutionary chance) and meaning (e.g., there is none but that which humans create for themselves) of the world and human history, then their statements are no longer statements of "fact" but of faith, and Christianity is under no obligation to discard its own affirmations of faith to concur with these. In this instance, the sciences do not possess a higher authority, only a different faith.

What is the nature of "faith" in this instance? Barth makes no effort to explain "scientific faith," but he does describe what sort of faith it is in Jesus Christ that "includes the perception of the secret of creation, the Creator, and the creature."[51] According to Barth, that faith is

> a very definite *attitude* and *decision*. It consists in the fact that one who has and confesses this faith [in Jesus] *takes seriously* precisely in that faith that God is the Creator of all reality distinct from himself. It consists in the *recognition* personally carried through by him that this reality is at the disposal of God as the theater, instrument, and object of his activity. It consists, therefore, in the fact that he reckons: God has exercised control over it, God exercises control over it, and God will exercise control over it. Faith in Jesus is still more and other than this. But it is necessarily this also: this taking seriously God as Creator, this recognition of his right and power to exercise control, this *taking into account* his actual control in past, present, and future.[52]

The thrust of Barth's thought is obvious: Faith in Jesus is not merely a matter of receiving certain bits of information available in no other

---

50. *KD* III:1, §41.3.
51. *KD* III:1, §40.
52. Ibid.

way, nor is it a neutral, passive, or merely private orientation. Rather, it entails a self-conscious "attitude" and "decision" about the source, nature, and purpose of the external world. By implication, "scientific faith" also requires a self-conscious attitude and decision about the world, though of a very different sort. One may not have faith in Jesus without a concomitant faith in the Creator, nor does one truly embrace the former without taking the latter "seriously." This means that the recognition of God as the Creator and of the world as creation requires certain determined ways of viewing God, the world, and God's historical activity in the world. One does not possess merely a general knowledge or noncognitive feeling that is then developed according to norms brought from elsewhere. Rather, the world that is the "theater, instrument, and object" of God's activity, and the God who exercises that activity, can only be recognized in a way that is consistent with, indeed based upon, one's primary faith in Jesus Christ.

Why is this so? Because the Christian's encounter with Christ itself makes it necessary. When the Christian responds in faith to Christ, he or she is granted "an absolutely new beginning." Indeed, when the Christian responds in faith to Christ, Jesus is there for the believer "as the Creator." The latter perception is a legitimate corollary of the former because "no creature can encounter another creature in so absolutely revolutionary a way."[53] In other words, the transformative power experienced in this encounter conveys not only a conviction about one's own new and personal re-creation; it also conveys a definite conviction and reveals a definite knowledge—albeit a "knowledge of faith"—about the external world and the "old" or original creation of the cosmos as a whole. That knowledge is not actually additional data about the world; rather, it is an interpretive framework for that world.

Yet why is this encounter between the Christian *and Christ* the necessary first step for a doctrine of Creation? Could not the community simply have faith directly in the revelation of the Genesis accounts? The answer can only be no, because the Bible on its own is ambiguous. It bears witness to God's revelation and is the attestation of this revelation, but this divine-human product is not itself the *event* of revelation. Barth describes his conception of revelation generally at the very

---

53. Ibid.

outset of his *Church Dogmatics*,[54] but he also summarizes his position later on in reference to the Genesis narratives:

> The biblical creation-histories are not dictums of the truth itself dropped from heaven, but human testimony to the revelation that has occurred in the creaturely realm. It is thus and only thus that they speak the truth. . . . In reference to their content as well as their credibility, they live wholly by their object and thus precisely by the self-witness of the Holy Spirit, to whom they alone owe their origin and alone owe their power. This is their certainty and their limitation, which may not be overlooked when they are assessed and interpreted. Their relation to their object is the supremely unequal one of heavenly treasure to the earthen vessels to which it has been entrusted for preservation and transmission. Yet precisely in this relation is their mystery and miracle. Precisely in this relation, and only in this relation, are they inspired, do they speak the Word of God.[55]

The task of the interpreter of these passages, as well as all others that pertain to the doctrine of Creation, is to be open to the Holy Spirit speaking through them. The revelation of God is not simply equivalent to these human writings, but it may and does make use of them in continually renewed "events" or "encounters" between the divine and human, or, more specifically, between Christ and humans. And because God may and does make use of them, Christians are obliged to return again and again to them. God can, of course, make use of other means of revelation. As Barth's famous quote has it, God may even speak to us through a dead dog—but the church's *special* commission is to proclaim the Word of God according to the biblical witness.[56] With the living Christ "in mind," as it were, one may approach these products of divine and human activity and derive from them a consistent and overarching message. But without the living Christ in mind, such a message becomes unattainable.

In this respect, the Bible bears a resemblance to the world around us, in that it lends itself to a variety of interpretations, some natural

---

54. See *KD* I:1, §4.2 and §4.3.
55. *KD* III:1, §41.1.
56. See *KD* I:1, §3.1.

and some supernatural. But just as Barth holds that one ought not
base one's doctrine of creation on a natural theology, so, too, one
should avoid basing it on what could be called a "natural biblicism."
Scripture displays a great variety of witnesses, and if we approach it on
our own, we will have no reliable means for rising above this diversity.
This is certainly the case with the historical-critical approach, which
tends to offer an increasingly atomized interpretation of the Bible. Yet
Barth implies that the same tendency can be found even in those who
approach the Bible with a premodern presupposition of its literal
inspiration. If that presupposition asserts a uniformity of inspiration
throughout the Bible, or, more precisely, equates the many words of
Scripture with *the* Word of God, then there is still no unifying principle by which one can rise above and tie together the Bible's overall
diversity. Each part is as inspired as any other, and thus the emphasis
of any segment over another can only be due to an arbitrary decision
on the part of the theologian. But if we understand God's revelation to
be displayed first and foremost in something more "focused" than the
diverse documents of the Bible, that is, in an unambiguous, conviction-
producing event, then we may approach Scripture with a unifying
principle that is not merely the result of an arbitrary human decision.
The subject of this more focused revelation is, of course, Jesus Christ,[57]
whose very name "Emmanuel" defines and comprehends all that the
Bible might say about creation: "Here God himself has made visible
the relation of Creator and creature—its basis, its norm, and its meaning. Here we are on secure ground in all directions. And everything
else that is to be learned from the Bible is precisely that which is to be
learned *in nuce* here."[58]

Jesus Christ acts as the assurance that one may indeed think of the
world as creation, because he himself embodies the Creator and creature. If God himself took the form of creature, then we have the surest
confirmation possible that creation does exist and that it does have
meaning. Indeed, Christ himself contains all that one need know

57. That is, "the Lord," and not simply "the historical Jesus." Cf. Sykes, *Identity of Christianity*,
197–98. Sykes notes that in contrast to Harnack, Barth "emphatically denied that it is the so-called 'historical Jesus,' as reconstructed by the biblical scholars working behind the text, which is the centre of
theology. The biblical object is not a human creation, especially not one brought into being by the
theological professoriate."

58. *KD* III:1, §40.

about Creation, and thus he properly serves as the hermeneutical key for unlocking the coherence and full significance of the various biblical narratives dealing with Creation. He is the "known quantity" that allows dogmatics to proceed in its exposition of this doctrine, giving it its legitimacy and its most fundamental content.

Hence, one must not suppose that the connection between Christ and creation is in any sense an artificial one. According to Barth, the church does not simply impose a christological hermeneutic on the cosmos; rather, it *recognizes* it as a result of the divine self-witness affirming the essential and intrinsic interrelation between Christ and creation. To be sure, Barth's first concern is to assert that the reality of creation can be *known* with certainty only in Jesus Christ. But he also states, "When such a genuine noetic connection does indeed exist, then one can always thereby reckon that it has an ontic basis."[59] From its encounter with Christ, the church learns that the first two articles of its Creed, which affirm God as the Creator and Redeemer, respectively, have an integral and necessary relation; indeed, it learns that the second is the foundation of the first. Thus, it is for this reason and on this basis that the doctrine of Creation—and the biblical narratives relevant to it—should not be thought of as separable from, or alien to, the remainder of Christian doctrines and sources. On the contrary, that doctrine and those narratives help to express the full reach and significance of the divine self-witness revealed to the church. Indeed, given Barth's supralapsarian position, this connection should not be unexpected. For if Christ is not an "after the fact" supplement to an otherwise independent creation but rather the basis, original instance, and ultimate goal of creation, then one could hardly expect Barth to expound a doctrine of Creation that does not reflect this position.

To summarize, then, Barth's complete doctrine seeks to be the recapitulation of a specific "message" given to the believing community. The task of dogmatics overall, and thus for this doctrine as well, is not to examine, organize, and give voice to general religious feelings or even a particular Christian consciousness. Instead, it is to examine, organize, and re-present in a disciplined manner the

---

59. Ibid.

church's distinctive talk about God—or to be more precise, the church's proclamation, the proper content of which is God's own "address,"[60] which narrowly understood is encompassed by Christ and broadly understood is contained in Scripture. To be sure, the church offers this proclamation in the hope that it will shape the Christian's consciousness in particular ways, but that does not mean the effect replaces the cause as the raw material of dogmatics. Indeed, to prevent any such "shift to the subjective," Barth makes clear that God's Word itself creates the capacity for its reception[61]—a position he maintains in order to eliminate the possibility of deriving doctrines from a consideration of human nature or "feeling," regardless of whether this is understood "in general" or in a specific historical manifestation. This distinction is, of course, a fundamental difference in the methods of Barth and Schleiermacher.

As one might expect, this difference in approach has a definite impact on their explicit doctrines of creation. In Barth's case, his doctrine is openly christocentric throughout. On the one hand, from the moment he considers the scriptural accounts of Genesis 1, Barth inserts Christ as the interpretive key for unlocking the meaning of Creation, rather than abstracting from Christian religious feeling certain limited and general theological axioms, which are then explicated in reference to the beginning and continuation of the cosmos. On the other, his christocentrism compels him to demonstrate how the diversity of Scripture is to be understood as a unified revelation, rather than as representative of two distinct pieties, divided between the Old and New Testaments, with the subsequent discarding of the former from dogmatic consideration. As he asserts:

> The whole Bible speaks prototypically and prophetically of him, of Jesus Christ, when it speaks of creation, the Creator, and the creature. If we want, therefore, to understand and value correctly what it says about these matters, we must consider first and foremost that—as with everything else it says—this too refers and bears witness first and last to him. . . . What is said in *prospect* of him can be understood in no way

---

60. See *KD* I:1, §1 and §3.
61. *KD* I:1, §6.2.

other than in *retrospect* from him; the whole circumference of the content of Scripture, and thus also the truth and reality of the creation of the world by God, [can be understood] only from this center.[62]

Thus, Barth uses a great deal of space examining christologically a great variety of biblical passages he deems relevant to Creation, which is to say, those describing its beginning or its ongoing nature or its ultimate goal. The prime example of this approach is, of course, his *Church Dogmatics* III:1, which devotes more than half its length to a christological consideration and coordination of the Priestly and Yahwist creation stories of Genesis 1 and 2 (§41.2 and §41.3, respectively). The same holds true for other volumes in this doctrine. Significant portions of III:2, where Barth presents his theological anthropology, concentrate on combining biblically derived concepts or themes with the notion of Christ as the prototype or ideal of humanity (especially §45.3 and §47.1).

Indeed, as he states in his preface to volume III, he was compelled to turn to the Bible because in this particular instance tradition proved silent: "Not even one of the older or more recent church fathers whom I surveyed was willing to select the path to a theological knowledge of humanity that I hold to be the sole one possible."[63] This path is, of course, Jesus himself, whom Barth understands as the implicit or explicit subject of all the biblical passages he considers. In the preface to *Church Dogmatics* III:3, which deals primarily with the doctrine of preservation, Barth points out that on this topic he was able to incorporate the categories offered by tradition more fully than he first anticipated. This might suggest a corresponding neglect of christologically understood biblical categories, yet an examination of the start of the first three subsections of this doctrine reveals that each is given a biblical basis and understood in covenantal—which is to say, christological—terms.[64] Finally, III:4, which seeks to establish an ethic for a doctrine of Creation, illustrates that many of Barth's subtopics come directly from biblical requirements and themes. Yet

---

62. *KD* III:1, §40.
63. *KD* III:2, p. vii.
64. See the opening exegetical excurses for *KD* III:3, §49.1, §49.2, and §49.3.

from the first proposition dealing with "The Holy Day" to the last dealing with "Honor," all are expounded in terms of the covenant relation established in Christ.

To put it succinctly, the task running throughout Barth's doctrine of Creation is the exposition of "the Word." In the first instance, this Word is Christ, while in the second it refers to Scripture, and Barth intentionally leaves the ambiguity in dialectical tension.[65] One is to use the former to reveal the meaning of the latter, and the latter to manifest the full reach and significance of the former. Of course, one should not equate this reciprocity with equality: "The Word" as Christ always remains Lord over "the Word" as Scripture. Yet if this authority is affirmed, then the two may properly and fruitfully interact. This is the principle of Barth's christocentrism, and also a description of how he interprets the various biblical passages and narratives related to Creation. Having said this, however, it should also be clear that in the first instance this principle does *not* derive automatically from these passages themselves, even in those instances where they explicitly link Christ and Creation. Instead, it is a principle brought to these passages from somewhere else, namely, from the faithful encounter with Christ *in the present* as made available in the event of the church's proclamation. Barth will indeed devote considerable ink to an exposition of biblical passages relevant to Creation, but only because he presupposes this encounter, which makes it possible, necessary, and worthwhile to do so.

---

65. See *KD* I:1, §5.

CHAPTER 4

Confirmation from Barth's Doctrine of Creation

———〰️———

Barth connects Christ and creation in the very first proposition of his doctrine of creation that is, in *Church Dogmatics* III:1 §40. He asserts that even the most primary claim about ourselves and the cosmos around us—namely, that we do in fact exist as the creation of the Creator—can only first be made through Christ. Solely on the basis of God's revelation made in Christ and accepted in faith can we know that the world exists. But once this epistemological issue is addressed, Barth then turns his attention to the much larger task of describing the ways in which Christ influences the character and course of Creation. If we know through Christ *that* the cosmos exists, we also come to know through Christ that it exists in *particular* ways. Barth describes these particularities over the course of his next ten propositions, as he presents his understanding of the Beginning, his theological anthropology, his notion of history, his doctrine of providence, and a theodicy, among other topics. The content of all of these are determined, sometimes more obviously and sometimes less, by what Barth affirms of Christ. This chapter and the next illustrate enough of them so that the conclusion of a "christological orientation" becomes clear. At the same time, these various topics display a sensitivity to both the inner norm of the Church's historic confession and the outer norm of the modern world's standards of intellectual coherence and plausibility.

Creation and Covenant

The first of these subsequent propositions, on the basis of our present relation in faith to Christ, enables and requires Christians to make the following affirmation about the origin of the cosmos:

> Creation is the first in the series of works of the triune God and thereby the beginning of all things distinct from God himself. As it also includes the beginning of time, its historic [*geschictliche*] reality eludes all historical [*historischen*] observation and reporting, and can be expressed even in the biblical creation narratives only in the form of pure saga. But according to this witness, the object and therefore also the meaning of creation is the enabling of the history of God's covenant with humanity, which has its beginning, its center, and its end in Jesus Christ. The history of this covenant is as much the goal of creation as creation itself is the beginning of this history.[1]

This proposition makes a number of points pertinent to my thesis. First of all, it clearly introduces Barth's claim that the connection between Christ and creation is not merely imposed "after the fact"; rather, the encounter with Christ convinces Christians there is an original and essential interrelation. To cite Barth's earlier formulation, we recognize a genuine noetic connection because there is first an ontic basis.[2] God undertakes the work of creation not as an activity independent of the work of reconciliation, but as the most fundamental prerequisite for it. Therefore, Christianity should feel no qualms about describing the whole breadth of creation in terms that are "narrowly" christological, as if it were merely and arbitrarily applying its own group impression on the external world. On the contrary, the "knowledge of faith" received through revelation requires Christians to affirm the actual and intrinsic interconnection of creation and reconciliation.

Secondly, this proposition also hints at how Barth will expound his doctrine in light of the internal demands of biblical and theological tradition and the external demands made by modern standards of

---

1. *KD* III:1, §41.
2. *KD* III:1, §40.

intellectual credibility. On the one hand, he clarifies that he will develop his doctrine within the framework supplied by the concept of the Trinity and the creation narratives of the Bible. Because God is a triune God, because the unity and integrity of Father, Son, and Holy Spirit is not to be sundered, then so too must the works of this God be understood as united and integrated. Although the creation, redemption, and consummation of the world may be distinguished in time, they are one in God's eternal decree and one in God's eternal act. As a result, the biblical witness to the chronologically first of those works not only may but actually must be understood in its connection with the chronologically later acts. Hence, it is this unabashedly "pious" presupposition, rather than some detached, "objective," or apologetic perspective, that drives his theological exposition.

On the other hand, Barth's characteristic "Yes, but . . ." method of simultaneously acknowledging and challenging external intellectual norms is once again evident. He readily concedes that the nature of "the Beginning" necessarily precludes any and all past or present assumptions that the Genesis stories of creation offer a literal account of how the world came into being. To the extent that Christian tradition views the Bible in this way, Barth presents an alternate reading. On what grounds does he make such a change? While he himself does not say at this point, it is obvious that modern intellectual assumptions and norms—and *not* the internally produced insights of theological tradition or pious impulse—lead him to include this observation in his proposition. He is, in essence, siding with Christian liberalism in allowing the restraining influence of the other sciences to keep him from viewing the Bible as a conduit for divinely given information on natural and historical occurrences.[3] However, at the very point where he seems to make a concession, he also implicitly challenges the sciences, primarily the natural ones at this point, to retain some humility. Recall what he wrote to his grandniece: Scientific theories such as that of evolution—and presumably of the big bang as well—deal with what has already "become," with what already exists in time. So when scientists extend their theories back in time, they must be careful not to overstep the boundary between existence and "basis of existence." If

---

3. See pp. 10, 48–53, 56–58.

they do cross over this line, then, according to Barth, they have actually abandoned their professed scientific method and are offering not
literal history or natural explanation, but only an alternative "saga,"
"myth," or—to use his earlier phrase—"pagan *gnosis*." The scientific
method, however fruitful it may be in explaining reality in its "inner
nexus," cannot of itself ascertain the *ground* of that nexus, and even
less "the *object* and therefore also the *meaning* of creation," because the
reality of the beginning "eludes *all* historical observation and reporting."[4] Thus, with reference to the big bang theory, I assume Barth
would say something like this: Insofar as it simply uses what we know
scientifically about the natural processes evident in the cosmos and
applies them retrospectively back to the point of the beginning, it is a
reasonable hypothesis and may be affirmed by Christians as legitimate. But insofar as it presumes to get "behind" the big bang to explain
its cause—or even to assert it has no cause—then it is not legitimate
science and Christians need not defer or feel bound to it.

If this reading is correct, then with this one introductory proposition we already have an indication of both the variety of items
included on Barth's agenda for this doctrine and the ways in which he
interweaves them. This variety and this rather intricate mix continue
throughout, so that his doctrine brims with passages both short and
long describing his christological orientation, as well as his response to
the inner and outer norms. Faced with the bulk of his comments, however, perhaps the best way to start would be to highlight the structure
he establishes in this opening part of his doctrine. Consider the last
line of the proposition heading up §41: "The history of this covenant
is as much the goal of creation as creation itself is the beginning of this
history." This brief formula encapsulates much of what Barth is about:
It asserts an intrinsic connection between the "general" (creation) and
the "particular" (covenant), it suggests that the meaning of creation is
to be revealed through history, and it lays the groundwork for how he
will describe the Beginning. Thus, following his initial comments in
§41.1, entitled "Creation, History, and Creation History," Barth then
presents two further subsections describing the interrelated, indeed,

---

4. *KD* III:1, §41; emphasis mine. This summary of his position stems from his letter to his grandniece and to §41. See the letter in Karl Barth, *Letters, 1961–1968*, ed. Jürgen Fangmeier and Hinrich
Stoevesandt, trans. and ed. Geoffrey W. Bromiley (Grand Rapids, Mich.: Wm. B. Eerdmans, 1981), 184.

symbiotic connection between creation and the covenant. The dialectic is obvious: §41.2 is entitled "Creation as the External Basis of the Covenant," and §41.3 is entitled "The Covenant as the Internal Basis of Creation." Creation and covenant are distinct yet inseparable; the former is the prerequisite for the latter, temporally and formally speaking, while the latter is the cause of the former, eternally and materially speaking. The claim is audacious: What the secular historian would view as but one "history" among many in the spectrum of human experience is here put forward as the sole, defining history of the world, indeed, as the very cause of that world and its histories.

But Barth's claim is actually more pointed than this might suggest, for it focuses not just on one history, but one being:

> The internal basis of the covenant is quite simply the free love of God, or more precisely stated, the eternal covenant that God on his own has decreed as the covenant of the Father with his Son as Lord and Bearer of human nature, and to that extent as Representative of the whole creation.[5]

The dialectic between creation and covenant is neither impersonal nor self-producing and self-sustaining, as if it were a blind historical force operating in an eternal cosmos. It is in the first instance a dialectic of love within God, between the Father and Son, which is then represented in the created realm, which in fact creates that realm precisely so that this dialectic may exist in a temporal as well as eternal sphere.

This dialectic transposed to the temporal realm, this love of God the Father for the Son in his capacity as Lord and Bearer of human nature and as Representative of all creation, gives Barth the structure for his description of the Beginning. And, not incidentally, it gives him his hermeneutical tool for expounding and also connecting the two creation narratives in Genesis. To be sure, on one level, Barth recognizes that each account is distinct, and must be understood as such. There can be no simple historical harmonization or synthesis of the two. In this respect, Barth simply adds his voice to the consensus of the scientific critics that these two accounts must be kept separate because they arose out of very different times and circumstances, have

---

5. *KD* III:1, §41.2.

very different styles and outlooks, and have very different purposes. He acknowledges these conclusions, and on one level abides by them.

But on another level, even as he concedes the point on the first, he also quite typically asserts that, dogmatically speaking, these historical-critical conclusions really have little bearing on the final interpretation of the Genesis accounts. Consider some general comments on the Bible and its interpretation Barth made during his Gifford Lectures of 1937–1938:

> These documents, the canonical writings of the Old and New Testaments, are human documents. Since this is so, we are given the unavoidable task of understanding them in a human way, and also enabled to do so. This task is performed by the scientific study of the Bible, which in recent times has developed into what is called the historical and critical study of the Bible. This is just the point where it is important for us to note that neither too little nor too much should be expected from such a study. One is entitled to expect from it that it will clarify the whole human form of the witness to Christ in the Old and New Testaments, throwing light on its linguistic, literary, historical and religious-historical aspects. But we should not expect it to set before us the object of this testimony, which is God's revelation and therefore Jesus Christ as the Messiah of Israel and the Lord of His Church. How could revelation ever be recognized as the divine content of that testimony except through revelation? But so to recognize revelation through revelation means to recognize it by revelation awakening one's faith. . . . Without that, the scientific study of the Bible will certainly miss the divine content of this testimony.[6]

These comments give a fuller explanation of what Barth meant when he said that the historical-critical approach to Bible study is concerned with "the preparation of the intelligence."[7] The dogmatician may learn a great deal from it, and have his or her dogmatic enriched thereby. But its method certainly, and even its results, are not to be thought of as directly transferable to the dogmatic task. The

---

6. Karl Barth, *The Knowledge of God and the Service of God according to the Teaching of the Reformation*, trans. J. L. M. Haire and Ian Henderson (London: Hodder & Stoughton, 1938), 66–67.
7. See p. 53.

approaches of these two concerns are distinct, so any "transfer" between them would require modification. If we look at what Barth does with the Genesis accounts, such modification is readily apparent. Barth uses critical study to help discern the distinct religious and historical backgrounds of the two Genesis creation stories, in effect giving himself more "resources" than a unified reading would allow. He also uses it to supply literary analysis and categories, as is apparent in his distinction that these stories may be classified as "saga" rather than as "myth." He then employs these categories as the springboard for asserting that, in contrast to myths, sagas present not "timeless truths" but "nonhistorical history"—a notion useful for supporting claims of a unique biblical faith. Similarly, Barth uses the distinctions in background of the two accounts as the springboard for presenting a dialectical reading of them. He recognizes that these accounts are not connectable through any obvious fit that they themselves possess. Theirs is not a literary or historical complementarity; rather, it is a *theological* one, made apparent through the encounter with Christ, that is, in faith. To Barth, it does not matter that the first presents, as it were, the large picture or the divine perspective, while the second offers a close-up view and a more human-sized perspective, because in a theological reading the first deals with the establishment of the external basis of the covenant while the second deals with the internal basis of creation. Barth understands the Priestly account as speaking quite directly to the "creation" aspect of his formula, and so he devotes §41.2 to a dogmatic exegesis of this saga. Similarly, he understands the Yahwist account as speaking to the "covenant" part of his formula, and so §41.3 is an exegesis of this second saga. Expounding these two accounts in light of this claim, and thereby asserting the meaning and purpose of Creation, is what occupies Barth for the bulk of *Church Dogmatics* III:1.

Christian Faith and Non-Christian Worldviews

But §41 is not Barth's last word in this first volume of his doctrine of Creation. To be sure, given his statements in the preface and the length of space devoted to a theological exegesis of the Genesis narratives, §41 clearly stands at the heart of this volume and his primary dogmatic responsibility. Yet the dogmatician has not only "inwardly oriented" responsibilities but "outwardly oriented" ones as well, and these are what Barth addresses in §42. Although he would likely resist calling it such, this section is essentially an apologetic theology. Having expounded the meaning and purpose of creation on the basis of the divine revelation given through Scripture, Barth will now describe the distinctive nature of creation "in itself and as such." Of course, this hardly means that Barth will formulate a neutral understanding of creation, that is, one derived from nonpartisan observation or rational conjecture. One must still presuppose Creation to be a divine work. Furthermore, knowing God through Christ to be of a particular charac-ter, this divine work must be viewed as having a particular character as well. This character, then, must be expounded and also defended in debate with those who would describe it differently—which is what Barth does in §42. In the proposition heading up this section, he asserts that the particular character of Creation consists in its being a benefit (*Wohltat*), that is, that it actually does *exist* and that it exists as *good*.[8] Creation is not a neutral realm or a blank slate; it is by nature beneficial. It has this character because that was the very "purpose and meaning" for which it was first brought into existence. We know this because it is visible in the divine-human covenant fulfilled in Christ. This is the Yes of God toward Creation; there is a No of God, a divine rejection, but it is directed not against Creation or any part of it, but against the "nonreal," against "nothingness," which is the topic of §50.[9]

In other words, the affirmation of the goodness of Creation is not based upon one's own conjecture and/or empirical observation. One may, of course, take this route, but Barth asserts that it is not the Christian one. Instead, Christians affirm the goodness of Creation because they first affirm the goodness of God the Creator, and they affirm the goodness of God the Creator because they have first *encoun-tered* the grace of God the Redeemer, who reveals and fulfills his covenant in the "God-man" (i.e., the unity of Creator-created), Jesus Christ. One may make the cosmological claim that creation is a bene-fit only after one has made the appropriate theological, which is to say,

---

8. See *KD* III:1, §42.
9. See pp. 103–6.

christological, affirmations. Method and content converge at this one point: the revelation of Christ—and necessarily so, according to Barth, because theology ought to start where God starts, that is, with the divine self-disclosure in Christ. That God chose to be incarnate in the man Jesus means there is an unbreakable covenantal link between the divine and the mundane, the Creator and creature. This is the Christian starting point, and this is the reason Christian affirmations about Creation are fundamentally distinct from, and independent of, all other worldviews and philosophies.

To support this last claim, Barth argues in his excursuses with a number of thinkers, mostly philosophers, whose views explicitly oppose or implicitly undermine these affirmations. In §42.1, he argues against the positions of Marcion and Schopenhauer; in §42.2, he debates Descartes; and in §42.3, he takes on Leibniz, his pupil Christian Wolff, and several of their less-gifted heirs. In other words, his task in this proposition is to elucidate, constructively and polemically, the uniqueness of the Christian view of Creation. Barth firmly believes that the Christian doctrine on this topic is fundamentally different from any conceivable *Weltanschauung* dealing with Creation, even those making apparently similar affirmations. As Barth writes in concluding §42.1:

The formal difference that the former, being theology, reckons only with God's revelation, while the latter, not being theology, reckons only with the perceiving and comprehending, which is feasible to humanity, is materially confirmed by both sides, because the former has to confess and to recognize creation as benefit because it is a work of God in Jesus Christ while the latter, according to its essence as a *Weltanschauung* and without forsaking itself as such, is precisely incapable of doing this. For it to have anything to do (even perhaps in other words) with the divine creation which has this character, a *Weltanschauung* would itself have to become theology. In the same way, theology would have to cease being theology, and become instead a *Weltanschauung*, the moment it were to apply itself to the problem of pure becoming *without* this character. In light of the determination regarding this character, it is as essential to a *Weltanschauung* as it is to theology that not only their grounds of knowledge but also their objects are *different*. Hence, it follows that the

Christian doctrine of creation must go its own *particular* way according
to its particular ground of knowledge and object, independent of any
and all known or yet to be made known *Weltanschauungen*.[10]

Here, as elsewhere, we can detect the move that Barth makes in
response to the outer norm: He takes for granted that the theological
and nontheological sciences simply operate in different spheres.
Moreover, the relation between the two is probably better characterized as a somewhat suspicious truce between self-sufficient and distinct realms than as a cooperative "eternal covenant." Theology has
its particular epistemological basis and ontological position, and all
other disciplines have theirs—and if each is to remain consistent
with its own given nature, then none may overstep its own norms or
seek, on the basis of those norms, to deny or employ those of another.
Of course, this hardly means that theology and various worldviews
cannot and will not speak of and to one another. They do—just as
Barth himself expends considerable effort in addressing "nontheological" philosophies.

However, judging from his excursuses in §42, he tries to do so from
within their own terms, rather than from some external, "superior"
viewpoint. That is, he attempts to show their weak points or limitations on the basis of their own norms and presuppositions, or by suggesting where they might be consciously or unconsciously relying on
assumptions brought in from elsewhere. Thus, for example, in his consideration of Descartes' proof of God's, and therefore the world's, existence, Barth points out that it is a variation of the ontological
argument. Then he goes on to assert that it works only if one also
includes Anselm's prior assumption that the whole argument is faith
seeking understanding in response to the divine self-disclosure in
revelation. And since Descartes does not ground his reasoning on this
assumption, then, according to Barth, his "proof" cannot possess the
certainty Descartes supposed it had.[11] In other words, Barth refuses to
acquiesce in the not uncommon assumption of his day, even among
Christians, that rational or empirical statements about the essential

---

10. *KD* III:1, §42.1.
11. See Barth's excursus in *KD* III:1, §42.2, and, of course, his book *Anselm: Fides Quaerens
Intellectum*, trans. Ian W. Robertson (London: SCM Press, 1960).

nature of creation are somehow more certain and accurate, while dogmatic affirmations about the same are less so. In fact, he argues the reverse of this position, and in so doing serves to reestablish, or at least reassert, the self-sufficiency and self-confidence of dogmatics in the face of modernity. In this way, he concludes the first volume of his doctrine of Creation.

Barth's Christological Anthropology

With his next volume, Barth moves to his consideration of "the creature," and here too he makes his christological orientation obvious. Even a brief examination of the headings in this segment confirms this. The wording of §43 is characteristic:

> Because man—under heaven, on earth—is the creature whose relation to God is revealed to us in God's Word, he is on the whole the object of the theological doctrine of creation. As the man Jesus is the revealed Word of God, he is the source of our knowledge of the human nature created by God.[12]

While it might first appear that his doctrine of Creation is engulfed in anthropocentrism, at second glance it becomes obvious that any anthropocentrism is absorbed into christocentrism. Barth does not first develop a general concept of human nature, or even a concept of that nature based on the original relation of Adam and Eve with God, and then apply it to humanity and thence to Christ. Rather, he first considers Jesus and then uses him to define "true" humanity, an approach made obvious in the way he structures *Church Dogmatics* III:2.[13]

Barth delineates his doctrine of "the creature" in five propositions, §§43–47. The first serves (as §40 did in *Church Dogmatics* III:1) to set the stage, while the next four present the main claims and exposition of the doctrine. Barth expounds them, both in relation to one another and in themselves, in a very definite order of priority. The first begins the definition of the human in terms of its relation to God, the second

---

12. *KD* III:2, §43.
13. See as well his brief work, *Christ and Adam: Man and Humanity in Romans 5*, trans. T. A. Smail (New York: Harper & Row, 1956), where Barth uses the same approach.

continues the definition of the human in terms of its relations to its fellows, the third defines humans as individuals made up of soul and body, and the fourth defines the human in terms of its temporality. In other words, Barth emphasizes the corporate over the individual or, more precisely, the dynamic capacity for relation over any static and internal attribute, as the key for understanding humanity. But of course, he also makes things more definite than this, for in each of these propositions, the starting point is Jesus. This means that human nature will not be defined in a neutral fashion, but in a very particular one.

Consider the way Barth structures §44. This proposition is entitled "The Human as God's Creature," and comprises three subsections, with the headings "Jesus, the Human for God," "Phenomena of the Human," and "The Real Human." One can readily guess from these headings that Jesus will have some sort of priority in Barth's exposition, and in fact he makes it clear from the outset that this will be his approach. Barth's initial question, a not unreasonable one with which to commence an anthropology, is straightforward: "Who and what is the human precisely in the midst of the cosmos?" Yet this is not the question he proceeds to answer, at least not in this subsection. Instead, he absorbs it into two other questions, namely, "Who is Jesus?" and "What is his human nature?" His point is obvious: One cannot define humanity generally without first considering that humanity in Jesus specifically. He shifts from any direct consideration of anthropology to the christological foundation of anthropology, and proceeds to outline what Jesus reveals in his human nature. What he reveals is that human nature should not be defined in static or substantial terms, but in terms of relation and activity. More specifically, this means (1) that in Jesus we immediately and necessarily "see," "think about," and "meet" God; (2) that in this revelation of God in Jesus we see not a passive relation but a God who is "resolute, hard at work and active in a specific direction," namely, in the history of salvation; (3) that in this revelation and saving work in Jesus, God does not diminish but in fact demonstrates his sovereignty, transcendence, and honor; (4) that in this demonstration, Jesus exists in and enacts the lordship of God; (5) that in enacting this lordship, Jesus is not simply a means: he *is* what he *does*, that is, he is God's salvation; he is the history of salvation; finally, in sum, (6) that Jesus is *for* God and God's work, and that in this we find the essence and distinctive character of his human nature.[14]

But how do these six points help clarify the essence and distinctive character of everyone else's human nature? After all, anthropology and Christology are hardly interchangeable in Barth's view. Yet neither are they totally dissimilar. There are points of contact between the man Jesus and all other human beings, so that with the proper modifications, what one asserts about Jesus can become the "indirect" basis or "criterion" for assertions about human nature in general. In fact, Barth uses the six christological affirmations just summarized as the springboard for six corresponding points about human nature, delineated in his second subsection of §44, "Phenomena of the Human." Barth makes a specific "if-then" correlation in each: (1) If we do indeed encounter God "immediately and directly" in the man Jesus, then every other person must be understood "at least mediately and indirectly" in his or her "belonging" (*Zugehörigkeit*) to God, that is, in coming from and moving toward God; (2) if we do indeed encounter God actively working out the history of salvation in the man Jesus, then every other person must be understood as a being involved in this history; (3) if in this redemptive work God does not "lose himself" in Jesus but maintains his freedom, sovereignty and glory, then the being of all other persons, inasmuch as it is involved in this history, is not an end in itself, but instead has its proper determination in the glory of God; (4) if, however, in the man Jesus, God does exercise his lordship, then we must understand that all persons exist under the lordship of God; (5) if it is the case that the very being of Jesus consists in the enacting of this redemptive history, then the being of all persons must consist in this history, in its participation in what God does for it; finally, in sum, (6) if the man Jesus is for God, then the essence of all other persons must be understood as being for God, as covenantally bound to God because God first bound himself to them.[15]

These are, according to Barth, the key affirmations that must be considered when conducting any theological exposition of human

---

14. See *KD* III:2, §44.1.
15. See *KD* III:2, §44.2.

nature. To be sure, they do not necessarily contain in themselves every-thing one may want to say, nor are they or theology itself the sole source of information for a complete portrait of the human. But they do and must serve as the criteria for interpreting whatever data or con-clusions one might bring from elsewhere, because without them theol-ogy risks losing sight of the fundamental assertion that a true understanding of the human is possible only in relation to God. For Barth, this is the sine qua non of any doctrine of the creature, and in this regard he sides firmly with the Reformation tradition exemplified so clearly at the very outset of Calvin's *Institutes*. Just as that work is based on the premise that the knowledge of man and the knowledge of God are unavoidably interconnected, so too is Barth's. What Barth adds, of course, is the immediate clarification that this man and this God are not to be understood in any general or speculative sense, but only as they are revealed in Jesus Christ.[16] Jesus Christ is the source for our hermeneutic; indeed, he *is* the hermeneutic by which all the dis-parate data and conclusions about human nature can be evaluated. With him, one can make sense of the human; without him, the human can only remain ambiguous and uncertain.

Conversations with Non-Christian Anthropologies

Having established his christological starting point, Barth can now engage in a critical conversation with alternate—and, in some cases, non-Christian—anthropologies (§44.2) and in a constructive exposition of his own (§44.3). The former serves to illustrate one aspect of Barth's attitude toward "the outer norm." Consider the following assertion:

> Given that about which we must here inquire, no definition of human
> nature could possibly suffice that deals only with a delineation and
> description of the characteristics of that nature accessible to our unaided
> perception and knowable to our unaided thinking, which man himself
> supposes he should regard as the nature of those like him and therefore
> as the nature of humanity. From the perspective of all our criteria,

---

16. See Barth's brief excursus, *KD* III:2, §44.2. His criticism and defense of Calvin are worth not-ing: He takes Calvin to task for not making this christological link explicit *at this point* in the *Institutes*, but he is also convinced that such a link really did exist in Calvin's mind.

human self-understanding on this basis must be characterized as a circle, in which we can never arrive at the real human.[17]

In essence, Barth makes the same argument here that is implicit in the
proposition with which he began §41.[18] Insofar as this passage has in
mind the natural and social sciences, it acknowledges that they may
discern the character of human nature, both in its individual and collective aspects, within the context of the "inner nexus," and to that
extent be able to "explain" human nature. Christians need have no
qualms about accepting such explanations, because they can truly
enrich one's understanding. But the sciences cannot, strictly speaking,
reach beyond or outside this nexus to offer an explanation of the
object and *meaning* of human nature, just as the big bang theory cannot offer an account of the object and meaning of the cosmos. In both
cases, Barth is saying, in effect, "It's not that the sciences are wrong; in
fact, what they tell us is quite enlightening—they are just not enlightening enough. More needs to be said. However, if that 'more' is based
on our own inquiries, whether scientific or philosophical, then it will
not be sufficient."

Here Barth proceeds to examine some examples of such "insuffi-
cient" interpretations. Judging from his arguments in this subsection,
autonomous self-understanding may take one of three forms. The first
may be labeled "the naturalistic," and can be found in Barth's analysis
of the Aristotelian theologian Polanus, by a number of nineteenth- and
twentieth-century theological apologists, and by Adolf Portmann, who
sought to counteract an excessively rigid Darwinism. This approach
seeks to define the human according to some distinct quality it possesses that none of the other creatures do, whether in terms of human
reason, some special spiritual attribute, or something else. The second
approach may be labeled "the ethical" or "the idealistic," and can be
found in Barth's analysis of Fichte. This approach seeks to define the
human not by what it *is* (or by what it *knows* or by what it *feels*), but by
what it *does*. The final approach may be labeled "the existential," and
can be found in the philosophy of Jaspers and, in a Christianized form,
in the theology of Brunner. It holds that the human is characterized by

---

17. *KD* III:2, §44.2.
18. See p. 76.

its ability to rise above not only its environment but even itself, recognizing in certain "frontier situations" a transcendent other.

The problem with all of these, even the last, is that they seek to define the human in isolation, as a self-contained reality whose distinctiveness can be identified through observation of the human alone. None seek to define the human from the perspective of, and in relation to, a very specific transcendent other. Even the existential approach— which sounds so amenable to Christian views—presupposes a human starting point, is based on human observation and induction, and can at best only point to a "generic" transcendent other. A truly Christian anthropology, however, ought to start with God: the God who creates human nature, who initiates and leads the relationship of the divine and human, and who reveals the essence of both the divine and human natures in the savior, Jesus Christ. Taking such an approach means one's doctrine of the creature will no longer rest on autonomous self-understanding, but theonomous self-understanding.

We must consider what Barth is doing with this assertion. In placing anthropology—or any other aspect of Creation, for that matter— within this larger framework, theology calls the other disciplines to account. But it does so not only on the basis of explicitly Christian norms—which of course they could legitimately ignore—but also on the basis of implicit modern ones that they presumably accept. That is, Barth challenges them with one aspect of their own ethos, namely, the modern assumption of historical and cultural relativism.[19] In effect, he employs this notion to attack any absolutist claims they might make, although he usually couches it in the traditional notion of God as the sole constant, the one true God. An example of this approach can be found in his Gifford Lectures:

> The gods so-called, which the proposition [in the Scottish Confession of 1560] about the "ane onelie God" was designed to combat, are, however, also the gods and godheads of all the human ideologies and mythologies, philosophies and religions. . . . [Man's] conception of the world and thus his world become full of ideas and principles, points of view scientific, ethical and aesthetic, axioms, self-evident truths social

---

19. See p. 10.

and political, certainties conservative and revolutionary. They exercise so real a dominion and they bear so definitely the character of gods and godheads, that not infrequently devotion to them actually crystallises into mythologies and religions. (Universities are the temples of these religions.) But each one of these claims at the moment to be the one and only reality with monopoly over all systems. . . . Service and honour are offered them also and it is believed that the hope of salvation should be put in them. To recognise the one and only God means to make all these systems relative. . . . Are they to be annihilated? Perhaps not at all, perhaps not yet. But the end of their authority is within sight.[20]

The tone of this passage and the Christian language in which it is clothed are hardly likely to win over the scientists and thinkers at which it is aimed, even if they agree with the necessity of restraining the claims made by their various disciplines. This is one more illustration of how Barth conceived the relation between theology and the sciences. At times, it may actually have more the character of *Realpolitik* than of an "eternal covenant" based on friendly mutual regard and common ideals. The openly cooperative spirit so evident in Schleiermacher is here replaced by one that is much more guarded. But this passage also illustrates how Barth adopts and adapts certain key assumptions of the modern era to serve his own theological ends.

So are all of these other approaches—these human conceptions, ideas, principles, points of view, axioms, and truths—simply wrong, perhaps even dangerous? Are they to be strictly avoided? Or might they still possess some value? And if so, how are they to be understood in relation to the "proper" approach? Barth makes some fairly concise comments on the distinction between theological and humanistic anthropologies that speak to this more general point:

Very generally stated, the difference must consist in the fact that humanity relinquishes the sovereignty in which it supposes it can know itself by itself, or rather, in the fact that this sovereignty is understood not as absolute, but as relative. It is therefore to be realized that the determinations of our autonomous self-understanding need not necessarily

20. Barth, *Knowledge of God*, 18–19.

be false, but in their own place and framework may well be correct and important, but that to the very last one they stand bracketed, and that the decisive instruction about humanity itself does not occur within these brackets, but can be expected only from a place and factor outside these brackets. This place and factor outside the brackets of human self-understanding is *God*. He, humanity's Creator, knows who and what the human is. For the human is his creature, and is therefore known to him—in the last analysis, to him alone. He must *tell* the human who and what it is in reality, who and what it is in itself, if this is in fact to be known to humanity.[21]

What humanity may learn about itself through its sciences and philosophies may well be useful and, in its own way, true. Such learning is not to be avoided, even, presumably, by theologians, for whom it can help "prepare the intelligence." But it must not supply the basis, nor these other disciplines the method, for what the theologian is about in his or her own sphere. That is, if one understands the "eternal covenant" as a relation between unequal partners, or as a relation in which a syncretistic intermixing occurs between the partners, then that conception does not reflect Barth's position. But if one conceives of that covenant as an association between equal and independent realms "keeping each other honest"—in part by recognizing the spheres of influence rightfully claimed by each—then one mirrors Barth's view.

In taking this position, Barth is once again simultaneously surrendering and claiming certain prerogatives for theology. He concedes to the sciences and humanistic disciplines the task of observing, describing, analyzing, and defining the "objectively" human. But he also asserts that this objective humanity is only "phenomenal" humanity, which means that what these disciplines say may be true, but not "true enough." To be that, their various claims must be undergirded by or fitted into a larger framework, that is, that of "the real human," which God reveals and with which theological anthropology is exclusively concerned. To summarize, Barth asserts that in relation to these other disciplines, theology is able to recognize the need for, and also furnish the presuppositions and interpretive framework required by, a full and true understanding of the human.

---

21. *KD* III:2, §44.2; emphasis his.

CHAPTER 5

Confirmation from Barth's Doctrine of Providence and His Understanding of Evil

—∿—

Barth presents his doctrine of providence in *Church Dogmatics* III:3, which comprises the eleventh chapter of his doctrine of Creation. This chapter is entitled "The Creator and His Creature," and it includes four propositions, §48 through §51. Respectively, these are "The Doctrine of Providence, Its Basis and Form," "God the Father as Lord of His Creature," "God and Nothingness," and "The Kingdom of Heaven, God's Ambassadors, and Their Adversaries." The most pertinent segments for understanding Barth's position are §48.2, "The Christian Belief in Providence," and §49.4, "The Christian under the Worldwide Lordship of God the Father." Moreover, what Barth has to say about evil in §50 is helpful not only for clarifying his own position but also for providing a key point of comparison with Schleiermacher.

The Christian Interpretation of History and the Natural Order

If one were to attempt to summarize in a phrase what Barth offers in his two segments from §48 and §49, it would have to be something like "a hermeneutic for history." What his doctrine of providence does above all is expound how the Christian is to "see" God working in the world, both in its human and natural spheres. Barth does not consider

93

the world directly, neither deriving his position from an examination of it nor making specific assertions about its inner workings. Instead, he describes how history—which, empirically speaking, should be the same for Christian and non-Christian alike—ought to be *interpreted* by the Christian according to norms revealed by God in Jesus Christ. Such interpretation stands one step removed from those made by the objective sciences (if they are being true to their own procedural norms), but in its own way it is also far closer to the heart of our concern with the world around us, namely, its ultimate meaning. For the Christian, the key to unlocking such meaning can only be Christ.

Typically, Barth's initial proposition offers numerous indications and hints about how he will proceed. He begins by stating that the doctrine of providence has to do with "the history of created being as such" as it proceeds "under the fatherly lordship of God the Creator." These comments allude to what he says in the first, brief subsection of §48: He gives a definition of the term "providence," explains his preference for following Reformation tradition in locating the doctrine in relation to the doctrine of creation rather than Scholastic tradition of placing it under the doctrine of God, and suggests how providence stands in relation to creation. Then the proposition makes it clear that this "fatherly lordship" is not to be conceived in neutral or general terms, but is instead to be encompassed in a progressively more specific focus: The will of this God "is done and discernible in his election of grace, and therefore in the history of the covenant between him and humanity, and therefore in Jesus Christ."[1] These comments hint at the two key points Barth will make in the second and third subsections of §48, namely, the "status" of providence in Christian life and thought—what it is and what it is not. Practically speaking, the belief in providence enables the creature to face all the events of life with confidence, even joy, and to do all that needs to be done not only obediently but willingly, because in all things it is "upheld, determined, and governed" by its living and sovereign Creator. For Barth, the "most splendid" witness to this point may be found in the Heidelberg Catechism, questions 26–28—and it seems obvious that the key point is made in the

---

1. *KD* III:3, §48.

Catechism's answer to question 27: We may be confident and obedient because we know that all circumstances, whether good or ill, "come to us not by chance, but from his fatherly hand."[2] In other words, for Barth and this strand of tradition, the central problem overcome by the belief in providence is meaninglessness. Christians may not always be able to elucidate the significance of specific occurrences, but in faith they can affirm that God "has his reasons," and therefore such occurrences must not be construed as utterly random and senseless.

Such are the practical benefits of a belief in providence, according to Barth. But having presented these claims, he also feels compelled to offer three definite clarifications or "delimitations." The first is the recognition that belief in providence is a matter of faith, that is, "a hearing, understanding, and accepting of the *Word of God*."[3] Thus, it is not based on rational deduction, empirical observation, or any personal experience or feeling. Secondly, it is always faith "in God himself," who alone exercises sovereign rule over all occurrences. Thus, it is not surreptitiously faith in historical forces or natural processes or some such creaturely power or hypothesis. And thirdly, this faith is always faith in Christ, who is, after all, the concrete Word one has heard, understood, and accepted. With this faith, the Christian is then able to "recognize" that the history of creaturely being does not simply run parallel to that of the covenant, but in fact "has its meaning in it, is conditioned and determined by it, serves it, and is, wholly and completely, in its reflection and splendor (and also in its shadow) in one way or another, the space, the domain, the atmosphere, and the medium of its occurrence and revelation."[4]

Secular history may indeed be broader than this particular "sacred" history, and from a neutral perspective one could label the latter as merely one strand in the fabric of the former. But, of course, a neutral stance is hardly what Barth asserts here. Instead, he claims that this one strand actually ties the whole fabric together, that without this history or, more precisely, without Jesus Christ, one simply cannot be certain

---

2. See Barth's brief excursus, *KD* III:3, §48.2.
3. *KD* III:3, §48.2.
4. Ibid.

of discerning any reliable pattern or order in the rest of creaturely history. The audacity of this claim is obvious, and Barth does not shrink from its implications. As he openly states:

> The belief in providence is not therefore something such as a forecourt or common ground on which the belief of the Christian church may come together with other conceptions of the relation between all possible denotations of the terms "God" and "world" . . . ; it is not a genus under which the rule of any other deity (freely chosen from any "religion" or worldview!) can be understood, except that of the Father of Jesus Christ, the God of the election and covenant of grace. It is, by virtue of its relation to what God has done once and for all in Christ, an occurrence *sui generis*.[5]

Where does this leave us? Barth seems to be promoting this Christian belief to a special status while simultaneously cutting off all possible conversation with, and support from, non-Christian sources. One can hardly be blamed for detecting in this move the chauvenistic attitude all too often evident in Christian history, and for concluding that this is an unfortunate way of continuing the Christian theological heritage. Might it not also be construed as a "retreat behind Chinese walls"[6] or, more precisely, a christological wall? Does Barth have any "outer norm" in mind when he asserts that Christianity possesses sole access to a true understanding of providence and implies thereby that it need not submit its belief to any sort of public (i.e., non-Christian) scrutiny?

The World Does Not Interpret Itself

Proposition §49, entitled "God the Father as Lord of His Creature," is by far the longest in Barth's exposition of the notion of providence, and it is the one most similar in function to the usual treatment of this doctrine. Its primary difference from these treatments lies in the fact that it proceeds only on the basis of the christological presuppositions

5. Ibid.
6. See p. 51.

outlined in §48. Thus, while it often deals with concepts typically examined under this heading (such as, e.g., the concept of *concursus* explaining the relation between divine and creaturely activity),[7] it always does so in accordance with Barth's christological starting point. Nevertheless, the very fact that he engages in this traditional exercise suggests that he may not be as obscurantist as the above citation might imply. In describing the divine preserving (§49.1), the divine accompanying (§49.2), and the divine ruling (§49.3), Barth presents an exposition that certainly does justice to the traditional affirmations of the faith. But he also presents modern Christians with a conceptualization implicitly compatible with the mindset that they inevitably share with their (non-Christian) contemporaries. Consider the following assertions from §49.2:

> We have to understand the activity of God and that of his creature as *a single* action. . . . If God the Lord accompanies his creature, then it certainly does mean that he is so present to the activity of his creature—that is, present in sovereignty and omnipotence—that his own event occurs precisely *in, with,* and *over* the creaturely activity. He himself does what Moses and David do. He himself, Yahweh, bellows out of Zion when his prophet speaks. He himself judges when the Assyrians capture Samaria and the Babylonians Jerusalem. He himself speaks to his congregations when Paul writes his letters to them. Yet according to the Old Testament witness as well as the New, there is no difference here between salvation history and general world history: He himself does what heaven and earth, what sun and rain, what lightning and thunder do. Hence, in the rule of God, we do not have to do first with a creaturely occurrence and then—somewhere above or behind, but distinct from it and with a content hidden from the senses—with one executed by God himself as well. The mathematical picture of two parallel lines would therefore *not* be suitable for describing the *concursus divinus.* Rather, as God acts, creaturely events occur. As he enters the creaturely arena—and he does not cease to enter this arena; he does it in every movement of every leaf in the wind—there occurs immediately in all

---

7. See Barth's long excursus, *KD* III:3, §49.2.

large and small creaturely occurrences *his* will, there descend and come
to pass *his* decisions. He would not be God, if he were not this living
God, if there were even only a single isolated point where he was absent
or inactive or only partly active or effective to only a limited extent.[8]

Although he would probably not admit it, this statement puts
Barth in virtually the same position as Schleiermacher, allowing him
to resolve in a quite similar manner the same apologetic issues faced
by his predecessor. That is, because he proposes no divine course of
events occurring alongside a broader creaturely history, no occasional
interruption of a mundane order by miracles, indeed, no existence and
interrelation of a distinctly natural realm and a distinctly supernatural
one, Barth can simply sidestep all the tensions associated with trying
to distinguish between divine and creaturely acts in the world around
us. The data available to the scientist and the theologian are the same,
and on the "creaturely level" the interpretation of the data must be the
same; indeed, the theologian ought to defer to the scientist on this level
of interpretation. In this respect, Barth shares liberal Christianity's
assumptions concerning natural cause and effect.[9] But he also argues
that nothing compels the theologian to concede this to be the sole possible level of interpretation. On the contrary, the event of divine revelation compels the theologian—indeed, all Christians—to recognize a
larger, more encompassing framework. It does so in a simultaneously
negative and positive fashion.

On the one hand, the event of revelation produces the conviction
that no creaturely interpretation suffices to explain the ultimate power
or purpose behind the world's ongoing existence. But that event does
so, on the other hand, only because it first presents Christ, the incarnation of the divine-human covenant and the "principle" determining
God's providential rule. That is, in light of Christ, the inadequacy of all
human attempts to explain the power or purpose driving the cosmos
becomes manifest. This is quite a claim, but is it really as audacious as
it seems? Yes and no. It is certainly audacious in the fact that, in spite
of the sensibilities of the modern, secular mind, it continues to assert

---

8. *KD* III:3, §49.2.
9. See p. 10.

the "objective" reality of the activity and rule of God. The traditional categories of the divine *conservatio, concursus,* and *gubernatio* are neither surrendered nor merely "privatized," but are still applied by the Christian community to the world around us because, Barth maintains, they reflect reality. We are in fact creatures ruled over by our Creator, and Christians cannot and need not avoid making this ontological claim, because the event of revelation requires it and the evidence of the world allows it.

However, this last comment suggests the qualification that also limits the audacity of Barth's position. Asserting that all other attempts to explain the world's workings are inadequate is based not on an assumption of the Christian's own superior technique or the non-Christian's inferior insights, or on data available to the former but not the latter. It is instead based on the assumption that the Word of revelation simply places the Christian at a different vantage point, giving him or her a different or rather additional perspective on, and therefore a different or rather additional interpretation of, the world and its course. Indeed, the reception of the Word itself *as revelation* actually *presupposes* this different vantage point and perspective (which is what Barth means when he says the Word creates the grounds for its own reception):

> The speech of God is and remains the mystery of God above all in its *secularity.* When God speaks to humanity, this event never so distinguishes itself from other events such that it could not also be interpreted at once as part of these other events. . . . Even the biblical miracles do not break through this wall of secularity: even as they occurred, they were already interpreted otherwise than as proofs of the Word of God.[10]

In other words, events and objects in the world will confront the Christian and non-Christian in the same way, but different evaluations of them can and do arise. One might be inclined *after the fact* to argue that one evaluation is better because it explains more adequately the object under mutual consideration or it is more compatible with its

---

10. *KD* I:1, §5.4.

myriad aspects. Apparently, this is what Barth himself does in §49.3, suggesting that one can engage "on and on, step by step" in a progressive "confirmation" of God's rule.[11] Specifically, he suggests that the history of Holy Scripture, the history of the church, the history of the Jews, and the limitation of human life can all be seen as "signs and testimonies" to the rule of God in the world.[12] However, he also insists that the confirmation received from such sources has the character of revelation, and not human discovery.

Moreover, arguments based on such data are not what *lead* a person to accept one position over another; they are not empirical deductions. In fact, by no neutral standard can anyone be said to possess a position capable of denying from the outset the possibility of the others. As the modern social sciences have made abundantly clear, there are no neutral or absolute standards in this sort of concern; everything is relative to its cultural and historical context. Different vantage points produce different perspectives. Some may be judged better than others—for example, by producing more conceptual clarity, by being more heuristic, by enabling more justice, by being more aesthetically or spiritually resonant—but such judgments can never be final or objective, because they are themselves always at root based on some form of faith. This faith may be associated with the creeds of a religion, or it may be associated with the accepted presuppositions and assumptions of a particular discipline, ideology, or community, but in any of these instances it remains faith.

This is the principle Barth uses to uphold the legitimacy of the Christian perspective in the face of any monopolistic claims made by modernity, but it is also the principle that prevents any resurgence of exclusivist Christian claims. In other words, the modern notion of relativism has actually made "faith" a necessary foundation for certain claims of science as well as religion, in effect putting the two on the same footing. Thus, the Christian will not be able to claim any special status over the non-Christian—but he or she will insist that the reverse is true as well. So when the Christian asserts on the basis of his or her faith that the Christian interpretation more truly comprehends

11. *KD* III:3, §49.3.
12. Ibid.

what is visible in the world, it will be done in both humility and self-assurance, even while non-Christians can and do interpret it differently on the basis of their faith. Barth speaks to this situation at length in §49.4, "The Christian under the Universal Lordship of God the Father," and his position may be summarized by citing one rather long passage:

> How is it that of all persons, the Christian comes to *confess* to the *veracity* of this claim? The answer can simply be: He *sees* something that the others do not see. The *world-process* in which he participates in solidarity with all other creatures could no doubt also be an unstable, uncontrolled, and purposeless shoving and tumult. Many see it so. The Christian sees in the world-process a *worldwide lordship*. Admittedly, the lordship could also be that of a supreme natural law, or of fate, or of chance, or perhaps even of the devil. Many see it so. The Christian sees that it is the worldwide lordship of *God*, indeed of the God who is the *Father*, who is to him his Father. He sees the constitutive and organizing center of the world-process. In fact, this makes him a Christian, in that he sees *Jesus Christ*: the Son of God in his lowliness, but also in the elevation of his humanity, and himself bound to him, belonging to him, his life saved by him, but also placed at his disposal. Seeing him, he sees the legislative, executive, and judicial *dominion* over all things and in all things, and this as the dominion of *God*, and this as the dominion of the *Father*—and himself, as one bound and belonging to the Son, as subjected to *this* dominion. Only the Christian sees this *center* of the world-process. Only the Christian sees in this center, as bearer of all dominion in heaven and on earth, the *Son* of God, and through him God the *Father*, and therefore on the circumference of this center himself as the *child* of this Father for the sake of that Son. This is in fact the Christian community: the assemblage by the *Word*, in which *this* is said and disclosed, through which *this* becomes visible—the assemblage of those whose eyes are opened precisely for this.[13]

In effect, Barth is asserting that ultimately the world and its workings do not interpret themselves, that they do not supply their own meaning.

---

13. *KD* III:3, §49.4.

In themselves, they are mute and ambiguous, lending themselves to a variety of interpretations and meanings. To be sure, there are those who deny this view, by assuming that their interpretations are the direct and necessary product of the object considered or by tacitly claiming for their theories a greater explanatory power than they can properly deliver. Recall, for example, Barth's comments to his niece regarding the biblical creation stories and the theory of evolution. He acknowledges the legitimacy and usefulness of the latter in explaining the world in its "inner nexus." But if it steps beyond this inner nexus of evolutionary processes to posit, say, the existence of an independent and ultimate force called "evolution," Barth would presumably say this is no longer legitimate science, but a "pagan *gnosis*" that can claim no greater prerogative in being accepted than any other view.[14] At this level of interpretation, and from a neutral point of view, no theory or explanation of the world and its workings is self-evident. They all work only on the basis of presuppositions or principles brought from elsewhere—and for Barth, obviously, the most persuasive and reliable elsewhere is God.

We may find another illustration of Barth's position in his exposition of Calvin's Catechism of 1545. In response to question 27 of that work, which describes how God is not just Creator but providential Ruler of heaven and earth, Barth writes:

> We have here the opposite of the parable of deism which says God made the world like the clockmaker a clock. Once all was finished, the clock works by itself, with no help from the clockmaker. On the contrary, God is maintaining his creation unceasingly. *Nothing in the world is independent of God; where there is order, it is God-given. If there be chance or fate, these are still under God's governance.* No necessity, no absolute action is independent of God, no freedom which is not God-granted (for he does grant it), no contingency which is not disposed by God. The order existing in the world has nothing absolute about it. It does not exist aside from him who ordains. *At bottom, both determinism and indeterminism are false: God governs and allows determinate and indeterminate things.*[15]

---

14. Cf. pp. 52 and 56–57.
15. Karl Barth, *The Faith of the Church*, ed. Jean-Louis Leuba, trans. Gabriel Vahanian (New York: Meridian Books, Inc., 1958), 50–51; emphasis mine.

These assertions do not adhere strictly to the "principle of parsimony." Then again, that principle would be persuasive in this instance not because it is self-evident, but because it appeals to a prior metaphysical or aesthetic sensibility that prizes simplicity over complexity.

Be that as it may, when Barth makes these assertions, he does not so much justify his starting point as simply assume it,[16] since in all of his writing he has not an apologetic, but a dogmatic purpose in mind. Nevertheless, the whole of his doctrine of providence—indeed, the whole of his doctrine of Creation—reinforces this one point: If one is to comprehend fully the ultimate meaning of the cosmos, a hermeneutical key is required, and for the Christian this key can only be Christ, whom the event of revelation shows to be the first Subject and Lord of Creation. The task of the theologian, then, is to explain, without embarrassment in the face of modernity and without the imperiousness of many past dogmatics, how this One determines the way in which Christians "see" Creation. Needless to say, Barth recognizes that the scientist might employ a different parable or hermeneutical key, and thereby produce an alternate interpretation of the meaning of the cosmos—and on one level, he would be willing to concede that this is entirely legitimate. But in Barth's view, it is legitimate only as an alternate faith, not as science. On this level, Christian theology need not defer to or maintain a covenant with science, because this "science" is a competitor not a partner, a rival not a complement.

Interpreting Evil

Barth also follows this line of reasoning when he discusses the problem of evil. The best summary of his position may be found, of course, in his initial propositional heading:

> Under God's providential disposal, there also comes to pass the threat to, and actual corruption of, the course of the world through the resistance of nothingness, which is hostile to the will of the Creator, and therefore also to the good nature of his creature. Having judged it according to the mercy appearing and powerful in Jesus Christ, he

---

16. Barth does occasionally present supporting arguments such as those cited on pp. 99–100.

determines where and how, to what extent, and in what subordinate
relation to his Word and work it may still come into play, until the general [*allgemeinen*] revelation of his *already-accomplished refutation and
abolition of it.*[17]

To clarify this proposition, Barth subdivides his exposition into four
subsections: (1) "The Problem of Nothingness," (2) "The Misconception
of Nothingness," (3) "The Recognition of Nothingness,"[18] and (4) "The
Reality of Nothingness." The crux of Barth's ideas about evil can be
found in §50.4. In this section, Barth responds to the question, "What
is real nothingness?" His answer consists of seven observations, the
first of which takes as its starting point a consideration of the word "is"
used in his initial question. Barth acknowledges that properly speaking, only God and his creature truly "are," but this must not be taken as
meaning that nothingness is somehow illusory. Nothingness is neither
God nor creature, and it has nothing in common with either, but it does
confront God as a problem and God does take it seriously. In being
taken seriously by God, we must recognize that in some way it "is."

However, second, we should not simply equate nothingness with
deficiency, that is, with what God is not and with what the creature is
not. We must avoid viewing the *limitations* of creaturely being (or of
God, for that matter, in the sense that "God is God and not creature")
as an imperfection. In fact, our finitude is "perfect," in the sense that
we were willed by God to be the creatures we are. The supposition that
we or the world around us could be "more" were it not for the
encroachment of nothingness must be rejected. What Barth calls the
"shadow side" of existence is not coterminous with nothingness, for
the former is a natural part of creation while the latter is not.

Barth then asserts, third, that nothingness "cannot be an object of
the natural knowledge of the creature."[19] We do not learn of it through
our own experience or observation. As with all other knowledge having to do with Creation, what we know of nothingness is a knowledge
of faith that comes solely through God's disclosure. Moreover, that

---

17. *KD*, III:3, §50; emphasis mine.
18. This subsection is by far the longest of the four, and it includes an excursus that deals at length
with Schleiermacher's position on the topic.
19. *KD*, III:3, §50.4.

disclosure does not come in isolation, but within the larger context of God's overall revelation regarding Creation and covenant. Thus, fourth, this broader picture forms the "ontic context" for nothingness. That is, in God's activity of election and Creation, we learn of nothingness as that which God rejects by *not* creating it—and in this rejection, it is "real," the "impossible possibility." Stated this way, the point may sound nonsensical, but one can still discern what Barth is driving at: God did not *create* nothingness; indeed, it was positively rejected. Yet this rejection means God takes it seriously, since otherwise it could have been ignored. It is in some sense "real," although it is not merely deficiency. Perhaps its reality is best described as some sort of negative, parasitical existence.

Moreover, it is not just neutrally negative, but actually evil, which is Barth's fifth observation. God rejects it because it is both alien and contrary to grace, going against him and his will for Creation. As Barth asserts:

> God's grace is both the basis and the norm of all being, both the source and the measure of all good. Measured by this standard, as the *negation* of God's *grace*, nothingness is as such *evil*, perverting and perverted. In this character, it therefore confronts God as well as the creature not as something neutral, some third other. Rather, it confronts both as an *enemy, offending* God and *threatening* his creature.[20]

Thus, just as we only first learn of the *existence* of nothingness through God's revelation and not our own observations and concepts, so too can we only truly define the *nature* of nothingness in relation to God and not our own observations and concepts.

In keeping with the above position, Barth's sixth point is that for all the impact nothingness has on the creaturely realm, "its overcoming, removal, and final disposal are primarily and strictly speaking *God's own* business."[21] This is so because of the covenant of grace. Creation does not exist in a vacuum, as some neutral arena produced by an arbitrary act of God unconnected with other areas of divine activity

---

20. Ibid.
21. Ibid.

and purpose. On the contrary, from its very origin it has been inseparably linked with God's gracious purposes, as Barth has maintained from the first chapter of his doctrine. Thus, any threat to God's creatures is in fact "first and foremost an offense against his own majesty."[22] Of course, in describing it as above all an affront to God, Barth does not intend to devalue in any way the very real suffering felt by creatures victimized by nothingness. Rather, his purpose is to make clear the affirmation that God has made the creature's cause completely his own. Indeed, one can be as sure of this as one is of one's own existence, because in actuality it is the basis of our existence, as the self-giving God reveals in Jesus Christ.

Barth's seventh and final point asserts that with this self-giving of God, with the death of Christ on the cross, nothingness is defeated and shown to have no perpetuity. Only God has perpetuity, although through the gracious fellowship God grants, the creature may share in it. Nothingness, however, is consigned to the past. It had power over the creature, but in Jesus it "struck at a prey that was too much for it and by which, in wanting to swallow it, it inevitably perished."[23] Should nothingness appear to be with us still, it is so not objectively but only to "our still veiled eyes."[24] For if in Christian *faith* we look back to Christ's resurrection and forward to Christ's coming in glory, we may *know* that nothingness is no more.

Even from this brief summary, one should be able to recognize that Barth's understanding of evil, of nothingness, displays many of the same characteristics apparent in previous parts of his doctrine of Creation. His christological orientation continues to be an obvious theme in his exposition. But which parts or themes from his description of nothingness can be said to show sensitivity to the "inner" and "outer" norms? Barth's consideration of these two norms appears most readily in two aspects of his exposition, namely, his exclusion of any possible dualism between God and evil, and his view that evil properly so-called is *not* to be equated with the "shadow side" of existence.

22. Ibid. Here is the reason for Barth's criticism of Schleiermacher: He believes the latter's "subjectivism" implies that for God, evil is not a concern, indeed, that it does not ultimately exist. See pp. 157–60.

23. Ibid. Barth's recapitulation of the ancient "fish hook" conception of the atonement is obvious.

24. Ibid.

Understanding Evil Christologically

In contrast to other segments of *Church Dogmatics*, one might wonder why Barth bothered to base his description of evil on revelation. Certainly the concept of an intrinsically evil "nothingness" is one that would have found a receptive audience among Barth's contemporaries, given their experience of the horrors visited upon Creation by two world wars. That one must neither downplay nor underestimate nothingness, nor attempt any sort of accommodation with it, either in one's action or in one's theological understanding of it, is a position that Barth's circumstances would seem to have made self-evident.

Regardless of this situation, however, he still did not open the door of his system to empirical confirmation or even, strictly speaking, corroboration. For him, the evil of nothingness remains a theological concept, based on revelation. Why? One could respond that Barth is simply maintaining methodological consistency with the rest of his work. Even though he is here dealing with a topic that could have easily used an approach based on empirical evidence, Barth had to continue with his previously established method lest he undermine his whole effort. But that was certainly not his only reason. To call nothingness a theological concept is to say something about content as well as method, namely, that it can be defined only in connection with the preceding theological concept of grace.

In this respect, Barth makes a move as old as the Apostle Paul, claiming that the true nature of sickness can be known only in light of the cure. To be sure, certain statements about that sickness may be analogous to certain affirmations made by the historian or the social scientist. But that does not mean those affirmations will contain everything the Christian must say, and it certainly does not mean those statements will be derived from historical and social observations or theories. To reach a complete and accurate understanding of nothingness, the Christian may only use revelation, for with this topic as with all others in theology, the source and substance of our knowledge derives solely from Jesus Christ. If we do not start here, we cannot hope to learn what we ought. If we do start here, then we will recognize the following "knowledge of faith": First, the real opponent of evil is God, and only subsequently the creature. Second, therefore, its defeat can only come at God's hand, which is accomplished in the incarnation, death, and resurrection of Christ. With this in mind, we may then recognize, third, that it must never be synthesized into our theology of Creation, for it always remains antithetical to Creation. Having established all this, Barth then acknowledges, fourth, that "in light of Jesus Christ, the *concrete* form in which nothingness is plainly effective and visible is most certainly human *sin*,"[25] which he explains as meaning that humans both are guilty of sin and are its victims. In other words, he actually concludes at the point that, for an empirical approach, would be the beginning.

Barth does not develop these themes in a strictly linear fashion, but in what might be called a musical way. With his initial noetic claim as the underlying melody, the other themes are played alternately as softer or louder harmonies. Each of the latter can be used to lead into the other, and all of them have a christological origin. However, it does appear that he intentionally introduces the fourth theme last, in order to guard against the perception that our own sin could be construed as a possible alternate starting point. He also repeats throughout and in various ways the point already mentioned, namely, that only in the event of healing—which happens in Christ—do we truly perceive the sickness.[26] His continued emphasis of this point serves two purposes: (1) It makes sure the good news of the gospel is always heard as God's first word, the word of grace, even as God speaks the second word of judgment; and (2) it is the means by which Barth maintains the proper scale of both grace and sin. Without such an emphasis, the seriousness of sin is inevitably downgraded, and with it the necessity and importance of grace. Both become domesticated, and humanity cuts itself off from faith in the grace of God to rely instead upon its own natural resources. In so doing, it decides, in effect, to settle for something other than that for which it was created, namely, its covenantal relationship with God.

In an effort to clarify both the christological method and content of his exposition, Barth debates a number of other thinkers in a long

---

25. *KD*, III:3, §50.3.
26. Ibid.

excursus in §50.3. The one who engages him the most is Schleiermacher, to whom he devotes nineteen of the forty-seven excursus pages in the German edition. He uses about the same amount of space summarizing Schleiermacher's position, highlighting his insights and *defending* him from his critics, as he does arguing *against* Schleiermacher's position. In fact, the fundamental charge Barth levels against him is that he was not true to his own best insight. Barth states that that insight can be condensed into one proposition with two interconnected parts: "[T]he essence and existence of nothingness consists in the fact that (1) it is that which God in his omnipotent grace negates, and therefore (2) it exists only in this relationship to grace."[27]

Regarding the first part, Barth commends Schleiermacher on his doctrine of sin because he holds that we only first *apprehend* sin through its conflict with our God-consciousness. Consciousness of sin does not come about by chance, nor do we deduce it from our surroundings, nor is it self-generated. It arises as a corollary tension with, or contradiction to, the sense of the proper relation to God previously and actually defined by the relation to the Redeemer. In this sense, Barth says, one can agree with Schleiermacher's claim that God is the "author" of sin, for he authors it in his negation of it. The metaphor may differ, but clearly Barth believes that he and Schleiermacher are making much the same point on this matter. However, in regard to the second part, Barth goes on to criticize Schleiermacher because he views sin as at root *nothing more than* a "consciousness," a merely subjective, human phenomenon. It has no objective reality, so ultimately it neither challenges nor affects God's own being—and if this is the case, then to Barth's mind, God's holiness and wrath, grace and judgment are all watered down, as is the role of Christ. Of course, when Barth himself first alludes to this "objective reality," he calls it "the impossible possibility"—a phrase that hardly seems suited to clarifying the discussion much. However, when one recognizes that it is simply Barth's shorthand or label for the seven observations made in §50.4, then its meaning becomes clear.[28]

---

27. Ibid; emphasis his.

28. Barth first uses the phrase in *KD* II:1, §31.2, and while he does not really employ it in his observations in §50.4, he certainly could have. See pp. 103–6. See also his defense of this phrase and others like it in an excursus in *KD* IV:3, §69.3.

Maintaining God's Omnipotence and Nature's Integrity

Be that as it may, this assertion by Barth, and Schleiermacher, that, on the basis of Christology, one may view God as the "author" of sin leads directly to another theme: Barth's exclusion of any sort of dualism between God and nothingness. This assertion is crucial for Barth because he develops it so as to maintain not only traditional affirmations of divine omnipotence and providence but also the modern assumption regarding the inviolability of the natural causal nexus. Barth begins his efforts in §50.1 by making it clear that, yes, nothingness is comprehended in God's providence—but not in the same way as other elements under God's lordship. It is an alien factor, and is governed in a way peculiar to it. But to make this claim is to raise up the classic dilemma at the center of all theodicies. Barth phrases it thus: "How can one, when dealing with the problem of nothingness, do justice simultaneously to the *holiness* of God and to his *omnipotence*?"[29] His response to this question presents a good illustration of his dialectical method, for he does not give a direct and conclusive answer, but instead establishes poles between which an answer must range. The first dialectic has to do with the derivation of nothingness. On the one hand, we should not understand nothingness "to be derived from the positive will and work of God, as if it too were a creature, and therefore incriminate the Creator himself and his lordship with the nullity of nothingness, while correspondingly excusing the creature from all responsibility for its existence, presence, and efficacy"; on the other hand, we are not to maintain that it "stems solely from the activity of the creature, in relation to which the lordship of God would shrink to a passive permission and observation, to an ineffectual foreknowledge, and to a mere after-the-fact endorsement."[30]

The second dialectic has to do with our evaluation of nothingness. On the one hand, we are to view it not as a demonic monster inspiring fear and respect, but through the joy of Easter, knowing it has already been judged in Jesus Christ and can therefore no longer kill or destroy. On the other hand, we should not suppose that this

---

29. *KD*, III:3, §50.1.
30. Ibid.

"victorious perception of faith" can be manipulated like some readily available principle; it is ours only in Christ and in the fear of God. In other words, we should avoid both "undue pessimism" and "cheap optimism," while maintaining a "commanded humility" and the "commanded confidence."[31] Barth summarizes and justifies this dialectical approach with the observation that all theology, including that dealing with the problem of evil, is *theologia viatorum*. As such, it does not possess its object so as to be able to put it on display once and for all within a final system; rather, it may only allude to its object in an ongoing report. To an extent, this conclusion merely echoes what Barth has already recognized, namely, that dogmatics is a historically relative activity. This means he once again shows acceptance of an assumption that had become canonical to modernity.

But it is also not hard to infer from this conclusion that Barth, like many theologians before and since, is simply unable to resolve fully the dilemma at the heart of theodicy. He wants to maintain the traditional pious sensibilities upholding both God's holiness and omnipotence. Thus, he does not dissolve the quandary, as, for example, the process theologians do when they redefine the notion of God's power. However, this does not mean Barth maintains a perfect balance between these two sensibilities. He does seem to tilt in favor of the divine omnipotence— as Schleiermacher did before him—by defining God's holiness "through" God's power. That is, he follows the same logic evident in Reformed understandings of providence, which I would summarize with the following line of reasoning: If it happened, God caused it; if God caused it, he had his reasons; because his reasons are always holy, then this event has to be just; therefore, we have no grounds for complaint. On the contrary, we are thankful that *all* things come to us from God's fatherly hand. Such a contrast echoes the passages from the Heidelberg Catechism and Calvin's Catechism cited earlier.[32] Indeed, Barth uses the former at one point to help expound the latter:

> From our point of view as creatures, there are "good" and "evil" things.
> But the certainty of the fatherly governance of God teaches us how to

---

31. Ibid.
32. See pp. 94–95 and 102.

be thankful for whatever he sends our way. For all things are under his governance. The Heidelberg Catechism puts it even more positively (27): "All things come not by chance, but by his fatherly hand." Therefore there can be no need for a theodicy, no need to justify God in all he does, since everything that happens is in his hand and since good and evil cannot be judged "in themselves," but in relation to his fatherly goodness.[33]

Yet in adopting this position, I argue that more than just traditionalism is motivating Barth—and Schleiermacher—here. This particular tradition, besides being a characteristically Reformed one, is also fully compatible with the modern demand that the integrity of the natural causal nexus be maintained. Because God is omnipotent, because God determines all that happens, the additional traditional suppositions that God sometimes governs by means of miracle or that evil likewise makes occasional supernatural incursions into the world become unnecessary. This idea also influences other themes in Barth's writing.

The "Shadow Side" as Natural

One of those themes centers on Barth's assertion that nothingness must not be equated with the "shadow side" of Creation. To do so is to commit a fundamental mistake, although it is often made. According to §50.2, this mistake takes one of two forms, both of which Barth guards against. The first form occurs when one comes to view this shadow side as itself evil, unnatural, and contrary to God's will and plan. Barth evaluates such a view as naively superficial in its estimation of the richness and diversity of real life. It is no accident that he enjoins us to consider Mozart and his music, for "real" life requires the harmony of the negative if it is to have any depth and fullness. He acknowledges that this negative aspect of Creation stands "so to speak *adjacent* to and *oriented* toward nothingness"—but it must not be equated with it.[34] In other words, Barth resolves part of the problem of evil by presenting what could be called an aesthetic understanding of at least some of life's travails. In this regard, his position is similar to

---

33. Barth, *Faith of the Church*, 51.
34. *KD*, III:3, §50.2.

Schleiermacher's. The second form of this mistake arises when one concludes that nothingness is actually not all that bad. Such a view adopts the aesthetic understanding toward *all* of life's travails, evil, and corruption. Barth condemns this attitude for what could be called its naive sophistication, for it assumes the desirability of all suffering and wickedness in life. Such a view is

> a masterpiece, even a triumph of *nothingness*. This is so not merely because it amounts to a slander on creation, to an act of stupidity and ingratitude toward the Creator who seeks his own likeness, but also because this act signifies the most refined *camouflaging* of *true* nothingness . . . [which thus] may cultivate its dangerous and pernicious being all the more undaunted and unchecked.[35]

In other words, while the first view fails to take seriously the diversity of Creation, this second view fails to take seriously the very evil and sometimes subtle power of nothingness. Paraphrasing Hannah Arendt's well-known quotation, Barth would likely say that the very banality evil can employ must make us all the more alert to its real character. To the clear-thinking Christian, both views must be rejected, according to Barth, because that is what God's self-manifestation in Jesus Christ requires.

Thus, Barth once again establishes a dialectic: He describes evil not by giving a straightforward exposition, but by establishing two poles between which any proper Christian understanding must move. So how does this help illustrate his concern for the "inner" and "outer" norms? The association may not be obvious, but his two poles themselves represent his implicit attempt to remain true simultaneously to tradition and modernity. On the one hand, his insistence that we take evil seriously, that we understand it in the first instance as an attack on God, and that we see its defeat as possible only through Christ are all affirmations continuing certain key traditional concerns. On the other hand, his insistence that we not equate evil with the "shadow side" of existence allows him to discard certain other traditional

---

35. Ibid.

associations that have now become rather awkward baggage for a contemporary worldview.

Consider, for example, the traditional notion that death was not an original aspect of creation, but only came into the world as the divine reaction to, and punishment of, Adam's and Eve's sin. This under-standing presents a whole variety of difficulties for both our concep-tion of the world and of God's causality. So when Barth begins his discussion of humanity's "ending time" (§47.5) by speaking of death as a sign of God's judgment, as an alien intrusion, as something that is felt to be (as it actually meets us) not an inherent part of human nature as God created it, he sounds quite traditional and almost unconcerned with the assumptions of modernity. Yet this is the case primarily because he devotes most of his initial exposition to an examination of the scriptural and theological resources available to him on this topic. However, as he approaches the end of this exposition, he begins to describe his own position. It may be summarized as follows: Death seems unnatural and evil because of our guilt and our fear of judg-ment. But the death of Jesus reveals that there are "two deaths," that is, our natural finitude and "the death of the reprobate." More to the point, it reveals that if we were unable to die the first death, then Jesus' redemptive death on the cross would have been, *ipso facto*, in vain. Thus, Jesus' death—which is to say, the fact that he *could* die—reveals implicitly that our finitude is natural and even good, an inherent part of God's Creation. It may confront us as something mysterious and strange, but we need not feel fearful or threatened. Ultimately, it is simply the mirror image of our beginning: From God we came; to God we will return.

Although Barth would probably bristle at the comparison, by describing death in these terms he has "subjectivized" the traditional account in virtually the same way as Schleiermacher. Death becomes a natural given, an aspect of the world's original created order. It points to no objective alteration or "fall" of that order, and it is not in itself evil. As Barth points out, "Death is not so much God's direct reaction against man's sin; it is rather God's abandoning of the men who have abandoned him."[36] Hence, the Christian should view it not so much as

---

36. Karl Barth, *Christ and Adam: Man and Humanity in Romans 5*, trans. T. A. Smail (New York: Harper & Row, 1956), 41.

a sentence to escape or as an enemy to defeat, but as a part of the divine design to which one should be, and through Christ can be, reconciled and conformed. In other words, the reality does not change, but our perception of it will—a formula that is applicable to the entire "shadow side" of existence and perfectly compatible with modern intellectual norms.

Yet Barth does not absorb all "evil," traditionally so-called, into this "shadow side" category, and in this respect he and Schleiermacher do differ. Some "evil" remains just that, and this is what Barth attempts to describe when he speaks of "nothingness." This evil is real,[37] and Christians must acknowledge it as such. Of course, such an acknowledgment is an acknowledgment "of faith," which means it remains, in non-Christian terms, a subjective affirmation or interpretation. Nevertheless, by designating it as in some sense real and not mere perception, by speaking of it as primarily an attack against God, Barth does grant it a theological status that has no counterpart in Schleiermacher's system.[38] And in so doing, Barth is not only more true to theological tradition[39] but also better equipped for adequately addressing the needs of his, and our, day.[40]

---

37. This is true in the sense described on pp. 103–6.

38. To Schleiermacher, such a move would presumably smack of Manichaeism. See *Gl*, §80, but also §81.3.

39. Cf., e.g., Anselm's *Cur Deus Homo*, book 1, chs. 11–15 and Calvin's *Institutes*, 1.14.15, 17, and 19. Consider also what Richard R. Niebuhr has to say about Schleiermacher's understanding of sin as presented in *Christmas Eve* and *The Christian Faith*:

> Psychological categories dominate the entire discussion, while political, social and purely mythical metaphors are conspicuously absent. Therefore, the reader necessarily misses the characterizations of sin as disobedience to God and as infidelity, not to speak of the mythical representation of sin as bondage to Satan, which are so typical of the Calvin whom Schleiermacher otherwise espoused and defended. The consequence of this limitation in the language of *The Christian Faith*—a limitation that is part and parcel of the "scientific" thrust of the whole enterprise—is an obvious impoverishment of the theology and piety Schleiermacher received from his spiritual precursors. (Niebuhr, *Schleiermacher on Christ and Religion* [New York: Charles Scribner's Sons, 1964], 200)

There is certainly a general difference in "mood" or imagery between Calvin and Schleiermacher on this topic. Niebuhr's more particular assertion that there are no political or social metaphors present in Schleiermacher's conception of sin is perplexing. True enough, he does not develop a notion of "institutional" or "nationalistic" sin comparable to that of Reinhold Niebuhr's (although his comments concerning patriotism in §70.3 seem to presage the logic of *Moral Man and Immoral Society* to a remarkable degree). Yet from as early as §6.2, Schleiermacher brings social categories into his discussion, while in §48.1 he explicitly states that the influence of moral evil is especially present in social evil. As a result, it is difficult to discern Niebuhr's precise point, and hard to avoid the conclusion that on this issue he was simply mistaken.

40. Cf. David Tracy, *Blessed Rage for Order* (New York: Seabury Press, 1975), 27–30.

CHAPTER 6

Confirmation from Schleiermacher's
Doctrine of Creation

What Schleiermacher himself labels as his doctrine of creation occupies only a small segment of his *Glaubenslehre*. Yet his "broader" doctrine of Creation includes not only his treatment of Creation, but of "preservation" as well. This "broader" doctrine also contains material on the divine attributes relevant to God as Creator, as well as Schleiermacher's thoughts on the "original perfection" of the world and humanity.

Legitimating the Claim of a "Broader" Doctrine

Schleiermacher divides the First Part of his *Glaubenslehre* into three sections. The first is entitled "Description of Our Pious Self-Consciousness Insofar as the Relation between the World and God Is Expressed Therein;" the second is entitled "On the Divine Attributes, Which Have Reference to the Pious Self-Consciousness, Insofar as It Expresses the Relation between God and the World"; and the third is entitled "On the Constitution of the World, Which Is Indicated in the Pious Self-Consciousness, Insofar as It Expresses the General Relation between God and the World." As the last phrase of each of these headings indicates, all three sections have to do in some respect with the relation between God and the world, that is, with describing some part of the relation of absolute dependence that creation has upon its Creator. The distinctiveness of the first section is that, as Schleiermacher states in §30.2 and reiterates elsewhere (§31 and §35), it describes this relation in its "fundamental dogmatic form" (*dogmatische Grundform*). That is, it is based on an *immediate* consciousness of God. To be sure, this same consciousness lies behind all dogmatic expressions, but in propositions of the second and third sections only indirectly or derivatively. Thus, the First Part of the *Glaubenslehre* produces two doctrines in the "fundamental form": divine preservation and creation. With these two doctrines, however, Schleiermacher does not intend to postulate the specifics of how the world began, nor does he intend to describe the mechanisms of that world in its ongoing existence. Such descriptions are the task of the natural sciences. Instead, he intends to offer a preliminary understanding of the world as the catalyst for the emergence and continuity of the fundamental feeling of absolute dependence as it is perceived by Christians. Thus, the propositions given will not offer specific data or knowledge about the world, but rather the Christian attitude toward and interpretation of that world's ultimate source, meaning, and destiny as revealed by a thorough exposition of the fundamental feeling.

On the basis of this exposition, however, one may then derive corollary forms producing doctrines that describe in much greater detail the character of the two poles in that relation, namely, God and the world. In the First Part, these doctrines describe those topics already mentioned, the "original" divine attributes and the "original perfection" of the world and humanity. However, as Schleiermacher's reference to pious self-consciousness in the latter two headings indicates, such doctrines remain subjective and secondary. Like the doctrines of the fundamental form, they too do not convey objective or immediate knowledge of either God or the world, even though they deal with realities external to the pious person. Nor does the latter describe some *historical* condition existing for some period at the world's beginning. Instead, they are simply logical deductions from the immediate and primary consciousness, elucidating what is implicit in the doctrines of the fundamental form and governed by the norms established in it. In other words, the material in these secondary forms is still not a direct description of God and the world; indeed, it is not even a direct description of a religious consciousness. Rather, these forms contain extrapolations derived from the description of the "imprint" of God found in the doctrines of the fundamental form. As such, they have a natural link to the doctrines of creation and preservation, complementing and clarifying many of the points raised therein. But as such, they are by definition dependent upon and subordinate to those first doctrines, because they are not themselves direct expressions of the pious self-conscious. Indeed, as Schleiermacher suggests to Lücke, dogmatics could do without them.[1]

Schleiermacher's goal in his doctrine of Creation is to offer a christological or Christian interpretation of the world, or, to put it more precisely, the world's purpose and meaning. What leads him to this task? Schleiermacher affirms that the world is a dynamic place, as the evidence of nature and history readily attest. But this dynamic character is not to be explained solely in a materialistic and deterministic manner. There is a spiritual element as well, which gives direction and meaning to the world. To understand this spiritual element properly, however, requires a careful delineation of its place and role in the natural order of the world. Is it distinct from, or an aspect of, the natural realm? Does it undergird, pervade, direct, and/or lead nature? Is it divine, human, or both? Leaving aside for the moment a consideration of the content of this spiritual element, how is it related to the natural order? Can it be characterized as a form of first, efficient, and/or final cause? Needless to say, Schleiermacher's explicit doctrine of creation will be one aspect of his answer, but just as clearly, he will not be content making only limited assertions about the world's beginning. To understand the relation of spirit to the created order properly, one should look not so much to the beginning of the world as to its fundamental structure, the basis of its development and, ultimately, its consummation. This Schleiermacher will do, starting with his explicit

---

1. Friedrich Schleiermacher, On the "Glaubenslehre": Two Letters to Dr. Lücke, trans. James Duke and Francis Fiorenza, American Academy of Religion Texts and Translations Series 3 (Chico, Calif.: Scholars Press, 1981), 70.

doctrine of creation, but also continuing through the whole course of his system. The first part sometimes plays a negative role, that is, it seeks to exclude understandings or beliefs that Schleiermacher views as unnecessary or inappropriate to the essence of Christian piety or as incompatible with modern intellectual assumptions. Alternately, it sometimes plays a preliminary role, that is, it seeks to expound certain general presuppositional beliefs that are to be embraced and completed in a specifically Christian manner in the second part. Such beliefs are thus positive or constructive, but they are also limited.

The Connection and Distinction between Creation and Providence

Let us now turn to what Schleiermacher himself specifies as his doctrine of creation. A brief consideration produces several impressions. We have already alluded to the first impression, namely, its brevity. Another obvious aspect of the doctrine is its link to his doctrine of preservation. On the basis of this linkage, Schleiermacher is able to assign the doctrine of creation a limiting, somewhat negative role, while giving the doctrine of preservation both a positive and negative role. Furthermore, his doctrine of creation gets its biblical basis from New Testament passages alone, using them in fact to forego any reliance on the Genesis creation accounts traditionally cited for this doctrine. This should come as no surprise, for as he stated in the second of his two letters to Lücke, Christianity must learn to relinquish much of what it traditionally conceived with regard to creation. By extension, this would also entail giving up the scriptural passages upon which that conception was based.[2]

How does Schleiermacher explain these various moves more fully, and what is the logic that leads him to take this approach? First of all, Schleiermacher yokes his doctrine of creation to his doctrine of preservation because they are the complementary parts of the more primary and original expression of the relation existing between the world and God, namely, that the world exists only in absolute dependence upon God. Secondly, because of Schleiermacher's understanding

---

2. Ibid., 60–61.

that this relation is itself made known to us through our own pious self-consciousness, the doctrine of preservation gains its larger, more positive role over the doctrine of creation because the latter presents something that is "simply not immediately given us in self-consciousness."[3] Rather, it is the self-consciousness of the *continuity* of our own existence, and by extension the rest of finite being, that is the basis for our recognizing God's sustaining of us and the world. In other words, we have an immediate sense of God's "preservation" of us and all finite being, in contrast to God's "creation," which is not immediately felt but is simply a logical presupposition of preservation. In itself, creation does not describe the total feeling of absolute dependence; it only describes its "beginning"—however that may be conceived—and it does so with the exclusion of any sense of continuity.[4] To repeat the analogy from geometry, creation is the point from which the line of time and the cosmos commences, but it is itself never part of the length of that line.

To be sure, this analogy may appear to overstate the distinction between creation and preservation, given what Schleiermacher writes in §38. In this proposition, Schleiermacher recognizes that the two doctrines could be presented in such a way that either could absorb the other without affecting what is contained in the "original expression." Presupposing "our increased knowledge of the world"[5]—gained, of course, through science—Schleiermacher points out the current recognition that the various heavenly bodies with their various living species, when viewed as discrete spheres of life, need not have come into existence all at once, but could have done so over a period of time. Yet if this is the case in certain instances, then from one perspective, it can only be due to an underlying continuity of formative powers in finite being as a whole.[6] Hence, one would consider this continuity the primary element, which enables the various individual creations to occur. If we were to express this relationship doctrinally, we would say that preservation is the source of creation, and that as such the latter could be entirely incorporated into the former. Considered from the

---

3. *Gl*, §36.1.
4. As I will discuss later, Schleiermacher uses this distinction as one point in his argument rejecting those who would conceive the "original perfection" of the world in temporal terms.
5. *Gl*, §38.1.
6. Ibid.

other perspective, however, these new spheres of life are just that, namely, new—each one a thing or effect that does not merely continue what preceded it, but that contains something not found in its originator. Hence, the key element would not be that which maintains continuity, but that which fosters innovation. If we were to express this understanding doctrinally, we would say that the ever renewing power of creation renders the notion of preservation superfluous.

That there is such an interrelation between these two doctrines, however, depends upon the underlying assumption that the divine activity, whether conceived as creating or sustaining, consists of *a single and uninterrupted act*. Thus, it is not that the doctrines say the same thing in different words; as we shall see from Schleiermacher's exposition of them, they each serve a different function. Rather, they are correlative because *both* are derived from the one fundamental religious consciousness that God is the sole immutable determinant of all that is, the all-encompassing "Whence" that Schleiermacher first referred to in §4. Recognizing this fact, we can see why he will later take such pains in his initial comments on the divine attributes to stress the absolute unity of God and God's causality. The multiplicity of attributes described in a dogmatic system should not be construed as reflecting any sort of actual multiplicity in God. Such differentiations are simply aids to our theological thinking. If we fail to understand this point, then God might be conceived as alternating between activity and inactivity, in one moment creating and/or sustaining the world while in another passively letting it run itself. Yet this would be lowering God into the domain of mutual interdependence, which would not only disparage the customary assumptions about the being of God but also disrupt the integrity of the natural causal nexus and destroy the reliability of the feeling of absolute dependence. This is the conceptualization that can and must be avoided in dogmatics, for it has its roots "not in Christian piety, but in a muddled worldview all too common in everyday life that accepts dependence on God only as a help in explaining the course of the world when the natural coherence of things is concealed."[7] If one does avoid such a conceptualization, however, then there are no necessary reasons, but only practical ones, for distinguishing the

---

7. *Gl*, §38.2.

divine attributes and the doctrines of creation and preservation in one's theological system.

One cannot ultimately separate the beginning and continuity of the world and its history from its end, either. If the divine causality is in itself a single, uninterrupted act, then God must have the consummation of the world in some sense "in mind" already at the creation of the world. There is, after all, but one divine decree. It is not amended or supplemented as time goes by, but is complete from all eternity, even though from a human point of view it appears to unfold progressively over the course of history.[8] Schleiermacher hints at this continuity or singleness of purpose in his discussion of the traditional distinctions made between God's "original" and "derived" attributes.[9] With the proper precautions, Schleiermacher allows that this distinction could be a way of differentiating those divine attributes considered in his First Part from those in his Second Part. His reason for allowing such a distinction stems from his desire to counter those who would group all the divine attributes in *one* dogmatic location. As he suggested in §31.2, such an approach too often conceals the link the divine attributes have with both the fundamental feeling in general and Christian piety in particular. By making this distinction in his presentation of the divine attributes, Schleiermacher gives himself a way to extend his doctrine of God over the whole of his dogmatic system, thus reflecting with the proximity of that doctrine to what he writes in his First and Second Parts—the underlying unity of those two parts. That is, if one recognizes the essential oneness of the divine attributes and activity, one cannot help but affirm the essential unity of the general fundamental feeling and specific Christian piety. Indeed, the divine attributes Schleiermacher describes in §§50–56 and §§79–85 are not only linked to, but completed by, the attributes described in §§164–69. What he writes about "omnipotence" in §167 may be said of the other "original" attributes as well: "We have certainly posited the whole divine act, but *without a motive* and thus as an absolutely indeterminate action."[10] In a very real sense, the attributes presented in the First

---

8. I will have more to say on this topic in chapter 9. Cf. Richard R. Niebuhr, *Schleiermacher on Christ and Religion* (New York: Charles Scribner's Sons, 1964), 248–59.

9. See *Gl*, §50.3.

10. *Gl*, §167.2; emphasis mine.

Part are strictly that, that is, descriptions of certain characteristics of God's *causality*, but not of the divine *essence*. They have form, but no content. They describe the basic mode of God's relation to creation, but offer no understanding of God's purpose. They tell us *how* God relates to creation, but not *why*. For that, one must turn to the Second Part of the *Glaubenslehre*, which retrospectively imbues the doctrine of God expounded in the First Part with a Christian "color and tone." In an identical fashion, all that is said in the First Part regarding creation itself must also be imbued with the Christian color and tone of the Second Part.

It is with all this in mind, presumably, that Schleiermacher explains his "practical" reasons for dividing creation and preservation in the proposition just prior to his actual exposition of them. Schleiermacher holds that we have no consciousness of a *beginning* of being, but only of a *continuity* of being. Hence, for the purpose of religious teaching, our resources commend themselves not primarily for a doctrine of creation, but for a doctrine of preservation. A doctrine of creation, strictly speaking, is derivative, and serves the supportive purpose of excluding any element that would undermine our fundamental con-sciousness, as expounded primarily in the doctrine of preservation. As Schleiermacher points out, "[G]enerally speaking, the question about the beginning of all finite being arises not in the interest of piety, but rather in that of the desire for knowledge, and thus it can also only be answered through the means that this desire offers."[11] Mythology, leg-end, and etiological tales are the means Schleiermacher has in mind here, which assert a form of "knowledge" and do not belong properly to piety, a form of feeling. Piety may have only an indirect interest in the question of finite origins, namely, the interest just mentioned regarding the exclusion of any element that would contradict our fun-damental feeling. As a result, his explicit doctrine of creation is almost inevitably brief.

In an effort to show that this is not just his position, Schleiermacher then states that this is also the position of the New Testament and all proper (*eigentlichen*) confessions of faith. This assertion presumably meets the requirement put forward by §27, which declares:

---

11. *Gl*, §39.1.

> All propositions that lay claim to a place in a compendium of Evangelical doctrine must prove themselves in part through appeal to Evangelical confessional writings and, in absence of these, to the New Testament writings, and in part through demonstration of the unity with other, already recognized propositions.[12]

The Old Testament, in contrast, with its creation stories in the historical book of Genesis, serves chiefly the desire for knowledge, and not the interests of piety. Thus, it is not just that these stories are to be excluded from a Christian doctrine of creation because they are Jewish; they are to be excluded because they are not even a product of religious feeling. This is one example of the negative role that Schleiermacher's doctrine of creation plays, maintaining what he views as essential in Christian tradition while deleting what he views as extraneous. One should also notice the way the "essential" is determined. On the one hand, he requires that material be compatible in the first instance with Evangelical tradition—the normative role of the New Testament apparently being only secondary, and sometimes unnecessary. On the other hand, he emphasizes the necessity of systematic coherence—a criterion any theologian ought to keep in mind, of course, but one that could lead to an overly streamlined rendering of the tradition.

Examining Schleiermacher's "Narrower" Doctrine

Schleiermacher then presents his doctrine of creation, explicitly so called, in two propositions. The first of these, §40, provides his understanding of what the doctrine should and should not say, while the second, §41, elaborates this understanding in particular ways. Evident in both propositions is Schleiermacher's desire to rein in the role of the doctrine in comparison to most traditional expositions of it. This limiting role is obvious in his wording of §40:

> The pious self-consciousness that here lays the foundation for our doctrine opposes every representation of the origin of the world that excludes anything whatever from origination by God, or that places

---

12. *Gl*, §27.

God himself under those determinations and antitheses that have arisen first in the world and through the world.[13]

Schleiermacher develops this proposition in three subsections. In the first, he states that the New Testament really requires of Christian dogmatics no more than this unadorned assertion about creation, and thus we may willingly defer to the natural sciences the task of elaborating the details of the origination of the cosmos. The New Testament passages cited[14] all take God's creation of the world as a given, without attempting to explain it any further. The implication Schleiermacher draws from this is that all Christians should do likewise, if they in fact accord the New Testament the authority they say they do. This rather limited given is the only essential element of Christian tradition that needs to be continued.

Schleiermacher also comments that Christians may "calmly await" a further explanation of creation by science. This stems from the passage already cited (§4.4), regarding the "Whence" of our feeling of absolute dependence. He assumes that science will not explain creation without positing a "Whence" outside the natural order that is comparable to, if not dependent upon, the "Whence" that Christian doctrine understands as God. Thus, there is little danger that the findings of science may conflict with the teachings of Christianity; indeed, they will likely complement those teachings, in a sense supplying the material data that Christianity interprets. To be sure, in certain brief asides and comments later on, Schleiermacher does suggest that there could be no complementarity between his system and strictly materialistic or reductionistic explanations of the cosmos.[15] But he also apparently assumed that such explanations would not be widely accepted by the scientific mainstream, so that his doctrine of creation would still be compatible with the intellectual givens of his age.[16]

In his second subsection of §40, Schleiermacher recognizes that, in spite of what he has just said, many dogmaticians have sought to

---

13. *Gl*, §40.

14. Acts 17:24; Rom. 1:19–20; and Heb. 11:3.

15. See p. 53, n. 27, for some of the passages in *The Christian Faith* that hint at this position.

16. Of course, such an assumption could not be taken for granted in Barth's age; from what we have learned of his position, aware as he was of Marx, Nietzsche, Freud, and others, it would seem that he certainly did not think so. The same is likely true of our age as well.

present a more detailed account of creation based upon the "Mosaic narratives" in Genesis. Any such attempt is a mistake, in Schleiermacher's view, based upon a confusion of the dogmatic task with that of philosophy. Moreover, nothing in the writings of the Reformers or in the confessions of faith requires such an undertaking. He acknowledges that while Luther and Calvin undoubtedly understood the Genesis account as a "genuinely historical narrative," they never made that assumption a required belief in their uses of it, which implies that neither should latter-day Evangelical Christians. Indeed, within the Old Testament itself, while reference is often made to the creation accounts, at times this is the case only so another, more important point could be made. At other times, these accounts may themselves be the central focus, yet they are still "very freely handled." Schleiermacher concludes from this: "We have no reason therefore to adhere more strictly to such a historical understanding than the Hebrews themselves did in their best days."[17]

Moving from this line of reasoning, Schleiermacher finishes this subsection on a different tack. He states that even if one were to grant that the Genesis creation stories were indeed genuinely historical accounts communicated in an extraordinary way, they would still be a "natural scientific insight," that is, a form of *knowing*, which as such could add nothing to a dogmatic, which is based upon a *feeling*. In other words, Schleiermacher's exposition up to this point conforms to all the legitimate demands of the church and the academy: It maintains what he views as the essential insights and affirmations of Scripture and tradition, even while weeding out peripheral accretions, and it does not overstep the bounds of proper dogmatic method, thus maintaining dogmatics in its rightful place among the other sciences.

In the last subsection of §40, Schleiermacher considers his proposition in light of its consistency with his own presupposition regarding the feeling of absolute dependence. Specifically, he tests the two "exclusions" of the proposition against this feeling, to ensure that they are legitimate representations of it. On the one hand, the proposition rejects any view that sees anything as coming into being apart from God's creation. Such a view would remove said thing from its absolute

---

17. *Gl*, §40.2.

dependence upon God, in effect elevating it to equal status with God and thus destroying the reliability of our feeling of absolute dependence. On the other hand, the proposition rejects any view that sees God as a part of that creation, involved with it in a way qualitatively similar to the creatures in it. Such a view would deprive God of absolute freedom, in effect lowering the divine status to that of creatures and again destroying the reliability of our feeling of absolute dependence. Thus, in asserting what it does, Schleiermacher maintains that the proposition as presented is a legitimate extension of the feeling of absolute dependence with regard to creation. As such, it establishes a solid starting point for his further elaboration of that feeling in the doctrines that follow.

Prior to such elaboration, however, Schleiermacher seeks to clarify two more matters regarding the doctrine of creation. This he does in §41. The first of these concerns the proper understanding of the traditional phrase *ex nihilo*, and the second concerns the relation between creation and temporality. Schleiermacher's purpose in explaining the phrase "out of nothing" is to ensure that it not be used in a way analogous to descriptions of human activity. Humans "create" all manner of things out of preexisting raw materials, but this does not mean God is to be conceived as creating the cosmos "out of" the preexisting stuff, "nothing." Nothing is exactly that. As Schleiermacher clearly states, "The expression 'out of nothing' denies that anything whatever was extant outside of God before the origin of the world, which as matter could enter into the formation of the world."[18] He then goes on to say that the phrase not only excludes any concept of a preexisting matter outside of God, but it also excludes any concept of a preexisting form within God. Citing Luther's objection to this understanding, Schleiermacher states that it violates the second part of his proposition, in that it cannot be conceived other than sequentially, which would make the divine activity a temporal activity, an understanding already excluded. In this matter, Schleiermacher aligns himself with tradition and affirms the propriety of the orthodox position, although it appears that he does so primarily as a result of his criterion that latter doctrines cohere with previously established ones.

---

18. *Gl*, §41.1.

Yet Schleiermacher accomplishes more than this. He has also established one principle by which he will later reject—in his doctrine of the "Original Perfection of the World"—the notion that God created "the best of all possible worlds." To assert that the world is "the best" and not merely "good" implies that at the moment of creation—and in each succeeding moment of the divine preservation—God selects from an array of different possible worlds the one that most closely fits the divine standards and purpose. But such a conception suggests that these worlds exist in some sense independently of God, either as possibilities within the divine mind or as some form of "actual potentiality" outside of God. However, the notion of creation *ex nihilo* already prohibits such conceptualizing, because it cannot be done without placing God in the determinations and antitheses that characterize the created realm.

At this juncture, Schleiermacher moves into the second part of §41, where he considers—or, to be a bit more accurate, explains why he need not consider—a number of the issues raised in the past regarding the relation of creation to temporality. He stakes out his own position at the outset:

> Now if we isolate the first creation as strictly as we did above, so that all that is not absolutely primitive is already reckoned to be part of the developing course of nature and thus brought under the concept of preservation, then the question whether creation itself occupied time is already settled with a no.[19]

Keep in mind that for Schleiermacher, a conception of creation serves its purpose primarily in what it excludes; it has a limited and limiting task. When one then combines this conception with his understanding of the intrinsic dynamism of the natural order, one can see why he felt no need to engage in speculations about various stages of creation. As a result, he will later be able to exclude any assumption of a golden age from which humanity fell. The developing course of nature he perceives in history represents real progress; it does not simply recover or seek that which it once had, but lost.

---

19. *Gl*, §41.2.

Another question that is not intrinsic to Schleiermacher's concern asks whether time existed prior to creation or whether it only began with creation. He nevertheless answers that it could only be the latter, for prior to creation it could only have referred to God. But this would place God within the temporal sphere, again a possibility already ruled out.

Schleiermacher concludes §41 with some thoughts on the controversy over the temporal or eternal creation of the world. His initial comments echo the attitude prevalent in the issues just discussed: The matter has no bearing one way or the other on the feeling of absolute dependence, and is thus in and of itself a matter of indifference to a proper dogmatic. Yet he then seems to suggest that certain ways of explaining a creation in time can indeed undermine the feeling of absolute dependence. He mentions Origen's formulation and briefly examines Augustine's position, and finds both of them wanting. From one perspective, both appear to bring God into the realm of change, while from another Augustine's could be construed as allowing the possibility of the world coming into being independently of the divine will. To avoid these problems, Schleiermacher appears to suggest that a conception of creation as eternal rather than temporal would be more conducive to maintaining the proper religious self-consciousness. To support this view, he links his earlier citation of Hebrews 11:3[20] with an allusion to John 1:1ff. He sets up a kind of exegetical syllogism: The world was created by the Word; the Word is eternal; therefore, the Word is eternally creating the world. Of course, this conclusion does not follow necessarily from these two premises alone, but given his immediately preceding references to Origen and Augustine, and what he will later say about the divine causality in §§51–55, we recognize the unspoken premise that it is inappropriate to think of God as making a transition from nonactivity to activity. Because the notion of temporal creation seems inevitably to entail such a transition, Schleiermacher finds that of "eternal creation" more intelligible. Perhaps this alternative is what he had in mind when he told Lücke that Christians might have to relinquish "the concept of creation itself, as it is usually understood."[21]

20. *Gl*, §40; cf. above, p. 126 and n. 14.
21. See p. 21.

But what are we to make of this conclusion? Is it not, after all, asserting a form of knowledge? If in fact Schleiermacher has left the explanation of creation to the natural sciences, then would not his task be to develop a doctrine that could fit either a "temporal" or an "eternal" creation? We must recall his definition of the task of a doctrine of creation as being primarily exclusive[22] and his remark about the indifference of dogmatics toward this particular issue. In that light, his comments on the matter appear to be simply an excursus on the problems implicit in some of the traditional arguments supporting a conception of a temporal creation. When one adds to that excursus the postscript attached to §41—which maintains "that God created the world through a *free* decree"[23]—one can see that Schleiermacher's primary concern here is simply to uphold the aseity of God.[24] One can conceive these matters regarding creation in a variety of ways, and in the view of a proper dogmatics, one may be as acceptable as another—as long as the one chosen does not conflict with the requirements just outlined in §§40–41.

Angels, the Devil, and Historical Progress

At this point, Schleiermacher ends his exposition of his explicit doctrine of creation and turns to two appendices dealing with, respectively, "The Angels" and "The Devil." As one might expect, he has little use for these two areas of traditional Christian belief—which could explain his consideration of each in an appendix rather than an actual doctrine. However, in a number of passages he makes comments that begin to offer limited yet revealing clues as to his understanding of, and assumptions about, the historical development of creation. With regard to angels, Schleiermacher acknowledges in §42.1 that we know far too little about the universe to assert once and for all that they either do or do not exist. Such spiritual beings may indeed exist as a part of the natural order. But if they do exist, and if they have made occasional appearances in our world, these appearances can be considered

---

22. See pp. 120–21 and 124.
23. *Gl*, §42, postscript; emphasis his.
24. Cf. *Gl*, §54, postscript.

"miraculous" not because they suspend the natural causal nexus (a possibility already ruled out), but only because they have been connected with "special points of development and revelation."[25] In §43.1, with regard to the notion of guardian angels, Schleiermacher points out that inevitably this concept is losing its influence among Christians, in that it belongs to a time when the knowledge of the forces of nature was still very meager and the dominion of humanity over the same stood at its lowest stage.[26]

We can draw several conclusions from these two excerpts. To begin with, Schleiermacher understands history to be developing, rather than static or cyclical; furthermore, it appears to develop not straightforwardly, with imperceptible yet steady progress, but in stages or epochs that can appear quite abruptly, with dramatic and disturbing force. In addition, history displays an increasing human understanding of and control over the natural realm—a development that apparently should not be viewed as morally neutral but as *good*. To be sure, this latter conclusion may not seem to have much support from what he writes about angels, but it does seem legitimate in light of a brief comment made in his appendix on the devil. In §45.2, Schleiermacher considers the phenomena of how often, with "a sudden development of the good," evil counteracts in such a tenacious manner that it seems to be a "kingdom and power" in its own right. In response to this perception, Schleiermacher argues, "The more the good consolidates itself, that is, as a historical totality, all the more seldom can such counteractions recur, and all the more must they splinter into isolated occurrences [*ins Kleine zerplittern*], so that here too the devil will be no longer thought of."[27] In other words, the primitive mind often made recourse to angelic and demonic forces to explain momentous historical events. The modern mind, however, understands such explanations to be unnecessary, in part because it possesses a clearer knowledge of the mechanisms at work in the world as a whole and in part because it views that world as inevitably, if not steadily, progressing, due to the increasing control it exercises over the world. Thus,

25. *Gl*, §42.1.
26. *Gl*, §43.1.
27. *Gl*, §45.2.

modernity's explanations can do without recourse to various supernatural agents and without recourse to any pervasive dualism between
good and evil, whether supernatural or natural, because it recognizes
God as the sole determinant of the world, enabling development on
the basis of one eternal decree.

Providence: The Start of the "Broader" Doctrine

Although Schleiermacher's explicit doctrine of creation is brief, his
broader understanding of the created order as a dynamic and divinely
sustained whole emerges in his doctrine of preservation. This is the
doctrine which directly expresses the relation between the world and
God, because unlike the doctrine of creation it is based upon an *immediate* self-consciousness, that is, our sense of the *continuity* of our existence in absolute dependence upon God. Only with this doctrine does
Schleiermacher really begin his explanation of our relation to and
understanding of the natural world of which we are a part. He states
his position in its fundamental form in §46, a proposition he then aug-
ments with his understanding of miracles (§47), theodicy (§48), and
free will (§49).

A brief consideration of §46 suggests that Schleiermacher seeks to
present a dogmatic interpretation of the created order compatible
with the norms of modern science. Indeed, insofar as any choice arises
between fostering such a compatibility or preserving various traditional dogmatic formulations, Schleiermacher is far more inclined to
the former than the latter. His proposition commencing §46 states:

> The pious self-consciousness, in virtue of which we understand every-
> thing that affects us and acts upon us as being in absolute dependence
> on God, coincides entirely with the insight that precisely all such things
> are occasioned and determined by the interdependence of nature.[28]

That is, we depend upon God in no way other than through the interrelated web of the natural order. We may not always be aware of this

---

28. *Gl*, §46.

connection, either because of occasional lapses in our pious self-consciousness or the limits of our experience and knowledge of nature, but these are the exceptions which prove the rule that "for each and every situation we *should* feel and acknowledge [*mitfühlen*] absolute dependence on God just as much as we conceive each and every situation as completely determined by the interdependence of nature."[29] Schleiermacher will describe more fully the basis for this "should" in his doctrine of the original perfection of the world.

In other words, he asserts that God works *only* through this natural order, even though Christianity has long held that supernatural incursions are at least occasionally God's preferred mode of activity. Schleiermacher recognizes the prevalence of this contrary view and argues persuasively against it. For him, a key problem with it arises in the way it creates an opposition between religion and science. Schleiermacher's description of the problem merits full quotation:

> It is said that the more clearly we conceive of something as completely conditioned by the interdependence of nature, the less can we come to the feeling of its absolute dependence on God; and, conversely, the more vital this feeling is, the more must we indefinitely leave undecided its interdependence with nature. It is clear, however, that, from our standpoint and in keeping with everything said up to now, such an opposition between the two views cannot be considered valid. Otherwise it would have to be that with the perfection of our knowledge of the world, in which case everything would always present itself in the interdependence of nature, the development of the pious consciousness in ordinary life would wholly cease, which is totally against our presupposition that piety is fundamental to human nature. And on the other hand, the love of piety, conversely, would have to struggle against any pursuit of research and every broadening of our knowledge of nature, which is totally against our proposition that the perception of creation leads to the consciousness of God. And besides, prior to the perfection of both tendencies, those knowing most about nature would have to be those who are the least pious, and vice versa. However, inasmuch as the

---

29. *Gl*, §46.1; emphasis mine.

orientation toward knowledge of the world is just as fundamental to the human soul as the one toward God-consciousness, it can only be a false wisdom that wants to dismiss piety, and a misconceived piety for love of which the advances of knowledge should be obstructed.[30]

The root of this false dichotomy, according to Schleiermacher, lies in that understanding of the religious consciousness which assumes our *occasional* experiences of the incomprehensible and the awe-inspiring are the *sole* source or stimulator of that religious consciousness. In addition, to use a phrase from a later time, in our encounter with the *mysterium tremendum*, we suppose that it is breaking through the natural order from "elsewhere." In contrast to this view, which attempts in fact to add a supernatural kind of knowledge to the initial experience, Schleiermacher does not so much deny the encounter with the *mysterium tremendum* as devalue it. It is not qualitatively different, but only quantitatively so, from all other encounters we have in the natural realm. Were this not the case, our understanding of how God relates to the world would be placed in a self-negating tension with itself: God's occasional interventions would be interrupting his own constant preservation of the world. To be sure, awe-inspiring occurrences may indeed seem better suited to awaken our sense of absolute dependence than the measured, familiar occurrences of our everyday lives, but there is no necessary cause preventing that sense from being awakened or remaining awake in that everyday life. All occurrences, whether awe-inspiring or commonplace, arise out of the interconnected web of the natural order, and whether they are incomprehensible or understood, each may excite the feeling that recognizes the *totality* of that order as existing only in absolute dependence upon God.

Problems occur for piety only when one seeks to consider an event in isolation from this totality. By their apparently unique characters, momentous events lend themselves to such a separation, but even trivial acts or events can create problems for one's sense of the whole natural order, when either too much or too little is made of their place in that whole. They may be given an inflated significance, as when one

---

30. Ibid.

supposes that because great events often evolve out of trivial ones, then even these trivial ones must be *directly* ordained by God. Such a view is too quick to see an immediate intervention by God, rather than looking for causes in the natural order itself. Or a particular event may be given a deflated significance, as when one fears it is sacrilege to attribute *any* divine ordination to something so trivial. The upshot of either view is to undermine the proposition that began §46, because both tend to divorce absolute dependence on God from the interdependence of nature.

Schleiermacher states this position most clearly in §46.2, where he writes that the feeling of absolute dependence "is most complete when we identify ourselves in our self-consciousness with the whole world, and yet, in doing so, feel ourselves no less dependent."[31] His point is not that God's sustaining power is sometimes exercised in supernatural events and sometimes in natural ones, nor that it is exercised only in certain key natural events while the remainder of them occur through their own mundane causality. To be sure, we may feel this sustaining power only from time to time, but this indicates a gap in our religious consciousness, not in God's preservation of the world. As the phrasing of the above quotation suggests, Schleiermacher's point is that our feeling of absolute dependence can be more or less complete depending on how far we identify our "horizontal" relationships in the natural realm with our "vertical" relationship with God.

> This identification, however, can only succeed to the extent that we unite in thought everything that in appearance is separated and isolated, and by means of this connection conceive of everything as one. In this "All-one" of finite being we then have conceived the most complete and universal interdependence of nature, and if in this case we feel absolutely dependent, then both have fully coincided, that is, the most complete conviction that everything is fully contingent upon and grounded in the totality of the interdependence of nature and the inner certainty of the absolute dependence of everything finite on God. From this follows at the same time the possibility of pious self-consciousness in every

---

31. *Gl*, §46.2.

moment of the objective consciousness and the possibility of perfect world-consciousness in every moment of pious self-consciousness.[32]

Not just we alone, not just occasional moments or events, but the whole interrelated natural realm exists in absolute dependence—and not just by means of a conglomeration of individual dependencies. Rather, it is precisely as this *whole*, with its mutual interdependencies and freedoms, that the finite realm exists in absolute dependence. Just as the divine activity can only be thought of properly as one—even though it might seem fragmented when reference is made to God's various attributes—so too must the created order, which stands in relation to God, be thought of as one, even with its great diversity of parts. As a result, the relation is of one to one. In other words, as Schleiermacher not unexpectedly states, divine preservation and natural causation "are both the same thing, only viewed from different vantage points."[33] Herein lies the reason for Schleiermacher's earlier claim that there can be no real conflict between religion and science—quite the contrary. When properly understood, the desire to promote both piety and knowledge of the world will foster but a single outcome. Schleiermacher formulates it thus:

> Now if we posit both tendencies as fully developed in a given man, then each would also evoke the other with perfect ease, so that every thought, as part of the world-comprehension [*Weltbegriffs*], becomes in him the purest pious feeling, and every pious feeling, evoked by a part of the world, becomes in him a total world-representation [*Weltvorstellung*].[34]

That the preceding demonstrates Schleiermacher's desire to make compatible his descriptions of the divine preservation compatible with the norms of science should be obvious. But that it also entails the rejection of certain traditional dogmatic formulations may not be as clear. Evidence for this rejection appears in his postscript to §46. He states that there is no place in his *Glaubenslehre* for past understandings

---

32. Ibid.
33. Ibid.
34. Ibid.

of God's "general," "special," and "most special" providence. Nor is there need to distinguish between God's "preserving" and "cooperating" work. And neither does it help to introduce the idea of "divine government" at this stage. Yet Schleiermacher does not view the elimination of these distinctions as in any way hindering his desire to maintain the essence of the tradition. Generally stated, Schleiermacher avoids such conceptualizations as not only unnecessary but inappropriate, and not just from the perspective of modern science but from dogmatics as well. First, they are unnecessary because they add nothing useful to Schleiermacher's position. For example, he observes that general preservation must include everything, so that any further subdivisions of it become superfluous. Similarly, certain points to be made with the idea of divine government, such as a "fulfillment of divine decrees or a steering of all things to divine purposes"[35] according to God's original and constant will, are already included in Schleiermacher's proposition. The implicit assumption operative in these two instances is that the more one subdivides one's conceptualization in these ways, the more one's conceptualizations are open to error and self-contradiction. Thus, nothing is gained, and a certain logic and coherence is lost by such expansions.

Secondly, they are inappropriate because they either violate other propositions already affirmed,[36] or lead to statements properly left to the natural sciences. Schleiermacher sees an example of the former in discussions of special and most special preservation which suggest that God's sustaining began or ceased at a particular time, which violates the principle given in §41 that God's activity not be conceived as temporal. Another example appears to arise inevitably from the concept of a divine cooperating work, because it implies that the finite may have an "efficacy [*Wirksamkeit*] in and for itself, thus independent from the preserving divine activity,"[37] which is an obvious violation of Schleiermacher's fundamental principle that all finite being is always absolutely dependent upon God. Schleiermacher sees yet another example of the latter problem in the further distinction made between special and most special preservation, "because it leads to the wholly

---

35. *Gl*, §46, postscript.
36. See *Gl*, §27.
37. *Gl*, §46, postscript.

natural scientific question of whether there is anything whatever in the world that cannot be brought under the concept of species."[38] Since individuals in fact always only exist as members of species, "most special" preservation can only be redundant. Moreover, these theological categories have in the past sought support in a correspondence to the natural world that science has shown can no longer be assumed. All animal species were thought to have originated with creation and remained constant, even though individuals within them came and went. Special preservation was thought to correspond to this originality and constancy, while most special preservation was God's sustaining will toward an individual for a given time. Yet science has discerned that even species may come and go, which means the assumption underlying the distinction between a general and special preservation no longer holds. Thus, if dogmatics wants to maintain intellectual integrity on this matter, it must relinquish its traditional way of thinking.

Finally, in reference to the notion of divine government, Schleiermacher does not so much suggest that it is unnecessary or inappropriate as that it may be developed more fruitfully later in his system. To be sure, he does recognize that some thinkers introduce the concept here to explain further the notions of God's preserving and cooperating activity. Yet if the introduction of the concept is meant to indicate that "by means of all the powers disseminated in the world and preserved in the same, everything only happens and can happen as God has originally and always wanted it," then Schleiermacher's proposition already makes the point and the concept is unnecessary.[39] However, if one introduces it in this dogmatic location so as to speak to the distinction between ends and means, then one must recognize that for the Christian religious self-consciousness, this end could only be "the kingdom of God established through redemption . . . to which all else relates as to its goal."[40] This matter belongs to the Second Part of Schleiermacher's system.

Yet this is the case not simply because this "end" is specifically *Christian*, but in the first instance because it is *specific* at all. Here— that is, in the First Part—Schleiermacher asserts that his concern is

---

38. Ibid.
39. Ibid.
40. Ibid.

only with the description of the feeling of absolute dependence in general. Such a description can assert the fact *that* all of creation is dependent upon God, and it can outline the fundamental structure or forms that logically must exist for the relation between the two to remain coherent. But it cannot yet suggest a purpose or content that gives meaning and "movement" to creation in that relation; it has no basis for lifting up one object as the actual end toward which all else ought to be oriented. Discerning such a movement or end comes only when one considers a *particular* modification of the fundamental feeling. That is, interpreting the ultimate meaning of creation presupposes a particular insight, which in turn presupposes or gives birth to a specific, living religious communion. Hence, if one's dogmatic structure is to reflect this distinction between the general and the particular, between fundamental structure and final purpose, between the capacity to develop and the actual course of development, then each topic should be expounded in its own distinct dogmatic location. What Schleiermacher indicates in this seemingly neutral discussion of end and means is that his doctrine of divine preservation will later be modified—indeed, completed—by the addition of a specifically Christian orientation in the Second Part of his *Glaubenslehre*.

In fact, Schleiermacher suggests the nature of this ultimate orientation even prior to that explicitly Christian Second Part of his work. What he writes regarding miracles, evil, and free will is largely implicit in what he has already written in §46 regarding the divine preservation of the world. Yet the three propositions (§§47–49) that follow §46 also develop it in ways that, if not already obviously Christian, seem capable of later fitting only a Christian position. Schleiermacher's descriptions of these three topics all appear to presuppose a Christian sensibility and to anticipate what he will eventually write in his Second Part. His understanding of miracles indicates that history is best interpreted as developing; his understanding of evil suggests its various instances are most appropriately viewed as opportunities for promoting that progress; and his understanding of free will comes across as the necessary presupposition for our true participation in that divinely ordained development of history. None of these understandings are really suited to any other religion than the most perfectly developed form of teleological monotheism, which is to say, Christianity.

CHAPTER 7

More Confirmation from Schleiermacher's Understanding of Miracles, Evil, and Free Will

———꿰———

The propositions considered in the preceding chapter serve as the fundamental expression of Schleiermacher's understanding of Creation. As such, according to his own stated approach, they could stand on their own without further clarification. Moreover, they also appear to meet his standard of being generically monotheistic rather than specifically Christian. Yet for various reasons, Schleiermacher recognizes the need to amplify the implications of these propositions, which is the task he undertakes in §§47–49 as well as in his doctrines describing the Original Perfection of the world and humanity. Hence, this chapter will concern itself with an examination of these various propositions, focusing primarily on §§47–49, and supplementing its consideration of them with references to the doctrines on Original Perfection. This examination will demonstrate Schleiermacher's seemingly generic doctrines of Creation and providence reveal not only a christological orientation, but in certain instances an implicit christological content.

On Understanding Miracles

In turning to §47, one is immediately struck by its recapitulation of the logic of §46. Schleiermacher himself presumably would not have included it had he not felt the need to counter the still common understanding and acceptance of miracles among many Christians. His task, as he describes it, is not to deny the inherent possibility of miracles, but only to relate the notion of miracle to his principle that our absolute dependence exists only within the interdependent system of nature. Of course, he does later write "that we should let go of the conception of the absolutely supernatural, because in no single instance would anything be recognizable as such by us, while additionally such a recognition is nowhere demanded of us."[1] So while Schleiermacher does not deny the possibility of miracles, he does deflate or dismiss their importance for Christian faith. Schleiermacher presents his evaluation of miracles most generally in §47.2. Put succinctly, he argues that any occurrence of an "absolute miracle" would necessarily entail the destruction of the whole system of nature, which, given the presuppositions described in §46, would also undermine our religious self-consciousness. A miracle would have this effect in a twofold manner. On the one hand, it would positively affect the future by introducing into the natural causal nexus an element that otherwise would not have existed, thus changing ever after the makeup and therefore development of the natural realm. On the other hand, a miracle would negatively affect the past by disrupting the whole natural concatenation of cause-and-effect that preceded it, thus abrogating any development of the natural realm up to that point. Moreover, if one supposes that God performs not just one but many miracles, then "every later miracle also negates all earlier ones, insofar as they have already entered into the continuity of efficient causes."[2] As a result, Schleiermacher suggests, we would be forced to choose one of two positions: Either God *did not* or *could not* so order the interdependent system of nature that the whole of the divine will would emerge therefrom. Yet the former position suggests a limitation of God's omnipotence, a fragmentation of the divine decree and activity, and the undermining of nature as a reliable system,[3] while the latter openly requires such a conclusion. Either way, the fundamental religious feeling is destroyed.

---

1. *Gl*, §47.3.
2. *Gl*, §47.2.
3. Cf. *Gl*, §47.1.

These problems cannot be avoided, Schleiermacher goes on to say, by establishing a distinction between God's "ordinary" and "extraordinary" cooperation, "so that the negative side of the miracle is the withdrawal of the ordinary cooperation, but the positive the entrance of the extraordinary."[4] This would seem to allow for the uninterrupted continuity of divine preservation in general, even though it might vary in its form. Yet it is precisely this alternation that causes a discontinuity in the natural order, thus leaving one with the same problem as above. Assuming that divine causality, whatever its form, may quantitatively wax and wane within the world fails to take into account the qualitative distinction between the divine and the natural. The divine preservation can only extend to the natural world as a whole; extending it to some parts of the world and not to others will only destroy our recognition of the world as that whole. For this reason, Schleiermacher mentions with approval those theologians who conceive of miracles as prepared by God "in nature itself"; these events are not divine interruptions of nature, but emerge out of divinely created nature, according to a schedule established in the original divine decree.[5]

Thus, far from buttressing the faith, miracles as commonly understood would actually serve to undermine it, at least insofar as they are "absolutely supernatural." Schleiermacher does seem to suggest that not all miracles fit within this category. His occasional reference to "*absolute* miracles" implies the existence of another category of miracle, namely, those that are not "absolute"—or at least one such miracle, namely, the mission of Christ. Schleiermacher does not develop a full-fledged theory to describe this miracle, but refers to it here only as a way of countering one explanation of absolute miracles. That explanation argues that God "has need of" miracles in part to compensate for the influence of free agents on the course of nature.[6] Schleiermacher finds this argument more sophisticated than most, yet he remains unconvinced. Its shortcoming lies in the implication that free agents are themselves somehow separated from the nature system, and thus objects of neither divine preservation nor creation. No Christian

---

4. *Gl*, §47.2.
5. Ibid.
6. *Gl*, §47.1.

would want to make such an assertion, just as none would conceive of the world as "the nature mechanism alone."[7] The world that is the object of divine preservation comprises this nature mechanism *and* freely acting beings. As such, the effects those beings have upon that mechanism are already encompassed within, rather than juxtaposed alongside, the divine preservation. Thus, God need not augment that mediate preservation of the world with immediate supernatural interventions.

Yet even if this explanation fails to justify belief in absolute miracles generally, its logic can be used in a more restricted manner to explain the particular task of Christ. Schleiermacher describes this particularity and its restrictions thus:

> Only the one miracle of Christ's mission indeed has this goal: to restore what free agents have altered, but in their own sphere, not in that of the nature mechanism and also not against the course of things originally ordained by God. Nor does the interest of piety require that the free agent doing this restoring in the realm of phenomena relate to the natural order differently than other free agents.[8]

What can we glean from this passage that pertains to the thesis of this book? It is, after all, only a brief aside in an argument that is not otherwise obviously pertinent to that thesis. To begin with, Schleiermacher speaks of a restoration of what free agents have altered "in their own sphere." He does not define this restoration, these agents, or their sphere of activity (although he will do that in part in §49). However, Christ's mission does not in the first instance "reinvent" the structure or workings of the nature system; there is no qualitative change in the world's or even humanity's basic constitution. Rather, it effects an alteration in humanity's understanding of and relation to the divine, an alteration that also inevitably changes humanity's understanding of itself, and then its understanding of and activity in the world.

It is, in other words, an alteration or evolution of human *consciousness*. One initial effect of this change is, of course, the emergence of the

---

7. Ibid.
8. Ibid.; emphasis mine.

church, which becomes for the redeemed a new "world" within the old.[9] To a certain extent, this new realm becomes both the midwife for and the recipient of the Christian's particular understanding and activity. That is, Schleiermacher presupposes that we are essentially social and historical beings who strive to establish definite fellowship with others. Such fellowships may arise centered around a variety of objects (e.g., the family and the nation), but presumably the most fundamental is one centered upon a particular consciousness of God. Once established, such a fellowship evokes and shapes—one might even say creates—its particular God-consciousness in the "pious potential" of individuals under its influence.[10]

But the new understanding and activity of the Christian will also reach beyond the church to external human society and the realm of nature. That is, as a result of the "miracle" of Christ, humanity will eventually influence the development of history and nature, though it will do so only by means of the nature mechanisms intrinsic to the world since creation. And both of these—the influence itself and the method by which it occurs—are to be understood as in keeping with "the course of things originally ordained by God." Hence, we see how this apparent shift cannot represent in any real sense a discontinuity in God's creation and preservation. Instead, it should be characterized in the first instance as a subjective rather than objective restoration. That is, it effects a reorientation of the human spirit, so that the promising capabilities with which that spirit was endowed at creation might become actualities aligned with and serving the eternal purpose of God. On this basis, it may then bring about a certain "objective" restoration, but one that is not to be thought of as the result of any supernatural redirection. As Schleiermacher later clarifies in §93.4 and §94.3 regarding the person of Christ, the Redeemer's appearance, and thus his mission, are miraculous only in the sense that they arise untainted by what preceded them in the corrupted progress of the human spirit. At most, they represent a suspension of the historical, but not the natural, order. Yet even as such, they are not something

---

9. Cf. *Gl*, §§60–61, "On the Original Perfection of Humanity."
10. See Friedrich Schleiermacher, *Christmas Eve: Dialogue on the Incarnation*, trans. Terrence Tice (Richmond, Va.: John Knox Press, 1967), 62.

absolutely new. They do not go "against the course of things originally ordained by God," but seek rather to fulfill God's eternal intention by bringing to fruition the original perfection that humanity received at creation and that it still possesses as a capacity.[11]

Thus, the benefit and impetus received from Christ may appear as something miraculously new from the finite perspective of human history, but from the divine perspective they are an original and eternal aspect of God's decree. And this reorientation is, in essence and in the means with which it is implemented, fully natural, in that Christ does not relate to the nature system any differently than do all other human beings. So the problems associated with belief in absolute miracles are avoided: There is no suggestion that God's omnipotence is limited, the divine decree and activity fragmented, or the stability of the nature system threatened. In other words, the general interests of both faith and science may be maintained, even as Schleiermacher lays more groundwork for the christological unfolding of his system.

These conclusions are reinforced when we consider Schleiermacher's reply to those who defend absolute miracles on the supposition that they are needed by God to answer prayer and to effect the "new creation" of regeneration. This supposition suggests that a suspension of the natural causal nexus must be possible in order for God to bring to pass something that otherwise would not have occurred. Schleiermacher recognizes the extent to which these understandings of prayer and regeneration have held sway among many Christians; indeed, of all the reasons he considers in support of miracles, these may be the most widespread. But he also observes that they "have never actually been established as church doctrine,"[12] hinting on the one hand that some inherent shortcoming in the idea has prevented this, while making clear on the other that in light of §27 he could forego the matter completely. They are not an essential aspect of dogmatic tradition.

Initially, it looks as if Schleiermacher will leave the issue dangling, stating that this is not the place in his system to consider these subjects.[13] But he does offer two comments on the matter based upon his

---

11. We will consider this "original perfection" more fully later.
12. *Gl*, §47.1.
13. One should presumably look instead to what he will say about regeneration in *Gl*, §§107–9 and prayer in the name of Christ in §§146–47, both in the second part of his system.

exposition of the divine preservation in this section. First, he states that "prayer and its fulfillment or nonfulfillment are only parts of *the same original divine ordination*; consequently, the view that things could have turned out differently is a meaningless conjecture."[14] Circumstances may appear to change course, but it is only a limited or misdirected understanding that attributes such changes to a supernatural *redirection* of the objective, natural order; from the divine perspective, everything occurs "according to plan" and by natural means. The proper human perspective, therefore, is to recognize this fact and align one's own interpretation and activity with it. Changes in the world should be understood in terms of the unfolding or development of the whole over time, rather than in terms of occasional discrete moments in which God chooses one course from among various options presented "from elsewhere."

Second, Schleiermacher refers to what he has just said about the mission of Christ: If the appearance and activity of the Redeemer are not themselves absolute miracles, then it would be illogical to suppose that the regeneration effected by him is such a miracle. The "new creation" of redemption is not something absolutely new; it is rather the realization and fulfillment of God's original decree for humanity. Hence, it need not be thought of as interrupting or correcting either the given order of the external world or human nature, for human nature and the world were made to receive it from the very beginning.

On the World's Original Perfection

In his description of the Original Perfection of the World, Schleiermacher makes this point in a fuller way. As he points out at the commencement of §57, in asserting the perfection of the world

> absolutely nothing else should be understood here other than what we must so designate in the interests of the pious self-consciousness, namely, that the totality of finite being—as it has an influence upon us, and thus also the human influences on the rest of being arising from

---

14. *Gl*, §47.1; emphasis mine.

our placement in the same—fits together in such a way as to make possible the continuity of the pious self-consciousness.[15]

Humans have the inherent capacity to maintain an uninterrupted
God-consciousness. If, in actuality, we experience moments in which
the pious self-consciousness has faded away, Schleiermacher's definition indicates that this cannot be attributed to some shortcoming in
the essential makeup of either the world or human nature. Instead, it
implies some shortcoming in the *realization* of those given capacities.
Yet is this not the same point maintained by theological tradition?
Allowing for the to-be-expected differences in terminology, one might
be tempted to take Schleiermacher's definition as a nineteenth-century
repetition of the ancient affirmation of the inherent goodness of
creation. In other words, the world was created a paradise in which
man and woman could be "at home" in pious relation to God, but
through the fall this original state, and the capacities that accompanied
it, were lost. Schleiermacher certainly affirms the original perfection
and goodness of creation, but he adds:

> By using the expression "original," however, it should be stipulated that
> we are not discussing some particular condition of the world or of
> humanity or the God-consciousness in humans, all of which would be
> a developed perfection that admits a more or less; rather, the discussion
> is about that [perfection], *in itself ever the same and preceding all tempo-
> ral development*, which is established in the inner relations of the finite
> being under consideration.[16]

In other words, "original perfection" does not refer to a historical
moment in the world's past, nor to a quality of being that has since
been "lost," but to a potentiality intrinsic to the nature of the world and
humanity. It represents an existential possibility for human spirituality
in the world that *objectively* is still available. Hence, Schleiermacher's
understanding of the topic to be addressed is clear: "We simply will
not be dealing here with some temporal condition of the world and

---

15. *Gl*, §57.1.
16. Ibid.; emphasis mine.

humanity, in particular neither past nor present nor future, but only with those *relationships uniformly underlying the whole temporal development and during it always remaining the same*."[17] For Schleiermacher, "original perfection" refers not to any particular actual state, but to the fundamental, underlying characteristics that make possible the actual, dynamic relations among humans, the world, and God.

One way of clarifying his position might be to consider the ambiguity present in the German word *Vollkommenheit*. English speakers may translate this term as either "perfection" or "completeness," and in selecting one or the other they choose different connotations. The former suggests the attainment of some ideal state that goes beyond mere completeness; indeed, it sounds like a goal beyond which one could not and would not want to go. The latter is not so value-laden, but does suggest something that is self-contained and in need of no additions. It also sounds not so much like a goal but a starting point. Which translation is more appropriate in this context? Given his use of the term *Vollendung* in some of his final propositions,[18] and the manner in which he employs the phrase *ursprüngliche Vollkommenheit* in this segment of his work, it seems "original completeness" and its connotations best fit his meaning. He wants to affirm that the nature system as a whole is always completely dependent upon God, and also that it was always complete, in the sense of being geared from the outset to be able to run its course without further external, that is, supernatural, additions. Schleiermacher recognizes that the most common position in Christian thinking and dogmatic tradition has been to conceive this *Vollkommenheit* as some original perfect state, as much an ideal for the end of the journey as a picture of its starting point. Yet he still views his understanding as being the more appropriate one, and as John Hick points out, he could have found support from at least one source in Christian tradition:

> Like Irenaeus, Schleiermacher has a two-stage conception of the creation of man. But instead of the terminology of the "image" and "likeness" of God, he uses that of the first and second Adam. The first Adam

---

17. *Gl*, §57.2; emphasis mine.
18. See, e.g., *Gl*, §§164ff.

possessed the potentiality for the full and perfect God-consciousness that has, however, become actual only in the second Adam, Christ, who is now drawing all men into a community of God-consciousness with himself. Thus Schleiermacher sees man being *gradually perfected*.[19]

It might appear that in refusing to define original perfection as an actual, temporal state, Schleiermacher has simply opted to follow the standards of the "outer" rather than "inner" norm, choosing to surrender theological tradition for a position more in line with the intellectual standards of his day. But in fact, he actually draws on parts of the tradition to suggest that the customary view makes assertions that are not only inconsistent with logic, but with proper piety as well. The approach he employs is to combine a reference to Genesis 1:31 with some deductions from his understanding of divine omnipotence. His reasoning is rather drawn out, but it merits full quotation:

> The original expression of this belief, only in another form, is the divine approval of the world [Gen. 1:31], which, with reference to the act of creation as such, has for its object not a temporal state arising out of another one, but solely the original essence [*Ursprünglichkeit*] of finite being, yet this, to be sure, as the source of the entire temporal development. Therefore, as little as this divine approval can be annulled by something temporal, *just as little can the diverse content of the temporal moments detract from the truth of our proposition, whether they appear in one instance more as an actualized perfection while in another more as a yet-to-be rectified imperfection.* When, in contrast, under this very designation dogmatics commonly deals with historical moments, that is, with a paradisical state of the world and a state of moral perfection of humanity, of which both are accorded a certain duration, it becomes clear that such a doctrine cannot assume the same place as the one advanced here. For an actual, and therefore to say the least changeable, state cannot be related to the divine omnipotence in the same manner as that which in finite being exists as the basis of all subsequent states, least of all one that has totally vanished, *because then the divine omnipotence*

---

19. John Hick, *Evil and the God of Love* (London: Fontana Library, 1974), 240; emphasis mine.

likewise could have no longer remained the same. By contrast, even if we should include something in the concept of original perfection that, upon closer scrutiny, showed itself to be something alterable, then this would be only an oversight owing to an erroneous subsumption, which, as soon as it was discovered, could be corrected without it changing anything in the doctrine.[20]

In other words, if one wants to maintain Christianity's long-standing affirmation of the world's inherent goodness, as well as a coherent understanding of the divine omnipotence, then one must forego a temporal definition of "original perfection." According to Schleiermacher, such definitions inevitably lead to the supposition that the fall effected some *qualitative* change in the nature of humanity and the world. Yet if this is the case, then one must also suppose that the Redeemer effects some sort of qualitative and supernatural restoration. But Schleiermacher has already indicated the intellectual difficulties in maintaining such a position. Hence, one ought rather to suppose that the fundamental *capacity* for an uninterrupted God-consciousness (which is how Schleiermacher defines one part of humanity's "original perfection") still exists in human nature; the task of Christ is to enable this capacity to flower. Thus, the Redeemer's work stands not as a "second" creation, responding to and correcting the failings of the first, but as the catalyst by which the capacities inherent to human nature may first attain fulfillment. In this sense, his effect is certainly unique, although not miraculous in the traditional sense of that word.[21]

Yet if Christ's work is not a literal second creation, but some form of eternally decreed catalyst influencing characteristics *already present*, then this tells us something about Schleiermacher's understanding of the originally created nature of human beings. It is not merely a "blank slate" or a neutral capacity that may be filled or led in any variety of ways. True, it may not have yet attained a particular temporal state or a particular consciousness of God, but this does not mean it was created without some intended end in mind. And this end, according to

---

20. *Gl*, §57.2; emphasis mine.
21. Cf. Niebuhr, who supports my reading here: Richard R. Niebuhr, *Schleiermacher on Christ and Religion* (New York: Charles Scribner's Sons, 1964), 206.

Schleiermacher, is indicated by humanity's "original righteousness." As a brief examination of §61.4 reveals, Schleiermacher finds unacceptable the customary understanding of this notion. On the one hand, as the term righteousness is commonly used, it would have to presuppose the existence of a broad network of social relations governed by a concrete structure of laws—conditions that could only exist in actual, and rather developed, temporal states. On the other hand, the term also usually refers only to an accomplished virtue, not a root condition. That is, it indicates the actual *result* of acting in a certain way, not the *starting point* from which one acts. Yet Schleiermacher's intention is to maintain the latter. He affirms that humanity has been created with the capacity for righteousness, but this capacity requires development. That this is indeed a legitimate usage of the term righteousness (*Gerechtigkeit*) is indicated by its other common usage: "inasmuch as we dub something 'right' [*gerecht*] which is suited to its definition."[22] On the basis of this etymology, Schleiermacher is able to reason further that

> if we reflect upon the divine decree of the whole development of the human species by means of redemption, and *that this was included in the idea of human nature from the beginning*, although unknown to humanity itself, then it will be precisely the attributes established in the previous proposition [i.e., the capacity for God-consciousness and religious fellowship] upon which this suitability for redemption depends.[23]

In other words, according to Schleiermacher, human nature *by definition* is intended for redemption. It was not created in this state, but it was created with the capacity to attain this state—and it is not fully itself, which is to say, it does not fulfill its true nature, until it attains redemption. Creation initiated human nature, giving it the attributes necessary for achieving its ultimate completion, but creation does not itself accomplish that end. That task, by divine decree, is left to the work of the Redeemer, and thus it is only with his appearance that we can for the first time truly define human nature. Redemption is not a divine supplement for a creation gone awry through human sin; it is

---

22. *Gl*, §61.4.
23. Ibid.; emphasis mine.

rather the keystone or goal of creation toward which humanity has been aimed all along. This means that theology should not look to Adam but to Christ for its anthropology. Why is this point so significant for our understanding of Schleiermacher? Because it indicates that the actual content of this segment of his First Part is influenced by, oriented toward, and completed by what he will write in the Second Part. His theological anthropology is neither neutral nor contained in only one dogmatic location; it is christological and extends from his First Part into his Second Part.

Schleiermacher concludes his treatment of miracles with some summary observations in §47.3. He first echoes what he had said earlier in §46.1, namely, that the interests of natural science and religion actually come to the same conclusion in this matter. Because we would not know how to recognize an instance of the absolutely supernatural, and because such recognition is not demanded of us, we may "let go" of the concept.[24] In other words, as should now be evident, Schleiermacher suggests that it is scientifically inconceivable and theologically unnecessary. Of course, this does not mean that Christians must henceforth discard all consideration of the New Testament miracles; rather, Christians must simply acknowledge that an explanation of their cause is not possible, given the current state of scientific knowledge. That knowledge is growing, so perhaps a future age will discover a natural explanation.

In the meantime, however, within the bounds just outlined, such miracle accounts may still evoke pious feeling—and they may continue to do so even if science eventually offers a natural explanation of their causes, for the religious significance of a miracle lies not in the means by which it occurs, whether natural or supernatural, but in its source and in the message or feeling it is able to evoke. Such a distinction even premodern theologians acknowledged, insofar as they assumed that miracles could be of diabolical as well as divine origin. The mere fact that its cause was supernatural was not enough to make it acceptable; its "message" had to be tested. If it conformed to the fundamental faith of the church, then it could be accepted as true and of

---

24. *Gl*, §47.3.

divine origin; if it did not so conform, it had to be rejected as false and diabolical. In his own framework, Schleiermacher says much the same thing, in that the message conveyed or, more precisely, the feeling evoked is primary. To be sure, he rejects the possibility of a diabolical origin, for the assumption of such a possibility would necessarily undercut the fundamental religious consciousness, which is monistic rather than dualistic. Thus, its source can only be God, the sole Creator and Sustainer of the natural realm. Yet even so, a miracle—or rather, one's conception of it—must be tested, for it may be construed as a supernatural interruption into that realm. Such a construal may not be diabolical, but it does not conform to the fundamental faith, and therefore it must be rejected as false. If, on the other hand, it is not so construed, and it does evoke a sense of God's creating and sustaining power, then a "miracle" has served its purpose and may be accepted— regardless of whether or not we can presently explain the mechanism of its cause in natural terms. With this bit of reasoning, Schleiermacher again stakes out a position that he believes is true to both the heritage of faith and the assumptions of science.

Understanding Evil

Schleiermacher's rejection of any sort of dualism between the divine and the diabolical in the explanation of miracles anticipates one of the points he will make in §48, where he considers the problem of evil. He will also return in this proposition to the point only suggested in his appendix on the devil.[25] In light of these two connections, it begins to appear that we should not assume his treatment of evil stands on its own. Instead, as with all the other segments of his system, it is an integral part of its overall unfolding. So let us turn to an examination of §48.

The heading to this proposition states the following: "Excitations of self-consciousness that express life's hindrances [*Lebenshemmungen*] are to be placed in absolute dependence on God just as completely as those that express an advancement of life [*Lebensförderung*]."[26] As with

---

25. See pp. 131 ff., above.
26. *Gl*, §48.

the previous proposition, Schleiermacher argues that one should not even need to make such a statement, because it is an obvious corollary of §46. But "imperfect piety" has had difficulty recognizing such a connection, because it has itself been overwhelmed by such hindrances or simply confused by skeptical and unbelieving presentations of the matter. As a result, according to Schleiermacher, Christian doctrine has the special task of showing the compatibility of sad and unhappy moments of life with the God-consciousness. Unfortunately, however, even when this task has been recognized, it has not been carried through satisfactorily. The problem, Schleiermacher seems to be saying, is that such sad excitations of feeling have been interpreted in doctrinal systems only in a vague and slipshod fashion. The motivation behind such halfhearted attempts has been, presumably, the desire to "protect" God from being the cause of such experiences, but the result has been the fragmentation of the fundamental feeling of absolute dependence. Needless to say, this is unacceptable to Schleiermacher. He counters it by presenting his own understanding of how one is to consider this aspect of life.

Schleiermacher begins by recognizing that such moments are not occurrences isolated from and unconnected with the rest of life. Were this the case they would not present such a problem to piety and doctrine (the implication being that they could simply be ignored as irrelevant anomalies). But in fact such moments carry with them a persistent, regularly renewed consciousness of life's hindrances, such that these hindrances are perceived to be as much a part of the fabric of life as more favorable or pleasant moments. The former are labeled "evil" (*das Übel*) while the latter are labeled "good," and both must be considered as absolutely dependent upon God. Otherwise, the fundamental feeling will be relying on a God whose causality is not absolute, because the power of that causality is limited, either in itself or due to some countervailing evil. Schleiermacher continues by saying that moral evil (*das Böse*), considered as a state, is to be included under this more general classification of evil (*das Übel*), "for wherever it is, it shows itself to be an inexhaustible source of life's hindrances."[27] A slightly different classification distinguishes between natural evil

---

27. *Gl*, §48.1.

(*natürliches Übel*) and social evil (*geselliges Übel*). Schleiermacher defines the former as a partial negation of human existence by the conditions of the natural world. He defines the latter as a partial subduing of human activity due to the conflicts of human interaction, which, as he will clarify in §§75–76, may be either the direct or indirect consequence of sin.

Having described the various species of evil, Schleiermacher moves on in §48.2 to the task he initially proposed. This task need not concern itself with teleological speculation about what has resulted from evil, nor with etiological explanations of the unavoidability of evil; rather, "we need only to show that apparent oppositions come together under the universal dependence."[28] He addresses these "apparent oppositions" in what I will call their "diachronic" and "synchronic" forms. The first has to do with "the relation of the changeably transitory to the constant in all finite being."[29] Schleiermacher observes that all individual beings display a pattern of development and decline between birth and death. This holds true in the natural realm and the social realm, and also when the "individual" is a single being or a collective entity. However, when taken as a whole, this continuous flow and ebb, rise and fall of many individuals actually produces constancy in that whole. Thus, individuals may come and go, but the species remains; species may come and go, but life continues; persons may come and go, but the culture remains; cultures may come and go, but human civilization continues to grow and expand. There is a repeated and random fluctuation between progress and arrest among individuals within the whole, and thus, insofar as humans are involved, a fluctuation in the consciousness of life as being advanced or hindered. But *as a whole* life continues as a constant, which to a properly attuned religious consciousness could only be possible on the basis of a universal and absolute dependence on God. Moreover, according to Schleiermacher, it should be recognized as well that that whole is progressing.

The second "apparent opposition," which I have termed the synchronic, has to do with "the relation of the only relatively self-existent and the corresponding mutual contingency of the finite."[30] That is,

---

28. *Gl*, §48.2.
29. Ibid.
30. Ibid.

having described the way that individual activities progress over the course of time, Schleiermacher then describes the interconnection of various activities in any given moment. His point is straightforward: "[T]here is no absolute isolation in the finite; each is self-existent only insofar as another is conditioned by it, and each is conditioned by another only insofar as it also exists in itself."[31] Every individual being is both actor and acted upon within the natural order, and this activity in all its diversity takes on one of two forms. The subject either progresses or is hindered in some way. When such activity then presents itself to consciousness, it does so only insofar as it presents both the subject and the object, the acting being and the conditioned being, and it does so regardless of whether life is being advanced or hindered. That is, such an opposition is inherent in the way that finite beings relate to one another within the nature system. As a result, the religious self-consciousness cannot but acknowledge that it is all equally ordained by God, as Schleiermacher first suggested in §46.

Stated plainly, this means that what we perceive as the obstacles and aids to life's progress, that is, the evil and the good, are *both* ordained by God. Indeed, according to John Hick, Schleiermacher was the first great Christian theologian "to affirm . . . openly" that "the *ultimate* responsibility" for evil lay with God.[32] The attempt to view it otherwise stems from the mistaken assumption that particular evils can be considered in isolation from their natural context, which leads to the false conclusion that evil, or rather "hindrances," could be excluded from the world. Schleiermacher has already stated that no such isolation is possible in the finite realm. Indeed, it would not even be desirable, for

> the same activity or property of a thing whereby, on the one hand, it enters as an evil into human life, on the other hand also produces good, so that if one would do away with that from which life's hindrances come, one would also be missing that by which life's advances are occasioned.[33]

Schleiermacher apparently sees us first as too prone to label a particular thing or event "evil" and then as too ready to construe such evil as

---

31. Ibid.
32. Hick, *Evil and the God of Love*, 234.
33. *Gl*, §48.2.

the fundamental essence of that thing or event. Were we to take our time and a longer view (which is to say, the *divine* view), we would see particular circumstances in the broader ebb and flow of finite existence, recognizing in them their positive as well as negative aspects, and hence their role in the divine preservation of the world. Brief reflection suggests how this is the case in our relations with nature, where the intractability of creation or natural disasters can spur us on to redoubled effort and advances. But it is also true in the social realm when we are confronted by moral evil. Such evil also has a good aspect, and not just in the accidental sense that circumstances sometimes fall together in such a way that a sinful act inadvertently produces a good effect on a personal or even historical scale. It has it rather in a "wholly general" sense, in that all human acts, whether good or evil, have their source in the inherent capacity of the human spirit to express itself in external action, to manipulate the world around it.[34] Thus, as the citation above suggests, we could not eliminate the source of moral evil without eliminating the source of moral good as well. Such reasoning comes across as almost Augustinian; moral evil is the product of a misused—or perhaps underused—yet fundamentally good quality of human nature. Hence, even in its sinfulness, evil is rooted in the good, and as such it can be considered ordained by God. What it needs is not elimination per se but redemption—which is to say, it needs to be understood in light of and employed for the divine purpose. In fact, the logic of grace requires it. As Hick observes:

> Looking at sin through grace, we see that redemption presupposes that from which we are redeemed. Thus, starting from the Christian experience of redemption, which expresses the immediate activity of God, and seeing this as occurring within the universal divine sovereignty, we can only conclude that the total event that culminates in man's redemption represents the outworking of God's purpose.[35]

Of course, in taking this position, Schleiermacher places himself one step removed from the assertion that God ordains particular and actual instances of evil. Having already asserted that evil cannot be so

---

34. Ibid.
35. Hick, *Evil and the God of Love*, 234.

isolated, he states that one is therefore justified in affirming that God does not ordain actual evil as such, because that ordination initially makes each thing or event capable of being either good or evil. For it to become one or the other in our actual experience depends upon how it is interpreted and used, as Schleiermacher's next comments suggest:

> Now with regard to our topic, this [claim that a thing or event is both good and evil] implies especially that it is an imperfection of self-consciousness, accompanying either the immediate consciousness or the activities of the objective consciousness, when a hindrance as such completely and exclusively fills a moment [of experience], and likewise an erroneous way of considering things when the causing of hindrances is taken to be the actual essence of any of the objects existing in dependence on God. *And even this imperfection is one disappearing with the increasing development of the good, just as every evil disappears into the good itself, that is, in the receptivity of the sensual self-consciousness in general for union with the God-consciousness.*[36]

With a slight variation in terminology, this comment reveals the same assumption of the good's progress evident in Schleiermacher's earlier statement concerning the "kingdom and power" of the devil.[37] In other words, to view some obstacle to life's progress as essentially evil is to miss not only its broader context but its underlying purpose, which is *to be put to use in the service of the developing good.* Schleiermacher is suggesting first of all that the essence of things be considered in dynamic rather than static terms, as befits a world that exists historically and not atemporally. Such an approach is only appropriate, given the fundamental feeling associated with the doctrine of preservation, namely, our sense of the continuity of all things in absolute dependence upon God. Yet Schleiermacher is doing more than saying we should take the "longer view" in our consideration of life's obstacles. In this and other passages, he is telling us to recognize the development taking place in history, and that *we should become a part of it.* To paraphrase his position, Schleiermacher holds that evil does not exist in and of itself, but only as a particular limitation of human life is

---

36. *Gl*, §48.2; emphasis mine.
37. See p. 132.

perceived as such. That it is so construed actually tells us more about the subject perceiving than the object perceived, namely, that that person's God-consciousness is not yet fully mature. Were it mature, that person would perceive this or any other limitation not as an evil per se nor even as a divine punishment for evil, but as an *opportunity* for some form of moral activity—for both nature and the social realm are meant to be developed by spirit.

To illustrate this point further, let us again consider some of the comments Schleiermacher makes in his treatment of "original perfection." He there considers the traditional explanation for our mortality. The inherited usage of the creation story has taken at face-value the claim therein that certain evils and death are the divine *response* to the original sin of the first human pair, and that it is logical to conclude that had they not sinned, these evils and death would not have appeared, and the world would have continued in its original "perfect" state. Schleiermacher has rejected a definition of original perfection as an actual temporal condition; here he also rejects any causal link between human sin on the one hand and evil and death on the other. Instead, he suggests that the latter was divinely preordained—either without regard for, or in the foreknowledge of, the former. One need not suppose that God had to *react* to human sin, or *alter* the world's nature in order to punish it. In fact, making either supposition would undermine the reliability of one's faith by implicitly denigrating God's power or the world's integrity. The only way to avoid this result is to recognize that our negative evaluation of mortality stems not from its intrinsic character but from our inappropriate perception of it. Hick makes much the same point:

> Schleiermacher states clearly the pregnant thought—*which we have also found within the Augustinean camp of Karl Barth*—that our finite and transient mode of existence as human animals, with the pain and eventual dissolution which it entails, is not in itself evil, being simply the mode of creatureliness which God in His love has appointed for us, but that it becomes evil through the sinful fear and anxiety of our self-centred reactions to it.[38]

---

38. Hick, *Evil and the God of Love*, 232–33; emphasis mine. Chapter 9 will address this similarity with Barth more fully.

Moreover, human life as we now know it would be inconceivable without the existence of evil and death. Schleiermacher contends that were we to imagine human nature as originally, and therefore essentially, created to be unencumbered with bodily decline, unthreatened by the external world, and unimpeded by the eventuality of death, we would in fact be describing a species unrelated to the present human race, unconnected with our own human history, and unable to give us a basis for development. In other words, it would be a conception quite useless for any dogmatic exposition of our nature and our purpose in the world. But in light of our actual experience, Schleiermacher observes that the consciousness of our mortality actually "belongs to the most powerful of motives for development, so that *because of mortality and the evils connected with it*, more human activities have developed in the course of our relations to the external world than could be expected without them."[39]

Here again Schleiermacher reflects at the very least the teleological orientation of his doctrine of creation. Hindrances and threats to human existence should be understood as *God-given opportunities* for the exercise of human ingenuity and progress in the natural realm. They should not be viewed only with fatalistic resignation or understood only as justified punishment for sin, as they would, according to Schleiermacher, in the faiths of Islam and Judaism, respectively. To be sure, such hindrances and threats may—indeed, will—overcome all individuals eventually, but as long as "the totality of human life increases rather than decreases," the *actualizing* of creation's original perfection will not be impeded.[40] And, in fact, the individual may still face such hindrances and threats in such a manner that they overcome him or her only in a physical sense. One may not always be able to use them as an opportunity for external progress, but one can always use them as an opportunity for spiritual maturation, by subsuming one's personal viewpoint and desires under the greater purpose of God. As a result, on both an individual and a communal level, humanity's dominion over the world will continue to develop, and the world will increase its motives for development [*Entwicklungsmotiven*] by fostering this particular consciousness of God.

---

39. *GI*, §59, postscript; emphasis mine.
40. Ibid.

There are occasions when Schleiermacher's position echoes Stoic sensibilities. Yet his emphasis on development in history, the dynamism of nature, and, through divine governance and human intervention, the gradual amelioration of the world's "evils" all point to the conclusion that his is not simply a Christianized Stoicism advocating public service and a modified *apatheia* in the face of an impersonal divine decree. Schleiermacher's theodicy suggests there is an evolution at work in nature and history that, while not predetermined by some *telos* (as that is usually understood) nevertheless intends human participation in a divinely ordained development. The failure to respond actively to such opportunities would appear to represent a failure to understand the nature of one's original perfection and one's divinely given role in the world and history, which is to participate in creation's progress toward the good. Of course, to have this particular understanding of one's divinely given role can only be the result of a particular variety of faith.

Interpreting Evil: The Influence of the Christian *Telos*

Schleiermacher deals in §9 with aesthetic and teleological monotheisms. He there states the following:

> Among the various forms of piety, the ones that distance themselves the furthest from one another are those that, with regard to pious expectations, oppose the one subordinating the natural to the moral in the human condition to the other subordinating the moral to the natural.[41]

Some form of subordination must take place. The active must subordinate the passive, as in teleological religion, or the passive must subordinate the active, as in aesthetic religion. To put it another way, one views the givenness of one's situation in nature as a call to action, or one views one's actions as the product of the givennness of one's situation in nature. It is not that the circumstances themselves differ; rather, it is that one's God-consciousness *predisposes* one to respond to those circumstances in one of two different forms. Schleiermacher

---

41. *GI*, §9.1.

spells out the contrast between these two forms in two passages that merit full quotation:

> According to the one position, this subordination is most strongly expressed when the passive [*leidentlichen*] states (whether pleasant or unpleasant, whether occasioned by external nature or by social relations) excite the feeling of absolute dependence only insofar as they are referred to spontaneous activity, that is, insofar as we know that *something is to be done by us* (simply because we find ourselves in relation to the totality of being, which is expressed in the passive state), so that the action corresponding to that condition and arising out of it has just this God-consciousness as its impulse. Thus, *where piety assumes this form, there the passive states, heightened to pious excitation, become simply the occasion for developing a definite activity explainable only in terms of a God-consciousness modified in this way.* In the sphere of such pious excitations, all passive relations of man to the world appear only as a means for evoking the totality of his active states, whereby the opposition between the sensually pleasant and unpleasant therein is overcome and recedes into the background—although it admittedly remains predominant in those instances where sensual feeling does not raise itself to pious excitation. This subordination we designate with the expression *teleological* piety, a term that, to be sure, is used somewhat differently elsewhere, but which here only means that *the predominant reference to the moral task* constitutes the fundamental type of the pious dispositions.[42]

A few lines further on, Schleiermacher presents his description of the other form of piety:

> In the opposing orientation, this subordination shows itself in its perfection only when the self-consciousness of a state of activity is taken up with reference to the feeling of absolute dependence such that the state itself appears as the result of those relations existing between the subject and the remaining totality of being, that is, in connection with the passive side of the subject. But in that case every individual state of activity is only a particular expression of the capacities common to the

---

42. Ibid.; emphasis mine.

whole of humanity [*Verhältnis der gemeinsamen menschlichen Kräfte*], existing in the subject and constitutive of the personal characteristics of the same. Consequently, *in every pious excitation of this kind that overall capacity itself is posited as the outcome of the divinely ordained influences of all things upon the subject*—in the elevating excitations thus as harmony, that is, as beauty of the individual life, and in the unpleasant or humbling excitations as discord or ugliness. Now this form of piety, in which every moment of self-activity is taken up into the feeling of absolute dependence *only as a determination of the individual by the totality of finite being*, that is, with reference to the passive side of the subject, we will term *aesthetic* piety.[43]

Schleiermacher is not suggesting that one form of piety is exclusively "active" while the other is exclusively "passive" in the sense that the teleological busies itself only with external tasks while the aesthetic occupies itself only with the inner spiritual life. Both have moments of work and moments of contemplation. The difference lies rather in one's consciousness of these alternating moments of activity and passivity, in how one's religious excitations or affectations understand them with reference to one's absolute dependence and to the relative extent of one's own agency in, and responsibility toward, the conditions existing in the surrounding world. In the passage immediately following his description of teleological religion, Schleiermacher offers a general example of how its "predominant reference to the moral task" affects it in actual moments of pious feeling. Given the presupposition that teleological piety relates to passive states as the occasion for something being done by the believer, if the action intended is "a practical [*werktätiger*] contribution to the furtherance of the kingdom of God,"[44] then the believer's pious disposition is an "elevating" one, regardless of whether the occasioning passive state was pleasant or unpleasant. If, by contrast, the action is "a withdrawing into oneself or a searching for help to overcome a marked hindrance to the higher life, then the disposition is a humbling one, whether the occasioning

---

43. Ibid.; emphasis mine.
44. Ibid.

feeling was unpleasant or pleasant."[45] Having been so humbled, however, the believer is presumably then to renew his or her efforts to contribute actively to God's kingdom.

Schleiermacher does not explain his description of aesthetic religion with such an example, yet he evidently means to fit it into the same sort of framework, only with an opposite tendency. Hence, we have warrant for saying that "aesthetic" is meant to signify simply that a predominant reference to "the natural"—rather than to the moral task—constitutes the fundamental character of the religious affections. Thus, one's pious disposition will be elevating if one perceives oneself as acting in harmony with—or in some cases, as resigning oneself to—external influences, while it will be humbling if one acts in discord with those influences.

Thus, while both teleological and aesthetic religions have an active and passive aspect, because these aspects have to do in the first instance with the religious affections, Schleiermacher also implies that the two types will produce correspondingly greater and lesser *amounts* of external work because of their differing attitudes. To phrase it another way, the teleological religious consciousness will understand itself as an active participant in and contributor to the external dynamic of the rest of existence. The aesthetic religious consciousness will understand itself as an individual product of that external existence, which requires not a contribution but a conformation, because the external exists according to immutable divine appointment. This view implies that the divine decree gives history a fundamentally static nature; the believer's ideal is realized in adapting to the present—not by adapting the present to promote some future end. Of course, teleological religion likewise sees external circumstances as divinely ordained, but this is not taken to mean that the believer is prohibited from attempting to improve those circumstances. Indeed, as our examination of §48.2 suggested, they are opportunities for precisely this, because history is viewed as fundamentally dynamic in nature, developing toward the good. Thus, while Schleiermacher observes that his use of the term "teleological" differs from its use elsewhere, he still retains some sense

---

45. Ibid.

of a *telos* in that for Christians, one's activity is oriented toward and motivated by the desire to help establish the kingdom of God, the "goal" of history. Aesthetic religion loses this historical dynamism, this moral imperative, because it subordinates the moral to the natural, the historical activity of shaping the natural or social world toward the divinely given future to the internal activity of molding one's spirit to the divinely given present.

Having outlined his conceptual division of teleological and aesthetic religion, Schleiermacher recognizes that the final validity of that division depends upon the fit between it and the actual historical monotheisms. This he seeks to demonstrate in §9.2. He acknowledges that only a general critical history of religions could fully accomplish this task, so his chief concern in this section is to show that the division actually serves to distinguish the three monotheistic faiths, rather than only distinguishing monotheism from polytheism. Schleiermacher sees this as a real issue, because the aesthetic religion that comes most quickly to mind as opposed to Christianity is not one of the other monotheisms, but Greek polytheism:

> In this one, the teleological orientation recedes entirely. Of the idea of a totality of moral ends and of a connection of human states generally to such a totality, there is neither in its religious symbols nor even in its mysteries a meaningful trace, whereas what we have termed the aesthetic view predominates in the most specific ways, in that even the gods are defined to represent primarily various relations in the activities of the human soul, and thus a characteristic form of inner beauty.[46]

Schleiermacher suggests that the contrast with Christianity is obvious. Not only does Christianity always connect its consciousness of God with "the totality of active states in the idea of a kingdom of God," it has also always regarded the conception of the "beauty of the soul" as completely alien to it.[47] That the latter is true even given early Christianity's widespread adoption of Hellenistic concepts makes it all the more noteworthy, and points out more clearly the determinative

---

46. *Gl*, §9.2.
47. Ibid.

influence of the former. Lest this determinative influence be missed, Schleiermacher concludes his brief comparison with yet another statement of its role and meaning:

> That figure of the kingdom of God, which in Christianity is so important, *indeed under which everything is considered*, is but the general expression of the fact that in Christianity all pain and all joy are pious only insofar as they are referred to activity in the kingdom of God, and that every pious excitation that derives from a passive [*leidentliche*] state ends in the consciousness of a transition to activity.[48]

Hence, Greek polytheism is distinct from Christian monotheism, and not just in the matter of level but in type. Yet is the type simply the product of the level? This question remains unanswered, and thus Schleiermacher's main concern unaddressed, for the final point of §9 is to place the historical religions of Islam, Judaism, and Christianity in their proper positions on the level of monotheism. Why has he bothered to contrast Greek polytheism with Christianity when it does not speak directly to that concern? Schleiermacher does not generally digress so easily. His purpose is to contrast teleological and aesthetic religion in the starkest terms with these two historical examples, so that the teleological and aesthetic tendencies may be more easily perceived in religions that are otherwise similar in being monotheistic. His comparison of Greek polytheism and Christianity certainly serves this purpose, which is the reason we have considered and cited it so extensively. Schleiermacher actually compares the three historical monotheisms only briefly, yet the several points he has just made are implicit throughout, serving as the basis for his comparison. Indeed, having just given a succinct outline of Christianity's teleological tendency, he makes the practical move of using it as the baseline for determining the tendencies of the other two monotheisms. If they both display the teleological tendency, then the question of level determining type will remain open. But if one or both display an aesthetic tendency, then it will be clear that level does not determine type, and some means for distinguishing between monotheisms will have been found.

---

48. Ibid.; emphasis mine.

What are Schleiermacher's conclusions? Consider what he writes:

> As for Judaism, even though it refers the passive [*leidentlichen*] states to the active more in the form of divine punishments and rewards than in that of exhortations and various modes of character development [*Bildungsmitteln*], still the predominant form of God-consciousness is that of the commanding will, and thus of necessity it turns to the active even when it proceeds from passive states. Islam, however, in no way shows the same subordination of the passive to the active. On the contrary, inasmuch as this form of piety comes to complete rest in the consciousness of unalterable divine decrees, so that even the consciousness of one's own activity unites with the feeling of absolute dependence only in such a way that its determination is understood as being based on those decrees, there is thus revealed in this fatalistic character a subordination of the moral to the natural.[49]

In other words, a comparison of the three historical monotheisms does answer the question of the relation between level and type: The latter is *not* simply the product of the former. Moreover, this comparison also enables Schleiermacher to categorize the three historical monotheisms: "Accordingly, the monotheistic level appears divided, the teleological type most strongly pronounced in Christianity, less fully [*vollkommen*] in Judaism, whereas Mohammedanism, just as fully [*vollkommen*] monotheistic, unmistakably expresses the aesthetic type."[50] It is hard to avoid the conclusion that Schleiermacher meant this to be more than a neutral statement of religious taxonomy; rather, he is ranking the three religions of the highest level in a relative hierarchy of perfection. He does not claim that Christianity is the one *true* religion, with all the others being false,[51] but he does suggest that Christianity is the most highly developed and refined of all known religions.

How does Schleiermacher support such an assertion? He does so explicitly by having previously drawn an analogy between the hierarchy

---

49. Ibid. For more on Schleiermacher's notion of "fatalism," see pp. 176 and 179.
50. Ibid.
51. Cf. *Gl*, §7.3.

of religious development, with its different levels and types, and the hierarchies of the natural realm, with its different genera and species.[52] While he acknowledges that one cannot categorize the former as precisely and consistently as the latter, he also maintains that this does not detract from the reality of the differentiation between levels and types, which is to say, the reality of a hierarchy of religions.[53] Again, this ranking of religions cannot be used to declare one religion uniquely true— for example, Christianity—and all others false, because the religions of the same level share by definition certain common features.[54] But the acknowledgment of such similarities does not negate "the conviction presupposed by every Christian of the exclusive excellence [*Vortrefflichkeit*] of Christianity."[55] This conviction, Schleiermacher implies, is not merely the assumption of group chauvinism, but is based on an analogy with the natural order:

> For we also differentiate in the realm of nature between perfect and imperfect animals as, so to speak, different levels of development of animal life, and additionally on each of these between different genera [*Gattungen*], which are thus equal to one another as an expression of the same level. This does not hinder the fact, however, that on a lower level one [genus] may more closely approach the higher [level] and is, to that extent, more perfect than the others. Now in the same way too, although several forms [*Gattungen*] of piety occupy the same level with Christianity, it can still be more perfect than any of them.[56]

Schleiermacher also supports this assertion implicitly, by so describing the doctrinal positions required to maintain a consistent description of the God-consciousness in relation to the natural world (that is, as described in his doctrines of creation and preservation) that only Christian doctrine meets them fully. To be sure, monotheism in general does a fundamentally better job of elucidating that relation than does fetishism or polytheism. But among the historical

---

52. See *Gl*, §7.2 and §7.3.
53. *Gl*, §7.2.
54. *Gl*, §7.3.
55. Ibid.
56. Ibid.

monotheistic faiths, he clearly ranks Christianity as doing a superior
job than Islam or Judaism.

However, the key concern is not the presumed superiority of
Christianity—although that presumption does have bearing on other
issues raised in the overall thesis of this book. Rather, it is the implication which arises out of that answer. If at the highest level of religion,
that is, monotheism, it is possible for particular monotheisms to exist
in one of two opposing types, then this suggests that in some manner
the "general" religious self-consciousness is always already modified in
a particular way. In other words, the "general" doctrines of a monotheistic faith—for example, as found in the First Part of *The Christian
Faith*—must already display at least the modifying influence of that
faith's *type*. When one then joins this with our discussion of
Schleiermacher's view of evil in §48 and §59, this conclusion seems
highly likely. Simply put, for Schleiermacher to claim that life's hindrances are most properly conceived of as divinely ordained opportunities for the human spirit to engage actively in promoting life's
advancement through modification of the natural world, rather than
as divinely ordained "tests" of humanity's ability to resign itself to the
given, he must be allowing the influence of the teleological type of religious consciousness.[57] Indeed, for him to describe life's hindrances
such that they evoke this sense of divinely given *opportunity* rather
than a sense of divine *punishment* suggests the influence of a Christian,
rather than Jewish, teleology. To be sure, Schleiermacher's discussion
of evil in §48 and the world's original perfection in §59 are not explicitly Christian, and certain aspects of them are portrayed in strokes
broad enough to be attributable to monotheism "in general." One
example would be his rejection of any sort of dualism. Yet §48 and §59
are also rather open-ended, made to be completed by the elements of
a more particular piety. And the only particular faith capable of completing them in *all* their aspects is Christianity. These particular
propositions are therefore not among those "which only articulate
monotheism in general, without distinguishing whether they belong
to the teleological or the aesthetic viewpoint."[58] Schleiermacher's

---

57. Cf. *Gl*, §48 and esp. §59.
58. *Gl*, §29.2.

understandings of evil and original perfection as described in the First Part of his system may appear neutral in their generality, but this is in fact a generality that only corresponds fully to the particularities of Christianity.

To support this conclusion further, consider the comments with which Schleiermacher finishes §59. He suggests that one point intended by the Genesis story—namely, the promotion of sinlessness as the key aspect of humanity's original perfection—is actually better illustrated if one portrays a role model living in a context where evil and death are present, rather than in a paradise where these do not exist. If present-day humans are to have such an ideal or role model, one who is relevant to their current situation, that person must have attained sinlessness tested by a context similar to theirs. The traditional description of Adam's sinlessness hardly seems suitable for emulation, since it was lost as a result of its very first, very trivial temptation. By contrast, that person who "bore evil and, by the union of God-consciousness with the love of the human race, overcame the attachment to his own life and submitted to death," would exemplify far more "powerfully" and "splendidly" the ideal of sinlessness.[59] Although Schleiermacher does not himself suggest the association, one cannot help but be reminded of numerous New Testament verses[60] and think that he is here alluding to Jesus as the true model for humanity's original perfection. Such an allusion could be construed as yet another example of how Schleiermacher's specifically Christian Second Part not only informs but also supplies some implicit content for the exposition of his ostensibly more generic First Part.

In light of all this, it should now be even more obvious why Schleiermacher described miracles in the manner he did. On the one hand, had he followed tradition and continued to define them in absolute terms, he would have undercut his ability to assert a developmental understanding of history and creation. On the other hand, by focusing on the one miracle of Christ, he establishes the basis upon which the divine agency can be said to intervene directly in creation: by promoting the active participation of humanity, the one creature

---

59. *Gl*, §59, postscript.
60. E.g., Matt 26:39–45; John 12:27–33; 15:13; Phil 2:6–8.

capable of God-consciousness, which is to say, the one creature created
in the divine image.[61] However, for human beings to be true and full
participants in God's purpose, one must presuppose more than just
the ability to recognize the opportunity presented by evil. One must
also be able to affirm that that participation occurs as a result of the
person's own volition, as a result of a person's own free agency.
Schleiermacher addresses this issue directly in the last proposition
(§49) of his doctrine of preservation.

Understanding Human Freedom

If one were to put a traditional label on this proposition, one would
call it Schleiermacher's doctrine of free will. Of course, his concern is
not simply to reiterate tradition, but to show how the concept of free
causality fits into his understanding of our absolute dependence on
God as it occurs in the interconnected system of nature. This is evident
in the heading that introduces this segment: "Whether that which
excites our self-consciousness and therefore acts upon us is to be
traced back to some part of the so-called nature-mechanism or to the
activity of free causes, the one is just as completely ordained by God as
the other."[62]

As with §§47–48, Schleiermacher views this section of his work as
being implicit in the "principal proposition" of §46. But as he did with
those preceding sections, he detects a number of problems, this time
with certain assumptions regarding the notion of free will and with
certain terms used in traditional formulations of this concept. He
therefore divides his consideration of this proposition into two subsections corresponding to these two sorts of problems, while clarifying his
own understanding of the freedom of finite creatures in both. In
§49.1, Schleiermacher seeks to counter the all-too-frequent assumption that our consciousness of free will somehow stands in opposition
to the feeling of absolute dependence. In fact, he asserts, the contrary
is true: Our consciousness of free will, and the action which that will
produces, can exist only as it is itself an aspect of that universal system

---

61. See *Gl*, §61.4.
62. *Gl*, §49.

"which is the actual indivisible subject of the feeling of absolute dependence."[63] Schleiermacher reminds us that he made this same general point as early as §4.3, and then reiterates the logic of that argument here. Briefly put, our freedom is not absolute, but depends upon the resources and conditions supplied us by the broader realm of nature. Once afforded this material, however, we are capable of exercising a limited control over it, thus displaying our relative freedom within the context of the natural realm. But the whole of that realm, of which we always remain a part, continues to exist only as it is absolutely dependent upon God.

Schleiermacher considers next the distinction between "free causes" and causality in general. He summarizes how this distinction is customarily explained, and observes that this approach, if taken to its logical extreme, must conclude that finite causality is actually an illusion, because free activity can only reside in God. He responds to this approach with adroitly understated sarcasm: "Fortunately, however, over the course of time only a few have been capable of this self-annihilating abdication, by which, having slain the rest of the world, they then also offer themselves in sacrifice to the completeness of such a conceptualization."[64]

To counter such an approach, Schleiermacher presents his own explanation of the distinction, in which "true causality" presupposes life, and vice versa. However, he declines to say how far this sphere of causality, and thus life, extends. He labels such an inquiry "foreign" to this task, even though the claim obviously implied in his approach is one a Christian theologian certainly should want to make, namely, that God is a living God.[65] That Schleiermacher backs away from this claim is due presumably to his desire to avoid "speculation," which he has already labeled as having no role to play in the dogmatic task. Instead, he can only say that our self-consciousness requires us to conceive of the finite world as a sphere of interacting freedom and dependence, the *whole* of which is maintained in absolute dependence. Were we to conceive of divine causation in terms equivalent to those of the sphere

---

63. *Gl*, §49.1.
64. Ibid. See p. 53, n. 27, for more references on the incompatibility of Christian faith with this particular tendency of the modern era.
65. See *Gl*, §55, on omniscience.

of finite interaction, then our feeling of absolute dependence would
lose its consistency. Logically, there would be three forms of causality:
that in which finite and divine causality were joined, that in which
divine causality alone acted, and that in which finite causality alone
acted. Taken together, all three would undermine the feeling of
absolute dependence, the first two indirectly and the last one directly.

The distinction Schleiermacher wishes to draw between past explanations of free will and causality and his own position may perhaps be
best illustrated by two different images of causal "direction." To
Schleiermacher's mind, traditional conceptions of divine causality
have described it in linear terms, either tracing *back* to God as the first,
unmoved mover, or *up* to God as the providential governor. The consequence of such a conception is that either God alone is free and active,
or the divine providence occurs only intermittently. Schleiermacher's
conception of causality replaces this linear imagery with that of two
concentric circles. The inner circle represents finite causality, in which
the various living agents have real, if bounded, freedom; the outer circle represents God, who empowers and sustains the inner as an integrated and enclosed whole.

In part, the problem of conceptualization stems from the terminology employed. Hence, Schleiermacher turns in §49.2 to an examination of the "prevailing dogmatic language" in this matter, which speaks
of God's "preservation" or "cooperation." Schleiermacher finds the first
of these terms not altogether bad, because it is able to comprehend all
that his own presentation has included. It is usually employed in a formulation such as: "God preserves each thing as it is, thus also free
causes as such."[66] To Schleiermacher's mind, this statement is correct—
yet all too often it is left to stand alone, without adequate explanation
of what it and its key concept, "preservation," fully entail. The second
term Schleiermacher finds even less adequate, in that it usually
describes the divine cooperation as being either "according to the
manner of free causes" or "according to the manner of natural ones."[67]
This mode of conceptualization he considers easily misleading,
because it can be construed as lowering the divine causality to the level

---

66. *Gl*, §49.2.
67. Ibid.

of finite causality. This would place God "in the realm of reciprocal action,"[68] a supposition excluded throughout Schleiermacher's system.

Propositions §47, §48, and §49, and the Claims of This Book's Thesis

With these observations, Schleiermacher concludes his treatment of the doctrine of preservation. All that remains is his "Postscript to This Doctrine," where he explains the reasons for including §§47–49 in his system, even though they were implicit in the "principal proposition" of §46. His reasons are of two types, addressing concerns that appear to correspond more or less to my categories of the "inner" and "outer" critical norms. The first set has to do with the concern that no one undermine or obscure "the right relation" between the doctrines of creation and preservation. Improperly conceiving miracles (§47), evil (§48), and free causes (§49) can make the relation of these two doctrines one of inequality or even opposition. Such a situation would not only destroy the logical consistency of his dogmatic system, it would also cast doubt on the fundamental feeling from which these two doctrines are derived. This would completely undermine his innovative approach to Christian theology. For instance, if miracles were viewed as absolutely supernatural, then they would be new creations suspending and negating preservation. The world and God would be felt unreliable, allowing no sense of continuity. Moreover, no sustained development could occur in the world because it would be cut short by the seemingly arbitrary incursion of "re-creations." Next, if evil were viewed as less ordained by God than other things, then the divine preservation would extend unequally to those things that are equally the product of the divine creation. Such a conceptualization would imply that some parts of creation have been forsaken by God—a notion obviously in conflict with the feeling that *all* things *always* exist in absolute dependence upon God. It would also eliminate the "raw material" of progress in creation. Finally, if free causes were described in terms that make their mode of acting appear too different from, or too similar to, that of other natural causes, it could suggest that the

---

68. Ibid.

former act in a manner that displays either independence from the
divine preservation or no particular evidence of having been created
in the image of God. If free causes are described as independent, this
could only drive a wedge between the two doctrines and into the unity
of the fundamental feeling. If they are described in merely animal
rather than spiritual terms, then God and Creation have lost their go-
between and their most active agents for the divine purpose.

However, if one conceives miracles, evil, and free causality properly,
then such divisiveness can be avoided. This Schleiermacher seeks to do
in his exposition of these three subsidiary propositions. As a result, he
is able to maintain the integrity of the fundamental feeling and the
cohesiveness of his two parts, which is to say, he is able to describe the
world as complete while also suggesting that it is capable of, indeed
intended for, progress and fulfillment through redemption.
Furthermore, he has been able to do all this while also remaining true
to what he considers essential in the witness of Scripture and dogmatic
tradition. To be sure, he has trimmed off many conceptions and
assumptions that his predecessors could have held or did hold as necessary. But he is rarely, if ever, cavalier in dismissing such things, and
generally attempts to incorporate into his own system the pious
impulse behind such conceptions and assumptions even if he discards
the previous formulation.

Schleiermacher's second set of reasons for expounding §§47–49
reflects his desire to demonstrate the "harmony" existing between
piety and science—the latter of which he defines as natural science and
history—and piety and morality. Each of his three propositions
addresses issues crucial to one of these three relations. Hence, the harmony that exists between piety and natural science would be destroyed
if miracles were construed as absolutely supernatural. Such a construal
would undermine the reliability of the natural order of things, thus
negating the basic supposition of the natural sciences and rendering
them impossible. Likewise, the harmony that exists between piety and
the science of history would be destroyed if evil were viewed as not
ordained, or less ordained by God than the good. History, which "has
to do especially with the opposition between good and evil," would
then "necessarily become fatalistic, that is, give up its reference to the

idea of the good," given the way good and evil "show themselves inter-
twined with one another" in the actual course of events.[69] In other
words, he would have to surrender the concept of a development
toward the good intrinsic to his historiography, and grant evil a degree
of independence which would negate the supposition that it may
always be subordinated to, and made to serve, the purposes of the
good. Life's hindrances would then not necessarily represent opportunities for progress; they could be debilitating and eternally insurmountable victories for evil. Finally, with regard to free will,
Schleiermacher states that the interests of morality "must always be
threatened or, for their part, must threaten those of piety, when absolute
dependence is so conceived that as a result free self-determination
cannot be maintained, and vice versa."[70] The whole notion of morality
would become meaningless if the agents it seeks to guide have no
capacity for choosing one course of action over another. Conversely, the
concept of absolute dependence would be nullified if finite agents were
capable of unlimited rather than only relative self-determination.

Schleiermacher's propositions, however, avoid any such conflict
between the interests of piety and the interests of science and morality
because of the way they explain the basic principle outlined in §46,
which describes the fundamental experience of absolute dependence
only *within* the context of the interdependent realm of nature. The
particular experience of miracles, of evil, and of freedom is not to be
explained through recourse to sources or causes outside of this natural nexus. Rather, each of these three is to be understood as one end on
a continuum of greatest and smallest that exists wholly within the natural realm. Thus, miracles are appropriately contrasted with ordinary
events, the good with the evil, and the free with the mechanistic; in
each case, however, the contrast is a matter of degree within the nature
system, and not of kind, which is to say between a natural and supernatural realm. Schleiermacher summarizes the first as a contrast
between "the greatest and least of the natural cycle."[71] Based on what
he said in §47.3, this distinguishes those occurrences that are most

---

69. *Gl*, §49, postscript.
70. Ibid.
71. Ibid.

readily understood as natural events from those that, given our current state of knowledge, are least easily explained as such. The second contrast, between good and evil, reflects the degree of harmony existing between individuals and the natural and social environment encompassing them. Insofar as that environment helps, or can be made to help, the purposes of the individual entity, it will be construed as good; insofar as that environment hinders or defeats the purposes of the individual, and is defined solely in terms of that opposition, it will be construed as evil. The third contrast, between freedom and mechanism, reflects the varying degree to which an individual's actions may be either self-consciously self-determined, and thus more individual and free, the product of spirit, or unself-consciously reactive or instinctual, and thus more a product of environment than personal will. In all three cases, then, Schleiermacher has offered an explanation restricted to the finite realm of interacting freedom and dependence, of natural cause and effect. In that way, he avoids any conflict with a modern, scientific outlook.[72] But it is also an explanation that not only avoids conflict with but actually lends itself to the fundamental religious feeling of absolute dependence. If properly conceived, neither miracles, nor evil, nor free will may call into question the complementarity of science, morality, and religion.

Thus, in his explicit treatment of the doctrines of creation and preservation, Schleiermacher clearly seeks to maintain what is essential in Christian tradition, while presenting it in such a way as to be compatible with the external intellectual norms of his day. The manner in which he has structured his doctrines and described their harmony with science and morality suggests that they could arise only in a Christian context. Because of his description of monotheism in general, what he has written in these two doctrines ought to be as applicable in a Jewish or Islamic dogmatic as it is to a Christian one. At least, as doctrines contained in the First Part of his system, their "expression" ought to "coincide most easily with those of other faiths."[73] Yet when

---

72. See p. 53, n. 27. Once again, we have here a suggestion that Schleiermacher's position, however compatible it might have been with most of the natural sciences of his day, would not be compatible with a completely deterministic or materialistic understanding of human agency.

73. See *Gl*, §29.2, and above, p. 26.

he describes the harmony between these doctrines—derived from a piety whose particularity is ostensibly at most only monotheistic—and history and morality, he slips into a definition of history (and by extension, morality) that according to his own account would exclude Islamic piety. Recall that he has designated Islam an aesthetic monotheism, which by his definition means it is fatalistic with regard to history and more concerned with the inner beauty of the soul than with outward acts of morality.[74] Thus, for all the apparent neutrality of §§48–49, it actually presents a treatment of evil and free will already influenced by, and most compatible with, a teleological understanding of history, that is, one in which human moral activity is encouraged as a response to God's will. Moreover, this teleological understanding also seems more specifically Christian than Jewish, in that the latter is apt to interpret evil as God's legally justified punishment for immoral acts, while only the former interprets it as an opportunity for life's progress. Indeed, for Schleiermacher Christianity alone best understands history, and thus creation, as *developing*, and Christianity alone best understands the role human beings are to play in furthering that development.

Hence, even though Schleiermacher seeks to present a set of doctrines "in which the characteristically Christian stands out less strongly,"[75] he still offers an understanding of the world and its dynamics that *Christian piety alone seems capable of producing*. To begin with, it promotes an interpretation of nature first as "developable," and then as developing, in part through the industrious efforts of persons attempting to act according to a certain religiously grounded moral imperative. Moreover, the logic of these doctrines is so tightly argued that they alone seem capable of fostering an understanding of creation compatible with the intellectual assumptions prevalent among the scientists and historians of his time and place—even though any other monotheism should be able to do the same. To put it another way, Schleiermacher has tailored his exposition of these various doctrines in such a manner that they present problems that

74. See *Gl*, §9.
75. *Gl*, §29.2.

can be fully met only by the answers given in Christianity. That is, to refer once more to his crucial passage from §29, their *expression* may stand out less strongly as characteristically Christian, but their *inner coherence* and *logic* is definitely Christian, because of the way in which they are ordered to, and completed by, the characteristically Christian Second Part of his dogmatic system.

CHAPTER 8

The Completion of Schleiermacher's Christological Orientation

———ᴍ———

Let me begin this chapter by summarizing the points I have established about Schleiermacher's doctrine of Creation as presented in the First Part of his *Glaubenslehre*. To begin with, Schleiermacher has been adamant in maintaining the unity and integrity of God's creation and preservation of the world. On the one hand, the divine creation and preservation are aspects of the same activity. Hence, what God's creative activity begins, God's preserving activity continues; the latter should be conceived not as in any way countering or "side-stepping" what the former establishes, but as actualizing and fulfilling what is nascent in the former. On the other hand, therefore, the world itself, in its origin and its continuing existence, forms a discrete and sufficient whole in its absolute dependence on God. It is neither proper nor necessary to conceive of God as intervening in its course by supernatural means. Instead, one should recognize that God governs the world only by means of the natural causal nexus established in creation.

Underlying this assumption of the unity and integrity of God's creation and preservation is the second point worth highlighting, namely, Schleiermacher's assumption of the unity and integrity of the eternal divine decree. Schleiermacher is quite traditional in his affirmation of the absolute oneness of God. From his standpoint, dogmatics must not construe the divine mind as separable from the divine will or of either of these as separable from the divine deed. Such a construal would not only disparage God—by describing the divine Being in terms appropriate only to finite and temporal beings—it would also undermine the reliability of the natural order by lowering God into the realm of mutual interdependence. As such, no guarantee could exist that the natural order would continue or the divine purpose would be fulfilled. But if we "let God be God," that is, in an absolute oneness of omnipotence, omniscience, omnipresence, and eternity (and as Schleiermacher later affirms, holiness, justice, wisdom, and love), then one can trust in the reliability of the natural order and the ultimate fulfillment of the divine decree.

What is the aim or purpose of the divine decree? This is the third point Schleiermacher has clarified. Stated generally, the divine decree gives direction and meaning to creation. To begin with, Schleiermacher has observed that the created order is not merely static, but exists historically. Moreover, this history is not merely a cyclical, perpetual-motion machine; it is developing or evolving, much as organisms do. And unique among the entities existing within that order and history are human beings, whose nature likewise is not merely static but intended for development. Schleiermacher does not describe explicitly the object of that development, but he does offer some hints that humans are meant to become "closer" to God, that they actualize ever more fully the potential for God-consciousness intrinsic to their nature. With this unique capacity, they are also to be active in the world, in effect acting as go-betweens in the relation of the created and divine realms. They can become the mouthpiece of nature and the agent of God in the development of creation toward its ultimate fulfillment.

Finally, Schleiermacher has proposed that in this development— and indeed, as a prerequisite for it—the obstacles that would appear to hinder or prevent it must no longer be construed as essentially or even primarily "evil," but as opportunities for the progress of the good. They exist as the catalysts for change and growth.

What makes all of these various assumptions or construals evident and possible? Why are these particular ones made, and not others? And inasmuch as they present a certain form, but no content, where will they gain that content? The answers lie in the appearance and work of the Redeemer. On the basis of what the Redeemer imparts, Christians may retrospectively interpret the meaning and purpose of all past history and creation itself, while being motivated to act in the created realm in ways intent on forwarding that meaning and purpose. The coming of the Redeemer brings a particular focus to certain general religious feelings that, if they could exist on their own, would do so in a vague and incomplete way. But in fact, Schleiermacher holds that such feelings only first come to exist in Christians in conjunction with the particular feelings evoked by the Redeemer. In other words, Schleiermacher has tailored at least some of his ostensibly general doctrines of the First Part so as to make the particular doctrines of the Second Part the only fitting ones to conclude his treatment overall.

Schleiermacher insisted that Christ can and does modify everything in Christianity that it has "in common" with the other monotheistic faiths.[1] These commonalities never actually exist in the historically living faith of Christians; they are merely intellectual constructs abstracted from that faith for the purpose of dogmatic exposition. So once that purpose is served—and even *as* it is being served—one must always recognize that they really only exist in the particular. They can be viewed as "commonalities" only because one has temporarily and artificially ignored their specific source and context. Eventually, one must see them again back in their proper place.

Schleiermacher's "broader" doctrine of Creation, like his doctrine of God, should not be viewed as confined to the First Part of his system, but as extending through the whole of it. To be sure, those segments of it located in his First Part do indeed downplay their characteristically Christian elements, so that their "expression therefore may also coincide most easily with those of other faiths,"[2] but those segments do not stand on their own. They must be completed by the propositions of the Second Part. In effect, this prevents Schleiermacher's system, or any part thereof, from being construed as a natural theology. His *Glaubenslehre* may commence with certain

---

1. See pp. 34ff.
2. *Gl*, §29.2.

general observations, but these ought not be taken on their own; one must allow the ordering of his system to carry one through to its conclusion, for only then can the full significance of his initial doctrines be manifested.

As a matter of fact, one could interpret the *unity* of Schleiermacher's First and Second Parts and the *development* of the First into the Second as actually corresponding to what he says about the relation of creation to redemption. On the one hand, the methodological progression of his work reflects his understanding of the historical progression between Adam and Christ. But on the other hand, one must also take account of it as a whole to understand truly any of its parts, which could reflect his understanding of the essential "nonsequentiality" of the divine activity. This approach allows him to maintain certain affirmations about the divine nature inherited from tradition while also offering an account of the divine activity in the world's history plausible to his contemporaries.

On the Unity of God's Activity and of *The Christian Faith*

The basic question, then, is this: Are creation and redemption one? From the divine perspective, the answer can only be yes. To respond in any other way would inevitably attribute to God a way of acting, willing, or thinking properly characteristic of only finite beings. There can be no division within God, nor any description of the divine activity that bespeaks a sequential mode of operation. To do so would make God's being and agency not only temporal but also reactive. Such a conclusion would undermine completely Schleiermacher's fundamental assumption of the feeling of absolute dependence. Hence, he emphasizes over and over again in a wide variety of dogmatic locations that God only relates to the world as one to a whole. Consider, for example, what he writes in §109.3, on the topic of the individual Christian's justification:

> If we want to speak as much as possible without figurative language and with dogmatic acuity, here no more than elsewhere [can we] assume a temporal act taking place in a particular moment, and just as little an

act directed toward an individual; rather there can be only an individual and temporal effect of a divine act or decree, but not an act or decree that is itself such. That means, only insofar as every dogmatic treatment derives from the self-consciousness of the individual, and in fact from the self-consciousness of the alteration of his relation to God, can we imagine the justifying divine activity in its relation to the individual. . . . [B]ut it may not be formulated as something in and of itself, as if the justification of each individual rested upon a separate divine decree—even if one wanted to represent it as prepared from all eternity and only entering into actuality at a particular point in time. On the contrary, there is but *one* eternal and universal decree of the justification of humankind for Christ's sake. This decree, moreover, is one and the same with that of the sending of Christ—otherwise this would have to be conceived and resolved by God without its result—and this, moreover, is but *one* also with the decree of the creation of the human race, inasmuch as human nature is perfected first in Christ. For as thinking and willing, willing and doing are not to be severed in God, so too is all of this only *one* divine act for the modification of our relation to God, the temporal manifestation of which takes its start in the incarnation [*Menschwerdung*] of Christ, from which proceeds the whole "new creation" of humanity. And from then on, the temporal manifestation of this divine act is also truly a constant one, although from its effect it appears to us to be, so to speak, broken into as many separate and distinct points as there are individuals presumed to be in union with Christ.[3]

His point is obvious. From the divine perspective, the individual's justification, the sending of Christ, the creation of humanity—indeed, creation itself—are all but a single decree and act. Of course, in actual human experience and for purposes of understandability and clarity, the Christian may conceive of them as sequential and need to discuss them in separate dogmatic locations. But this must not be taken as indicating that they are actually separate acts, purposes, or thoughts on the part of God.

---

3. *Gl*, §109.3.

However, from that human perspective—indeed, in the actual order of history realized under God's rule—an evolutionary or progressive sequence of events does occur. Thus, one can speak appropriately of a "first" and "second" Adam, or a "first" and "second" creation, or of an "old" or "new" creature when one attempts to describe these stages. To be sure, one must not overextend the implications of this division. As Schleiermacher points out:

> Although the communication of the Spirit to human nature occurring in the first Adam was an insufficient one, in that the Spirit remained sunk in sensuousness and barely looked around fully at moments presaging something better, and although the work of creation is perfected only through the second, equally original communication to the second Adam, nevertheless, both moments go back to *one* undivided eternal divine decree, and establish even in a higher sense only *one* and the same natural order, albeit one unattainable by us.[4]

There is a single divine purpose and a single, continuous natural order, but the implementation of the divine purpose for human nature within that order takes place over time. There is no *essential* change, only one from potential to actuality. Human nature was endowed at the first creation with all things needed for development, which is to say, the elemental capacity necessary for a true and constant God-consciousness. But the "perfection" or fulfillment of that nature and its capacity became possible only with the second creation, because it was decreed originally that they should undergo development or maturation on the basis of this second event.

However, in order for this second creation to have its effect, certain preconditions have to exist. Human nature must be prepared, so that it can receive what it was always intended to receive. What form does this preparation take?

> God has ordained that the earlier insurmountable impotence of the God-consciousness shall become for us, as our own act, the consciousness

---

4. *Gl*, §94.3.

of sin, in order to sharpen that yearning without which even Jesus' tal-
ent would have found no living receptivity for the assimilation of what
he communicates.[5]

That is, Schleiermacher has formulated matters in such a way that each
of the creations has an intrinsic need of the other—which is only reasonable, given his assertion of their underlying unity. On the one
hand, reference to the first Adam indicates that human nature is, at
root, endowed with all that it needs for God-consciousness; the coming of Christ does not effect, by supernatural means, a qualitative
change in that nature. It does not add a previously nonexistent capacity, but rather fulfills an imperfectly used one.

Yet this could be taken to imply that Christ's assistance was not
strictly necessary, but only helpful, that the first Adam could have
attained on his own what the second Adam merely brings about
sooner. Schleiermacher rejects this view, in part because it is not in
keeping with the church's testimony about Christ's influence and in
part because, given the pervasive sway of sin, it is as logically impossible as pulling oneself up by one's own bootstraps. Thus, on the other
hand, reference to the second Adam indicates that human nature cannot, in itself, attain that stage of God-consciousness for which it was
preordained; it can attain it only with the help of the Redeemer. That
is, the decree preordaining this result was made simultaneously with
the preordination of the Redeemer as the means. Hence, the appearance and effect of the Redeemer is not a supernatural incursion into
the ongoing history of the created order, but neither is it merely a
product of that history. It is rather a sort of "time delayed miracle"
embedded, as it were, in nature itself by God at creation, a conception
Schleiermacher first mentioned under his doctrine of preservation in
§47.2.[6] God created human nature to undergo a process of development, to reach ever higher stages of spiritual maturity. But the means
by which human nature attains the (at present) highest stage, that is,
Christianity, is not itself a product of that process, coming into

---

5. *Gl*, §89.1.
6. See p. 143.

existence merely as the result of an accidental or naturally generated set of historical circumstances. It is rather the product of a direct and eternal divine decree, a decree fully embedded in the natural order at the moment of the first creation, but only fully manifested after the second.

Of course, the preceding should not be taken as meaning the two creations are isolated moments of divine activity in an otherwise natural flow of history. Even if one understands that activity correctly (i.e., as embedded in nature itself), one must also affirm the inherent connection between the two creations. The latter does indeed effect something new in human history, but it is not new absolutely. Rather, it effects a modification or consummation of an already existing being. To underscore this point, it is appropriate to also call it a "preservation." Consider what Schleiermacher writes in §89, in partial explanation of his claim that the appearance of Christ and the establishment of the new collective life in relation to him are to be regarded as the only just consummated creation of human nature:

> Here again the concept of creation must be explained in terms of preservation. For not only is the man Jesus called the second Adam, which can only mean the second called into being by God, but all those born again are called the new creature, the result being that even that gets construed [*aufgestellt*] as creation which we, with complete justification, describe originally as preservation, namely, as preservation of the ever broader saving strength of Christ for redemption and blessing; by the same token, the appearance of Christ himself is likewise to be viewed as preservation, namely, as preservation of the receptivity of human nature—implanted in the beginning and developing continuously— for assimilating such an absolute potency of God-consciousness. For at the first creation of the human race, only the uncompleted state of human nature made its appearance, although as such the appearing of the Redeemer was implanted in it already in a nontemporal manner.[7]

This passage reminds us that the relation between the First and Second Parts of Schleiermacher's *Glaubenslehre* should be conceived in

---

7. *Gl*, §89.3.

organic or biological terms, rather than architectural ones. Here, Schleiermacher's use of such images as "implanting" and "developing" suggests that the change wrought by Christ not be conceived as God's mechanistic imposition upon, or addition to, the natural, but as an ongoing, divinely guided evolutionary culmination of the natural. Whatever seeds there are, God planted them at creation, and they contain within themselves all the genetic potential needed for full growth. But for the final stage of that potential to come to fruition requires—just as it does in the parts of the botanical realm—an external (yet still natural) source of "germination." This, of course, is what Jesus accomplishes.

The value of this "evolutionary" explanation should not be underestimated, for it enables Schleiermacher to address quite well the demands of theological tradition and modern standards of intellectual plausibility. He wants to avoid any formulation of the divine activity in Christ that would reduce it to a merely natural causality or portray it as actually needing or reacting to human sin. He also wants to avoid any formulation of it as interrupting the natural causal nexus. He accomplishes all this by interpreting the scriptural image of Jesus as the "second Adam" in a thoroughly developmental manner. It is, of course, anachronistic to suppose that Paul himself understood the image this way. His faith did not include the belief in the inevitability of progress so often attributed to the nineteenth century. Nevertheless, this Pauline nomenclature does suggest very concisely that what God does in Christ is both "new" and "not new," both a part of the original creation and also an advance from it. In that sense, one can certainly see how it could be used to suggest that creation and preservation—indeed, creation and redemption—are but aspects of one and the same divine activity.

Christ and the Christian Interpretation of Nature

Yet certain matters still remain unaddressed. Schleiermacher asserts that Christ, as the "second Adam," brings into being a "new creature" and a "new creation." But a brief examination of how Schleiermacher employs these latter two terms suggests that they refer primarily to

Christians and the church. What about the rest of the world, in particular the realm of nature? Does the coming of Christ have any rele-
vance in fostering a new understanding of the rest of creation? Or does
it exercise *only* a personal influence, that is, only changing the way
Christians understand themselves? Does Schleiermacher even much
concern himself with the external world once he begins consideration
of the church? The answers to these questions are crucial to this book,
for if Schleiermacher is now using the term "creation" in a very limited
way, that is, in reference only to the "new creation" of the church, then
proving its christological orientation will be no great insight. One
would be surprised only if his doctrine of the church lacked such a
focus. But if the coming of Christ is described as effecting not only the
"new creation" of the church but also a new understanding of the
nature and purpose of the rest of the world, then the scope of that orientation must be much greater. Indeed, it will modify or complete all
that he has said previously.

When we turn to Schleiermacher's discussion of the work of
Christ, which commences in §100, it first appears that he describes
the Redeemer's activity in strictly psychological and sociological
terms. He does at one point describe that activity as "world forming,"
but then goes on to say "its object is human nature, in the totality of
which the powerful God-consciousness shall be implanted as a new
life-principle."[8] This would seem to suggest that Christ's work focuses
only on the human sphere, effecting a transformation in human feeling but no direct change in the world. Yet it could also be taken to
mean that this transformation occurs "miraculously," that is, for all
humanity all at once, since the object of Christ's activity is human
nature in its "totality." We must avoid this conclusion, however,
because of what Schleiermacher says next regarding the realization of
the Redeemer's influence in the lives of actual individuals. These

> he makes his own in connection with the totality, wherever he has an
> impact on those in whom his activity not only remains, but from whom
> also, through the revelation of his life, it can affect others. And thus the

8. *Gl*, §100.2.

total efficacy [*Wirksamkeit*] of Christ is only the continuation of the creative divine activity, out of which even the person of Christ emerged.[9]

The points to be drawn from this are several. First, the Redeemer's influence spreads in a fully natural manner, being realized in the lives of actual persons only as they come in contact with, and are incorporated into, the life of the Christian community. Thus, secondly, reference to the "totality" of human nature does not indicate that Christ's work effects an immediate and actual transformation of the human race, but that such a change is the ultimate goal of that work. The human species is not to be divided finally into two "subspecies"—the redeemed and unredeemed—although for the time being humanity will comprise these two groups. It also indicates that the ongoing increase of the church is not the result of direct, special acts of God. It is, rather, the result of the ongoing operation of natural mechanisms employed by Christ and the church. Therefore, thirdly, it is appropriate to say that the Redeemer's activity is not a new and different form of work, and it does not have a goal for humanity different from that first established at creation. Instead, that activity continues—in fact, makes truly efficacious—the original divine work toward the original divine goal, which is that humans have a full and uninterrupted consciousness of God.

But does all of this suggest that creation, understood as the natural realm, gets left behind? Does it suggest that Christ has no final relation to, or power over, the world? Does it mean that Schleiermacher will simply deny those scriptural and traditional affirmations describing Christ's lordship in relation to the world? If so, how will he justify his position? Will that position serve to suggest that Schleiermacher's doctrine of Creation—understood as including the natural world—does not, in the end, have a christological orientation?

If we begin by turning to some of Schleiermacher's christological doctrines, the news for the thesis of this book does not seem to be good. For example, consider some excerpts from his description of Christ's kingly office. A quick survey of this doctrine reveals that

---

9. Ibid.

Schleiermacher does indeed describe Christ's power as being exercised only within certain clear limits. Of those relevant to our investigation, the first one stems from a passage found in the Gospel of John. As that passage relates, Christ's kingdom is not of this world (John 18:36). Schleiermacher interprets this as asserting in part "that his kingly power does not immediately rule over and order the things of this world—which means therefore that only the inner life of persons in themselves and in their relation to each other is left as his immediate domain."[10] The second limit stems from Schleiermacher's insistence that Christ's kingly power not be construed as encroaching in any way upon either the general divine government of the world or the various secular governments of the world.

Both of these limitations would seem to preclude any lordship of Christ over the world. In effect, they keep him human, with his influence operating by natural means and confined to the realm of piety. It might seem initially that Schleiermacher has simply opted for a modern, privatistic description of Jesus' power, so as to avoid the intellectual difficulties associated with certain past affirmations, such as those portraying him as the "God-man." These sorts of concerns certainly play a role in Schleiermacher's thinking, but just as certainly they should not be viewed as stemming solely from norms external to theology. Schleiermacher is also compelled to present a formulation consistent with what he views as the essential witness of Scripture and the prior assertions and underlying assumptions of his dogmatics. Schleiermacher displays all of these factors in the following quote, which also serves to delineate further Christ's sphere of influence:

> The customary division of the kingdom of Christ into the kingdom of power, the kingdom of grace, and the kingdom of glory accomplishes little here. To begin with, we must break it up in such a way that under the latter two is comprehended the characteristic object of Christ's kingly efficacy, namely, the world that has come to partake in redemption, while under the kingdom of power the world in general and in

----

10. *Gl*, §105.1.

itself will be understood. In asserting such a view, however, the unwarranted corollary too readily emerges to the effect that a kingdom of power inhered to Christ, as it were, prior to the kingdom of grace and independent of the same. Now such a kingdom, at the very least, could not possibly belong to his redeeming activity; and if the apostles had known of such a thing from the Word (John 1:2–3), then this would be at least a knowledge that, lacking a connection with redemption, could not belong to Christian piety either. If one believes, however, that one must interpret expressions that the apostles use referring to Christ as the Word become flesh, the God-man and Redeemer (Heb. 1:2–3), or that even Christ uses in reference to himself (Matt. 11:27, 28:18; cf. John 17:5, 22–24), as if they imputed to him the whole government of the world, then one gets caught in a contradiction not only with all those passages where he himself submits petitions to the Father and refers to that which the Father reserves to himself, but also with all those that express the intention of establishing as well an immediate relation of petition and bequeathal between believers and the Father.[11]

Schleiermacher's position is clear. One ought not ascribe to Jesus more status or power than proper piety, dogmatic systematizing, and Scripture allow. Christianity relates to Jesus always and only in conjunction with the feeling of redemption. Were it to present a dogmatic exposition of him apart from this feeling, it would not only be straying from the realm of piety into that of speculation, it would also be encroaching upon its previous exposition of the feeling of absolute dependence. This latter consequence is unacceptable for two reasons: First, it brings to dogmatics a certain redundancy, if not an outright self-contradiction; second, it conflicts with Scripture by making greater claims for Jesus than he reportedly claimed for himself. Hence, Schleiermacher concluded, if we are to assess Jesus' lordship in the world correctly, we must affirm that that lordship is

a power over the world only insofar as believers are indeed taken out of the midst of the world, and the communion of believers or the kingdom

---

11. *Gl*, §105.2.

of Christ can increase only as the world—as the antithesis of the
church—decreases, and its members are transformed gradually into
members of the church, so that evil is overcome and the domain of
redemption extended.[12]

This passage obviously reflects a modification of Schleiermacher's use
of the term "world." Here it refers not so much to the external natural
order as to the various distractions and assumptions that retard spiritual maturation. Despite the shift in connotation, however, the point
remains that Christ's power is restricted to the "subjective" sphere. He
can affect the world only insofar as he influences members of the
Christian community to exercise their powers in the world. The ongoing divine government of the world, that is, divine providence,
remains the prerogative of God "the Father."

Does this mean we have reached a dead end? Does this mean that
Christ is not the key for unlocking the true and full meaning of
Creation, according to Schleiermacher? It might appear so. In light of
the passages just considered, Schleiermacher seems intent on describing Christ's influence in very restricted terms. He is portrayed as having no direct control over the natural realm, and any indirect influence
he might exercise could be construed as merely a veneer of activity on
an otherwise independent world. Reinforcing these conclusions is the
way Schleiermacher uses, or chooses not to use, the various scriptural
references attributing to Christ creative and providential agency.
Throughout his doctrine of Christ, Schleiermacher portrays him in
strictly human terms.

Yet denying such agency of Christ and ascribing it rather to the
Father alone does not preclude the assertion that the Father orders all
things *with the Redeemer in mind*. That is, Christ may not be the direct
cause or power creating and sustaining the world, he may not himself
exercise divine agency, but he can be construed as the one creature
capable of being the "epitome" of creation. He *completes* creation by
establishing the means by which nature can realize and express its
relation to God, namely, through perfecting the God-consciousness
of its representative, humanity. This is indicated by Christ's role as the

---

12. Ibid.

"second Adam," consummating the "first" creation and initiating the "second." Once one is incorporated into the life of the second Adam, one also gains a new perspective and understanding of God's purpose in the world. One recognizes that the original creation did not merely establish a static world; it initiated a dynamic world. One also recognizes that this was not to be an open-ended dynamism, but one tending toward the coming of Christ. One should also recognize, therefore, given the nature of God's being and activity, that this development toward Christ had to be eternally ordained by God, and that development on the basis of Christ should naturally continue. In other words, understanding the full significance of Christ's mission inevitably entails the modification of all previous observations made about creation and its meaning, for only with the coming of Christ is God's eternal purpose made clear.

Christ: The Determinant and Goal of History

The most explicit statements supporting this reading are located at the end—or, given Schleiermacher's comments to Lücke, the climax—of Schleiermacher's *Glaubenslehre*, in those propositions expounding the divine attributes that relate to redemption. The first of those propositions, §164, makes the following claim: "When we trace our consciousness of fellowship with God, reestablished through the efficacy of redemption, back to the divine causality, then *we set forth the planting and propagation of the Christian church as the object of the divine government of the world*."[13] Schleiermacher begins his elaboration of this proposition by stating that this particular conclusion is really the only one Christians can offer in explaining the divine government. The reason for this lies in the fact that for the Christian consciousness "all other things exist only in reference to the efficacy of redemption, either belonging to the organism in which the reawakened God-consciousness expresses itself, or given as the stuff that is to be first cultivated by this organism."[14]

It may appear that Schleiermacher is making a new assertion here, but he is actually only filling in the blanks of a formula established

---

13. *Gl*, §164; emphasis mine.
14. *Gl*, §164.1.

earlier. To begin with, that Christians view all things only through the lens of redemption is a principle first hinted at and described generally in §10, and stated explicitly in §11. The God-consciousness only becomes *actual* by adhering to "some relation" of the self-consciousness. Once this is done, it subordinates all other relations to it and imparts to them "its color and tone." This primary relation is, for Christians, the one established by the redemption accomplished through Jesus of Nazareth. As a result, Schleiermacher's statement in §164.1 that "all other things exist only in reference to the efficacy of redemption" becomes inevitable, because a *Christian* consciousness could interpret them in no other manner.

But what about the continuation of that statement, and the manner in which he classifies all those "other things" as either internal to or external from the Christian subject? Here Schleiermacher simply builds on what he has said previously in §59 about the original perfection of the world. That proposition described in general the dynamic relation existing between the human spirit and the world: The world's stimuli (which includes a human being's "bodily aspect") fosters the emergence of the God-consciousness, but the world also "lets itself be manipulated by that spirit, in order to serve it as an instrument and as a means of expression."[15] What Schleiermacher adds here in §164 is again simply particularity, that is, the particular "color and tone" brought by the consciousness of redemption. In other words, the Christian's understanding of his or her "give and take" with the world will be formulated in all respects according to the interpretive principle established by redemption. That means, among other things, that the Christian will understand the world as having been ordered and sustained by God in such a way that from the very beginning the appearance of the Redeemer and the emergence and spread of the church were inevitable.

Here Schleiermacher recognizes that misinterpretation might arise with regard to this divine activity, and his proleptic comments serve to illustrate just how far the consciousness of redemption colors the perception of all other things. One can readily detect his earlier affirmation of the unity of the divine creation and preservation, but now it

---

15. *Gl*, §59.1.

also becomes clear that the divine activity of redemption must likewise only be understood as the key to a larger, undivided activity. Indeed, for the Christian consciousness it stands as the motive and determinative influence in God's creation and preservation of the world. Consider the following comments:

> Since "govern" means first of all to set in motion and to direct forces that are already present from another source, this expression very easily tempts one to think even here of a divine directing of already existing forces, and to separate the government of the world from the creation in such a way that that government appears to be something arriving in the middle of or after the fact, while also making it appear as if, from creation on, everything could have gone otherwise than it has. In the Christian belief that all things were created for the Redeemer (Col. 1:16), it is implied, however, that with creation itself everything preparatory and retroactive is arranged in reference to the revelation of God in the flesh and to the most complete possible conferral thereof to the whole of human nature for the formation of the kingdom of God. In the same way, we also do not regard the natural world as if, by dint of the divine preservation, it could follow its own course, with the divine government exerting an influence on it only through special isolated acts in order to bring it into union with the kingdom of grace. On the contrary, to us both are completely one, *and we are certain of the fact that indeed the whole arrangement of nature, from the beginning on, would have been different, if the human race had not been ordained for redemption through Christ following its transgression.*[16]

Overall, Schleiermacher describes a seamless unity: creation, preservation and redemption, the natural world, and the kingdom of grace all stem from a single, eternal act of God. From our temporal perspective and for the purpose of dogmatic exposition, they may appear sequential and be logically distinguished, but, ultimately, their fundamental unity must also be affirmed.

This being said, what more specific points might we draw from this passage that serve to clarify Schleiermacher's understanding of the

---

16. *Gl*, §164.1; emphasis mine.

relation between Christ and creation? One is discernible in his reference to the Colossians passage. Schleiermacher only uses half of the
affirmation made in that verse stating that all things were created *for*
the Redeemer, but not *in* or *through* him. This deletion seems to show
the same concern voiced above with regard to the proper description
of Christ's kingly office,[17] which Schleiermacher also addresses at the
close of his doctrine of the person of Christ. He there observes that
Scripture ascribes a variety of titles, attributes, and activities to Christ,
a number of which seem to confuse the line between the human and
divine. Schleiermacher implies that such confusion was virtually
inevitable, given the profound impact Christ had made on the authors
of Scripture. But he also implies that any current dogmatic reading of
these passages ought to resolve their ambiguity in such a way as to
reestablish the distinction between the human and divine. For example, in reference to 1 Corinthians 8:6, Colossians 1:15–17, and Hebrews
1:4, Schleiermacher observes that "creation and preservation are
ascribed to Christ only in such a manner that the question remains
whether he is not active cause only insofar as he is final cause."[18]
Needless to say, this was not still an open question to Schleiermacher.
The divine activity upon which creation, preservation, and ultimately
redemption depend is to be traced back solely to God; not Christ. For
Schleiermacher, Christ does indeed possess a perfect consciousness of
God, but he is not to be thought of as himself divine. Hence, he does
not "share" in the divine activity, nor does God delegate to him tasks
that belong properly to the Father. But this Fatherly activity is nevertheless "oriented" toward Christ, so it is proper to assert that all things
were created "for" the Redeemer and the role that he could play in
bringing about the kingdom of grace in the world. Christians understand Christ to be the *telos* or goal of Creation, and thus the key for
unlocking its meaning.

Schleiermacher makes it clear that the Redeemer is the goal of
creation in neither an accidental nor supplemental sense, but in an
original and essential sense. That is to say, first, Christians do not view
Christ as merely a brilliant and productive improviser, capable of taking

17. See pp. 191–93.
18. *Gl*, §99, postscript.

the independent givens of the world and pious feeling and interpreting them in a manner more insightful, comprehensive, and fruitful than any "competitor." Such a construal would be too superficial, implying there is no necessary or intrinsic link between Christ and creation, only a subjective and de facto one. Secondly, according to Schleiermacher, Christians do not view Christ as God's response to a creation gone awry through the fall. This would imply not only that God bumbled in the act of creation, but also that creation and redemption are two distinct acts. Both implications are, of course, unacceptable to Schleiermacher. The former is not merely unflattering to the divine dignity; it could also suggest that alternative creations were available but remained unchosen, a supposition that violates the affirmation of creation *ex nihilo*.[19] The latter implication has also already been ruled out, because God is not to be construed as acting in a sequential or reactive manner. Therefore, given the above—and all else previously said about the divine being and activity—the only possible option is to recognize that Christ is indeed the essential and eternal goal or "final cause" of creation. In one way or another, all things are aimed toward or made to serve the divine purpose of redemption, and not merely in a coincidental sense, as if God gave them an independent existence and purpose that could however lend itself to the emergence of redemption. Schleiermacher makes this point when he states that otherwise the "whole arrangement [*Einrichtung*] of nature, from the beginning on, would have been different,"[20] and when he rejects the view that the divine government uses only isolated events in an otherwise independently preserved natural world to serve its special redemptive purpose.[21] Indeed, to avoid implying any duality in the divine, one should maintain that God only undertook creation in the first place as the necessary initial step in achieving this end, and that God only maintains the divine preservation so as to enable the emergence of the kingdom of grace.

All of this leads to but a single conclusion. In spite of the seemingly neutral coloring Schleiermacher gave his doctrines of creation and preservation in the First Part of his system, one must not suppose that

---

19. See pp. 128–29.
20. Above, p. 197.
21. See *Gl*, §164.2.

Christians understand Creation, from its beginning and its continued unfolding, solely in generic terms. The complete content and meaning of Creation only becomes apparent when it is understood in light of the "color and tone" supplied by Christ. In a sense, the sequential unfolding of Schleiermacher's system from general to particular mimics what an outside observer would see were he able to watch the historical progression from creation to the coming of the Redeemer. But this does not mean that Christians themselves start with a generic or "primitive" feeling and then supplement it with their own "ending." Actual Christian experience does not mimic this temporal perspective; it mimics the divine perspective. It has learned the goal of Creation, and thus understands retrospectively the full and particular significance of God's initial creation and ongoing preservation of the world. It has, as it were, the eternal view, even as it recognizes its place and task in the temporal evolution of the world. It understands not only the bare structure and dynamics that must logically exist in God's creation and preservation; it also understands the purpose motivating that activity, and therefore its own part in its realization.

Its part is an active one, as one should know from Christianity's status as a teleological religion. It recognizes humanity's role as the "mouthpiece" of nature, and it also recognizes its role as the agent of Spirit in nature. For if Christ's task was to realize and make available for the first time the completion of human nature, the church's task is to continue and expand this "new" creation not only to all humanity, but in some sense to the whole world. Humanity serves as the mediator between the realm of Spirit and the realm of nature. In fact, it was created to serve this role. Yet it only first became capable of actually fulfilling it through the intervention of Christ. With that intervention, however, it is now "complete," and able to make use of whatever circumstances may arise. In this way, the advance of Spirit may continue, and the reign of blessedness grow to include the whole world.

CHAPTER 9

Comparisons, Observations, and Concluding Comments on the Common Ground between Schleiermacher and Barth

—⁓⁓—

Both Schleiermacher and Barth use a "christological orientation" in their respective understandings of Creation. Such an orientation can be seen not just in the method by which they expound their doctrines, but also in the content of those doctrines. Indeed, the two are linked. Because their approach to explaining the world is in some form christological, what they actually say about that world is also (less obviously in Schleiermacher and more obviously in Barth) christological. To use and also modify Calvin's analogy, Christ serves as the eyeglasses through which we view the world. Yet this necessary assistance is not neutral; these eyeglasses are "tinted," which inevitably affects the perception of that world. The Christian will always see the world, in Schleiermacher's phrase now, with a particular color and tone.

An Overview of the Argument of This Book and the Evidence Found

Both theologians actually presuppose a uniquely religious experience as the basis for what they say about creation. On the basis of this presupposition, both Schleiermacher and Barth demonstrate a certain compatibility with the external norm. That is, neither of them simply turns to the world itself and attempts a "natural theological" and unmediated description of Creation. Nor do they turn in the first instance to an unmediated consideration of the scriptural accounts of Creation, as if these offered objective and unequivocal descriptions of the origin and character of the world. Instead, each theologian posits a prior, "religious" experience, and only then, on the basis of that experience, does each turn to his own dogmatic description of Creation. Of course, in insisting on the necessity of recognizing this starting point for each theologian, I am not suggesting that either of them does his dogmatic work directly from some nebulous and "raw" experience itself. For Schleiermacher, the experience produces a certain feeling or pious consciousness, which manifests itself most characteristically and concretely in the various credal formulations of each particular communion. For Barth, the experience is an encounter or event, which manifests itself most characteristically and concretely in the church's preaching of the Word. Thus, the root experiences are themselves mediated before becoming a source for dogmatics.

Schleiermacher and Barth understand these root experiences in very specific ways, that is, in christological ways. Schleiermacher's "fundamental feeling" of absolute dependence is "fundamental" primarily in a logical or theoretical sense, and the specifically Christian feeling determined by the antithesis of sin and grace made known in Christianity has primacy in actual experience, because the fundamental feeling only first exists in particular ways. It never exists on its own, but only as it has been given a certain "color and tone" by an actual, historical community of faith—a color and tone that, to a greater or lesser degree, pervades all aspects of that feeling.[1] For Barth, the word of revelation is always in the first instance *the* Word, Christ. Thus, regardless of the topic preached or considered in the words of the scriptural text, the reception of revelation, which must itself be understood as possible only through the agency of the Holy Spirit, should always be construed as an encounter with Christ. That is, the presupposition for all dogmatic statements regarding Creation will be this prior, transformative event and the conviction that, among other

---

1. See appendix A, which examines Richard R. Niebuhr's interpretation of Christ and Creation.

things, this encounter epitomizes all one need know about the meaning of the world and history.

Why are these starting points significant? And how is it that in spite of Barth's frequent criticisms of Schleiermacher, they are actually quite similar? To answer the first question, they are significant because each in its own way enables its author to overcome the challenges posed by modern science and by Kantian criticisms of traditional metaphysical assumptions. Neither Schleiermacher nor Barth claims that his assertions about Creation are direct assertions of "knowledge," as that term came to be understood in the modern era. Schleiermacher makes clear from the very outset that *The Christian Faith* is not rooted in a "knowing" or a "doing" but in a "feeling," in particular the pious feeling binding together one given religious communion, Evangelical Christianity (which is to say, the German Protestant Church of his day). Of course, as the *exposition* of a particular form of pious feeling, *The Christian Faith* does claim to be empirical and factual; it claims a "knowledge" about what this community believes. But just as obviously, this means the various assertions it makes about Creation are one step removed from being *themselves* empirical and factual. Similarly, Barth makes clear, in spite of what one might infer from his frequent use of such terms as "noetic" and "knowledge," that what he will expound is a knowledge *of faith*, received through revelation. In other words, neither theologian is doing an apologetic nor attempting to prove the objective veracity of his claims to a larger, non-Christian audience. In a sense, neither is trying to "prove" anything. Rather, each understands himself as presenting a dogmatic exposition of what he takes to be the essence of a particular faith, even though certain parts of those expositions do have apologetic implications. This is why both Schleiermacher and Barth strongly reject all natural theologies and deny that their work bears any resemblance to such an approach. Neither argues *from* anything external *to* their particular theological assertions (e.g., that the order perceptible in the world implies the existence of a divine governor); rather, both start from within a religious given and seek simply to explain that given and clarify its assorted implications. In this sense, both are engaged in "faith seeking understanding."

The similarity between the two consists of more than just the fact that they both reject the approach of natural theology. There is at least one positive similarity as well, in that both are not so much making assertions about the world as they are about what Christians "feel" or "believe" about the world. In other words, they describe not the world per se, but the Christian *interpretation* of the world, or more precisely, the world's meaning. For an understanding of the world in itself, one may turn without hesitation to the natural and social sciences. They have much to teach. However, Schleiermacher and Barth both assume that these disciplines cannot supply everything needed to explain the full meaning of the world, of "Creation." Objective knowledge must be fitted within a more encompassing interpretive framework. But from this point of agreement, Schleiermacher and Barth then appear to diverge quite starkly in their methods: Basing that interpretation on "feeling" is one thing, but basing it on a particular revelation is quite another. After all, no less a figure than Barth himself has said so.

Yet is this methodological divergence really that great? Is Barth correct? If the issue is framed in certain ways, we can agree with him. For example, basing an interpretation of Creation on "revelation" (i.e., a long-accepted set of specific documents) certainly seems the more concrete or objective approach—or at least the one most capable of maintaining continuity within the Christian community over time—whereas basing it upon "feeling" seems by definition fluid and subjective, a method capable of producing a multitude of idiosyncratic interpretations. The dramatic differences evident in their explicit doctrines of creation seem to confirm this. Schleiermacher's treatment excludes consideration of the Old Testament creation narratives and foregoes many traditional affirmations, while Barth's bulges with biblical expositions and credal restatements.

Yet framed in another way, the notions of "feeling" and "revelation" almost literally abut one another. According to Barth, revelation is in the first instance the Christian's *encounter* with Christ, a variety of existential experience in which an individual "meets," primarily through the preaching of the gospel, the risen Lord and acknowledges his sovereignty. Only then, on the basis of this encounter, does the individual go on to accept the authority of the rest of revelation, that is, that which is contained in Scripture, including passages pertaining to Creation, and the affirmations of the creeds.[2] In other words, at the heart of everything he writes, Barth posits an interpersonal experience and what could be called a "transferal of allegiance" by the individual *from* all previous lords and outlooks *to* Christ. Then, as a result of this experience, there will also be a practical transferal of allegiance to the norms of the Christian perspective, as handed down by previous generations.

Similarly, according to Schleiermacher, the particular feeling felt by the individual Christian is neither self-generated nor effected in isolation. It grows in the individual only as that person is a part of a larger community, which has itself inherited its feeling from its predecessors, tracing back to Christ himself.[3] The locus of this feeling may well be each single Christian, but Schleiermacher's use of the term makes it clear that it is not so much an individual as a group concept. Thus, Schleiermacher did not produce *The Christian Faith* simply by analyzing his own personal feelings. Moreover, he did not produce it by conducting some sort of opinion survey of a random group of individuals within the community. Indeed, it is not the product of any sort of *direct* analysis of pious feeling. Rather, using the general and particular God-consciousnesses of Christianity as his interpretive touchstone, he described this "collective consciousness" of a particular historical community primarily through a consideration of the various creeds and confessions produced by its "group feeling" and normative for that feeling.[4]

With this reference to a group consciousness, one might be tempted to conclude that Schleiermacher was simply reflecting the Romanticism of his day, while Barth's "encounter" and "decision" talk was simply reflecting the existentialism of his day. Such influences are, in fact, present in our two figures, yet in themselves they do not necessarily produce antithetical positions. Instead, they could simply represent the differences one would normally expect between theologies

2. See p. 46.
3. See *Gl*, §24.4.
4. B. A. Gerrish, "Nature and the Theater of Redemption: Schleiermacher on Christian Dogmatics and the Creation Story," *Ex Auditu* 3 (1987): 122.

written by different persons in different eras. Taking matters a step further, one could then argue that "revelation" refers to *that which makes
the impression* upon individuals in a given community, while "feeling"
refers to the *impression made* upon those individuals in that community. Thus, the former could be said to concentrate more on the
"object," while the latter concentrates more on the "subject." But from
a perspective outside this community, they would be viewed as adjacent rather than antithetical, with neither approach producing what
an outsider would call an objective or self-evident description of the
meaning of life and the cosmos.[5] Both interpretations presuppose
one's prior incorporation into this particular group and the acceptance of its hermeneutical norms. Of course, for both Schleiermacher
and Barth the preeminent norm is Christ, so that in effect each is
claiming he is merely explicating the self-evident: Once one has
accepted Christ, then this particular understanding of the world must
follow. Yet from an outside perspective, this simply begs the necessarily prior question as to why one should accept Christ rather than some
other interpretive principle or standard. As a result, Schleiermacher's
"subjectivity" and Barth's "objectivity" would likely be perceived as
either equally arbitrary (to give it a more pejorative cast) or equally an
act of faith (to give it a more sympathetic cast).

To be sure, when Schleiermacher and Barth then proceed to spell
out in detail what this particular understanding entails when applied
to the world, they do produce doctrines of Creation that differ in a
number of respects. For Schleiermacher, the most fundamental source
now available to Christians for dogmatic exposition is the "impression
made," that is, the consciousness of the living community. As a group
mentality, this consciousness first belonged to the original disciples,
and it was not merely arbitrary or idiosyncratic in origin or character.

---

5. Cf. Langdon Gilkey, *Religion and the Scientific Future* (Macon, GA: Mercer University Press /
Rose Reprints, 1970), 31–32. Gilkey's general assessment is that neo-orthodoxy, insofar as it locates religious authority in experience, is as subjective as theological liberalism. But practically speaking, in comparison to Schleiermacher, Barth's work is also shaped to a relatively greater extent by the written
(which is to say, public) norms of Scripture (including the Old as well as New Testaments), the creeds,
and the like. To be sure, Schleiermacher also appeals to the creeds, confessions, and the New Testament
as the primary sources for his dogmatic exposition. But he also "tests" them by his standard of the fundamental feeling. Thus, I would also maintain that within the realm of the community, there can be
varying degrees of "subjectivity," with Schleiermacher's position representing a greater degree and
Barth's a lesser.

Rather, it was the direct product of the Redeemer's own consciousness. That consciousness was impressed upon them, and as a result a distinctive, new religion was formed, with its own unique and enduring spirit. Thus, even when the founding generation had passed from the scene, including Christ himself, this consciousness or spirit continued, serving as the constant maintaining the particular essence of the community. Indeed, for Schleiermacher this spirit is *the Spirit*, embedded in the church's history from the era of Christ to the present day, yet unaffected by that history inasmuch as it simply continues the original impulse of its founder.

However, in another sense, that Spirit is anything but "above" the influences of history. Since it actually exists only in the particular communions that have arisen in different ages and places, and since its essential content, limited as it is to a rather general consciousness of sin and grace, virtually demands to be further clarified and expanded, its actual manifestation has come in a variety of ways. In other words, the "Spirit" not only influences, but is influenced by, the communions it animates, which means the consciousness of those communions will not simply consist of a reproduction of Christ's consciousness. They will contain that consciousness, but much more besides. In effect, one could posit two types of "Spirit": the original individual Spirit of the historical founder of Christianity, which produces the consciousness of sin and grace, and the subsequent and ongoing collective spirits of the various Christian communities, which both define further and add to that original consciousness. Theoretically, the only norm one need meet to be classified a "Christian" is a consistency with the original consciousness. Adherence to the subsequent creeds and confessions of the church, or even to the Scriptures, seems not to be strictly necessary. In actuality, however, one is never a Christian "in general"; one is always located in a particular time, place, and communion. Therefore, one will rely especially upon the creeds and confessions produced by one's church and then upon the Scriptures.[6] As B. A. Gerrish observes, Schleiermacher sought to produce a *Protestant* dogmatic, and "for this purpose, the most immediate data will be the Reformation confessions of faith, used less as tests of orthodox belief than as the primary

6. See *Gl*, §27.1.

expressions of the evangelical Christian spirit."[7] In other words, these inheritances from the past are not themselves the *original* "object making the impression," that is, Christ's own consciousness; rather, they are products of persons upon whom the impression has been made. These products may witness to the influence of the Redeemer, but they are not the immediate creations of Christ himself nor of his Spirit. Indeed, his Spirit no longer exists in any discrete or personal form, but it does "exist" in a residual and historicized form, namely, as the animating spirit of the church. To employ one of Schleiermacher's earlier formulas in a rather different way, it appears that what he would call the Holy Spirit and a sociologist the collective spirit of this particular human religion "are both the same thing, only viewed from different vantage points."[8]

Thus, the various confessions of the church are the creations of the collective "living" Spirit of a particular community attempting to extend the implications of Christ's consciousness to all aspects of its communal life. If that Spirit is to remain "living," each new generation must take on the responsibility of explicating, and adapting if necessary, the implications and corollaries of this consciousness for itself. If it embraces this responsibility, then it sends out the next shoot in the growth of Christian tradition while maintaining its historical rootedness in the founder. However, if it rejects this responsibility, whether through a desiccating traditionalism, a shift into one of Christianity's "natural" heresies, or mere neglect, then it actually risks killing this Spirit—and also ending this branch of the church.

There is a tremendous contrast with Barth here. For him, the source for dogmatic exposition is not the "impression made" but the object making the impression, that is, that which stands over against the community, in a sense independent of it, constant over time, and spelled out in specific ways. Ultimately, Barth understands this "object" to be the Word of God, that is, Christ himself, but in a secondary sense he understands it to be the Word of God proclaimed in preaching and sacrament according to the witness of Scripture. Thus, while it is conceivable that in the divine freedom God could speak through some other, nontraditional means, it is nevertheless the church's "special commission" to engage in proclamation according to

---

7. Gerrish, "Nature and the Theater of Redemption," 122.
8. See *Gl*, §46.2 and §116.3.

this biblical witness.[9] All of these—Christ himself, the proclaimed Word, the Word of Scripture—certainly make an impression on the Christian, but this does not mean that that impression then becomes the source or supplies the data for one's dogmatics. There may indeed be a distinct group "spirit" within the community, but for Barth this can never be equated with the Holy Spirit. That Spirit always exists apart from any historically mediated collective consciousness, and solely by its power do preaching and Scripture—which are, Barth acknowledges, human products—become vehicles of divine revelation. In his preface to his commentary on Romans,[10] Barth shows little concern over the distance separating the birth of Christianity from the present day, and we can see now that this is due in part to his assumption that the Spirit allows the church to bypass all of those years and encounter Christ in virtually the same way the early Christians did. If there is a difference, it consists in the fact that the Christ encountered is not the "historical Jesus" of the past or even a "historicized" Spirit communicated through the life of the church. In comparison to Schleiermacher, Barth is relatively unconcerned with explicating the life, teachings, and influence of Jesus—his Christology is simply too high. Instead, he emphasizes the risen, eternal, and actually present Christ, and the one represented in most creeds and catechisms. In sum, the dogmatician can undertake his or her task with far more immediate, concrete, and public resources than those provided by a relatively unspecified consciousness of sin and grace ostensibly communicating itself from generation to generation. To be sure, each new age must produce its own dogmatic, but in Barth's view far more of both content and framework are already supplied by the Bible, and, derivatively, the creeds and the confessions, than one detects in Schleiermacher's approach. As a result, the balance of authority is weighted far more heavily in favor of tradition than innovation.

Conclusions about Methodological Similarities

First of all, Schleiermacher and Barth both begin with the assumption that their statements about Creation are based not on a consideration

9. Cf. *KD* I:1, §3.1.
10. See p. 45.

of the world itself, but on a consideration of something within the community, something uniquely "religious." For Schleiermacher, this is the pious *feeling* of the community, and for Barth, it is the *revelation* given to the community. Secondly, neither this feeling nor this revelation is to be understood as immediately and actually concerned with Creation; rather, both have to do in the first instance with Christ, the divine mediator for God's purposes in the world. Thus, all statements regarding Creation are subsidiary to this original feeling or revelation, being interpretations of Creation determined by a christological hermeneutic. Thirdly, however, because of the very different manner in which Schleiermacher and Barth define the content and extent of this christological norm, the way in which it is conveyed, and its authority, they end up producing doctrines of Creation with many obvious differences.

For example, Schleiermacher's explicit doctrine of creation is necessarily brief because absolute beginnings are not immediately accessible to consciousness and because he construes the Genesis accounts as speculative attempts to satisfy the desire for knowledge rather than as expressions of pious feeling. Hence, by his own definitions he leaves himself almost no raw material from which to develop a more involved interpretation of the world's origins and no apparent basis for linking its content to his Christology. For instance, he does not use the Genesis stories, and nowhere does he describe Christ as the actual agent of creation.[11] By contrast, Barth's doctrine of creation uses the Genesis accounts extensively, because his understanding of revelation allows—indeed, requires—him to turn to these sagas as a perfectly legitimate source for the "nonhistorical" history of the world's creation. Moreover, because he presupposes that Christ stands at the heart of all revelation, Barth is able to interpret these sagas in a thoroughly christological way. While this approach is nothing if not anachronistic in the eyes of the historical-critical method, it is completely in keeping with the approach of certain New Testament passages.[12]

---

11. This is demonstrated in Schleiermacher's interpretation of Col. 1:16. See pp. 197–99, but also pp. 191–94.

12. See his excursus in *KD* III:1, pp. 54ff., which, not surprisingly, employs both affirmations made in Col. 1:16.

But does this final divergence in method alter everything, so that the content of their respective doctrines of Creation differs in every respect? Certain variations, even substantial differences, do in fact exist between Schleiermacher and Barth in this regard. Yet because of their common orientation to Christ, their actual treatments of some of the subthemes or topics customarily associated with Creation display some remarkable similarities, including sensitivity to balancing the demands of the "inner" and "outer" norms. The subthemes or topics we will consider are theological anthropology, the fall and the status of evil, particularly "natural" evil (including the implications these have for the relation of divine and creaturely causality), and the divine purpose "behind" creation. In many respects, these topics are interconnected, so that affirmations made in one inevitably influence affirmations made in the others. Schleiermacher and Barth make the content of each christological, either directly—by making Christ the primary referent in topics usually framed generically—or indirectly—by making a christologically expounded topic the presupposition of a seemingly generic topic.

Content Similarities: Christ as the Archetypal Human

First of all, Barth and Schleiermacher think in similar ways regarding human nature. Neither places Adam (or Adam and Eve) at center stage. For Schleiermacher, Adam represents at most only a logical preliminary in his theological anthropology, while for Barth he is not even this. Schleiermacher's Adam, to whom he does not much refer, preferring instead to speak of the "original perfection" of human nature, is complete only "in potential"; the *actualization* of that potential in human nature occurs for the first time in Christ the Redeemer. Moreover, the fact that this actualization does indeed take place, and that it is Christ who accomplishes it, is due to more than just historical serendipity, according to Schleiermacher. Viewed from the perspective of the divine decree, one will recognize that humanity was ordained for development by means of redemption and that therefore this end was "included in the idea of human nature *from the beginning*, even if unknown to humanity itself."[13] Thus, in the development of

---

13. *Gl*, §61.4; emphasis mine.

human nature over time, "Adam" may be said to have a certain logical priority, in that his "original perfection" supplies the necessary raw material for this actualization, but in terms of the divine decree and any *definitive* understanding of human nature, preeminence can only belong to Christ. For if the distinguishing characteristic and "original perfection" of that nature is its capacity for God-consciousness, and if Christ was eternally ordained to be the first to realize that capacity purely and consistently, then not only is he, rather than Adam, the first actually complete or fulfilled human being, he is also the archetype and source for all true humanity. Christ does not represent a re-creation of human nature, but the historical fulfillment of the first creation. As Schleiermacher writes in the very last sentence of the First Part of his *Glaubenslehre*, "[W]ere everything that can develop out of such original perfection to be synopsized in a single human appearance, this would not be sought in Adam, in whom it would have to be lost again, but in Christ, in whom it has brought gain to all."[14] In other words, the content of Schleiermacher's theological anthropology starts out as indirectly christological; it appears generic, but in fact is framed in such a way that it leads inevitably to Christ. By the time he reaches the transition from his First Part to his Second, he becomes more direct, deriving his understanding of human nature from his understanding of Christ.

In comparison, Barth's theological anthropology is directly christological from the outset. Like Schleiermacher, he holds that Christ is the first to reveal—because he is first to embody—the true nature of humanity as created by God. However, as the eternal Son of the Father, this "first embodiment" should not be understood in merely historical or evolutionary terms. As the eternal Son, Christ was prior to Adam, and thus may be affirmed as the model even for him. What is the key characteristic in this model? A particular, constant *relation* to God, in contrast to Schleiermacher's emphasis on a particular consciousness of God. Humanity at large has and knows of this relation only through Christ, although Barth's distinction between *de jure* and *de facto* means human nature is established upon this relation even if individual humans are not aware of it. In this respect, Barth's position sounds

---

14. *Gl*, §61.5.

similar to Schleiermacher's, when the latter states that redemption was included in the idea of human nature from the beginning even if this was unknown to humanity itself. That is, a specifically Christian affirmation is made of human nature in general, in spite of the fact that that affirmation is not universally known, let alone universally accepted.

However, Schleiermacher and Barth differ in one key respect on this issue: The former's position conceives of this completed nature as being made available to exercise its transformative influence by wholly natural and historical means. It only first becomes a possibility for human nature with the appearance of the historical Jesus, and it is only now available through the church. By presenting matters in this way, Schleiermacher is able to avoid the problems an assertion of miraculous intervention would bring. But strictly speaking, it also means that some proportion of the human race must inevitably be viewed as having never attained "fulfillment." While Schleiermacher's personal attitude obviously tended toward universalism, his method placed distinct restrictions on how far he could let this attitude exercise its sway. Specifically, he believed that the church would indeed come to embrace all persons one day, so in that sense redemption will indeed be universal. But his naturalistic and historicist assumptions also mean that all those who lived prior to Jesus' appearance, as well as all others who remain outside the church's influence, whether in the past, present, or future, are necessarily excluded from this end. To be sure, certain teachings of Christ and the church could be used to suggest that another chance at redemption might be offered even after death, and evidently Schleiermacher would have liked to draw upon them and develop them for his own theological purposes.[15] However, he would not do so if it required him to be inconsistent with his own dogmatic logic. This is indicated in part simply by the classification of §§160–63 as "prophetic" doctrines, rather than as doctrines in the strict sense of the word. But it becomes readily apparent in Schleiermacher's very candid discussion of the deletions and modifications required of these traditional teachings if they are to become a part of his dogmatic system. So in the end, they do not really help him avoid or overcome the

---

15. See, e.g., *Gl*, §163, appendix, where Schleiermacher argues against the notion of eternal damnation by suggesting that the blessedness of the redeemed would actually be diminished knowing that others are suffering.

problem of exclusion. This also suggests that to those whose pious sensibilities find the concept of double predestination unsatisfying and unfair, Schleiermacher's position will hardly be viewed as an improvement, even though the "unredeemed" proportion of humanity decreases with each year the church extends its sway. In either case, the element of arbitrariness seems unavoidable.[16]

Barth's position, which is equally if not more universalist in tendency, does not display such historical dependency, because it is based on the affirmation that in the *eternal* Son, human nature is *already* and always complete. As a result, this nature is also already and always *redeemed* in the eternal Son. In other words, the proper relation to God has been established by Christ, and it is that relation which is judged to define true humanity. In this respect, Schleiermacher and Barth make much the same point. But this judgment is held to apply not just to humanity or human nature "in general," but to all humans individually, regardless of their time and place in history. Thus, according to Barth's schema, neither a transformation nor evolution is required of human nature, regardless of whether understood corporately or individually. The only change that can and may occur is an alteration in how that nature is *perceived* in light of God's grace revealed in Christ. That is, it is a noetic, and not an ontological, change that distinguishes Christians from non-Christians. And this distinction does not exclude non-Christians from access to redemption.[17]

---

16. Cf. John Hick's observations: In contrast to the tradition represented by Augustine and Calvin, Schleiermacher rejected any notion of an absolute double predestination. One should only use it in a tentative sense (i.e., of a given individual, one can only say God has *not yet* regenerated him or her) while also maintaining ("undogmatically," according to Hick) the belief in the eventual universal efficacy of Christ's redeeming work. Hick, *Evil and the God of Love* (London: Fontana Library, 1974), 240–41.

17. The contrast between Schleiermacher and Barth on this point raises an interesting question: Whose position is more in keeping with Protestant tradition? In certain key respects, I would argue that Barth's position remains more true to that heritage than Schleiermacher's. Indeed, we would suggest that the "psychologism" and "naturalism" of the latter's method actually leads him to certain positions more in keeping with Catholic tradition, despite his explicit statements to the contrary.

While it may oversimplify the distinction too much, consider the following points: In Protestantism, the notion of grace is used primarily as a way of describing God; on the basis of his graciousness, embodied in Christ, God offers us redemption "while we were yet sinners"; hence, "redemption" is primarily a juridical concept, i.e., descriptive of God's decision and not of what we are or become. In Catholicism, the notion of grace is often conceived as a gift, as a self-communication of God. On the basis of this gift, bestowed through Christ, a "divinization" of the human occurs; hence, "redemption" is primarily an existential concept, referring to the transformation and restoration of human nature (cf. e.g., the entries on "Grace" in Van A. Harvey, *A Handbook of Theological Terms* [New York: Macmillan Publishing, 1964], 108–111 and Karl Rahner and Herbert Vorgrimler, *Dictionary of Theology* [2d ed.; New York: Crossroad Publishing, 1981], 196–200). Obviously, this summary describes the distinctions between

Despite this apparent difference between Schleiermacher and Barth, however, we should not lose sight of the more important similarity that has just been indicated: their decision to define human nature not in neutral but in specifically religious, even christological terms. That is, instead of basing their respective theological anthropologies upon Adam and Eve, or on some hypothesized original humanity, they base it upon Christ, for it is he who embodies and reveals our true and essential character as human beings.

Moreover, Schleiermacher and Barth both seem to recognize the advantages to be gained from this approach, not only for the topic of anthropology as such but for other theological topics as well. It may oversimplify matters somewhat, but in one sense, everything else these two theologians have to say about Creation is influenced by, and perhaps even deducible from, what they say about human nature. That is, based on their descriptions of humanity, certain corollary affirmations about the world and God seem to follow almost inevitably. In Christ, both Schleiermacher and Barth see the true definition of the human creature, and each in his own way then uses this definition as the lens through which to view and interpret all other creatures, Creation as a whole, and ultimately God.

Protestantism and Catholicism in a very elementary way. But assuming it does not oversimplify them, what does it suggest about the respective positions of Barth and Schleiermacher? In Barth's case, when he describes the difference between Christians and non-Christians as a noetic, rather than ontological one, i.e., asserting that in Christ God *pronounces* for all the divine Yes rather than the divine No, even if knowledge of this judgment is limited to the faithful, then he clearly echoes that aspect of Protestant tradition described above. (Of course, his universalism is hardly traditional, but that is another matter.)

In Schleiermacher's case, however, things are more ambiguous. On the one hand, in §109.3, he openly acknowledges that viewing the divine act of justification as "declaratory" is one of the key ways Protestantism differs from Catholicism. To be sure, his assumptions about God's activity prevent him from maintaining the conception of each convert being "declared just" in a discrete and special divine act. Nevertheless, he does say the notion itself can be maintained if it is simply understood as an aspect of the original divine decree and an outgrowth of the original creative act.

On the other hand, Schleiermacher also clearly differentiates Christians and non-Christians on the basis of *consciousness*, and in this respect one could argue that they are thereby distinguished by a "quality" of their own human makeup. Indeed, as I have made clear in this book, Schleiermacher views the attainment of this consciousness as the very fulfillment of human nature. Moreover, in spite of the distinction he made in §24, it is hard *not* to see his position as making "the relation of the individual to Christ dependent upon his relation to the church." Consider, for example, his formulation in *Gl*, §113.1: "[T]he new life of each individual emerges from the collective life [*Gesamtleben*], although the collective life emerges from no other individual life than that of the Redeemer." And, of course, both of these moves come across as rather Catholic.

Thus, when Barth takes the approach he does, he avoids not only the problems associated with assertions of supernatural transformations of human nature, but also any apparently arbitrary division of the human race and any charges of being truer to Catholic than Protestant tradition.

Content Similarities: The Fall and the Natural

A good example of the impact of this approach can be found in the next subtheme of Creation to be considered, namely, Schleiermacher's and Barth's respective understandings of the fall. To modern sensibilities, the traditional assumption that the fall brought about a qualitative change in, or diminution of, human nature on the one hand and the external natural order on the other is one that can no longer be maintained. There are simply too many scientific (not to mention theological) problems raised by supposing that God intervened to alter those attributes and that order in response to the fall, or that they could be so altered at any time by a supernatural incursion of the divine causality. And insofar as neither Schleiermacher nor Barth understand the fall narratives in literal, historical terms, they are able to sidestep these obvious difficulties associated with the traditional view, showing themselves in fact to be aligned with modern sensibilities.[18]

Yet even if one reads these narratives in a poetic, existential, or some other nonliteral manner so as to avoid threatening the integrity of the natural order, one must still take care that they not be interpreted in such a way that one's theological consistency is threatened by an implicit and ultimately irresolvable dualism. Such a threat to the integrity of one's dogmatic thinking is possible as long as these narratives are still viewed as presenting some sort of "before and after" portrait of humanity and the world, in which the distinction between "before" and "after" is interpreted as indicating an essential discontinuity in either human nature, the world's existence, or God's causality. These distinctions might include those within "generic" humanity (i.e., between "original" and "fallen" humanity) as well as between "generic" and "redeemed" humanity, those between a "paradisical" natural world, the current natural world, and some future utopian world, and also those between a presumably omnipotent, omniscient "proactive" God at creation and an apparently less-than-omnipotent or omniscient, "reactive" God punishing original sin. But insofar as Schleiermacher and Barth both approach the fall from a christological starting point, beginning with their theological anthropologies and

---

18. See pp. 103ff., 128–29, 147–54, 160–61 and 181ff.

then interpreting the rest of Creation and God through them, they are also able to avoid the dualistic tensions that can arise from even a figurative reading of the fall narratives.

They do not suppose there are two essentially distinct human natures, the first modeled after Adam and the second "remodeled" after Christ; rather, there is only one, and it is embodied by Christ. Then, taking this particular creature as representative of all creation, they are able to conclude that the essential character of the natural order and existence is likewise unitary and constant. Our current world and nature are not essentially less than they could or should be; they are not in any sense objectively "fallen." Rather, they are only perceived to be such by sinful humanity. Once one gains the proper christological perspective, the falsity of this perception will be unmasked and the underlying integrity of the natural order will be made manifest. And once this becomes clear, then the underlying unity and constancy of the divine causality will likewise become apparent.

According to Schleiermacher, Christians can indeed affirm that from its very inception, human nature has been complete, even perfect. However, this "original perfection" was never an actual temporal state. Instead, it is simply the capacity for God-consciousness logically presupposed to inhere in human nature as such. Yet this does not mean it was something humanity could attain on its own during its historical infancy. A maturing was needed, and the first to reach this state was Christ. Thus, in effect, Christ simply fulfills the divine process of Creation with regard to humanity. Hence, one need no longer understand the fall as effecting a qualitative diminution of human nature, nor the appearance of Christ as effecting a miraculous restoration of human nature. Christ does not represent a divine reaction to a creation gone awry; rather, he represents the goal toward which humanity was aimed from the beginning.

If this is the case, then the Christian may understand the divine activities of creation and preservation not as separate from the divine work of redemption, but as united with that work. Indeed, the Christian may affirm that they are actually but one divine act, which consequently enables the Christian to keep God above the fray of reciprocal activity, where Schleiermacher insists he must remain. If this is the case, then *no* divine act need be described in terms of a supernatural interruption of history or the natural order, for they can all be described in terms of development or the gradual unfolding of the eternal decree. Thus, Schleiermacher can maintain not only his insistence on the self-contained character of the natural causal nexus but also the integrity of God.

Now consider a summary of the corresponding points made by Barth with regard to human nature and the fall. For him as for Schleiermacher, the "original perfection" or archetypal definition of human nature is not something found first in Adam and Eve. Instead, it exists first in Christ—an assertion made inevitable by his conjoining of Creation and covenant at the outset of his doctrine because Christ is portrayed as the embodiment and epitome of both. As a result, he essentially precludes describing the fall as anything other than an ulti-mately impotent occurrence. Of course, this hardly means he refuses to take it seriously. He certainly does, as §50, "God and Nothingness," indicates. But as the relatively early appearance in his schema of §42, "The Yes of God the Creator," and the relatively late appearance of §50 suggests, the impact of the fall must not—in fact, cannot—be con-strued as interrupting or even ultimately challenging the divine rule and purpose. Nor can the fall be understood as effecting some quali-tative change in human nature or the world. The fall did not produce an ontological change, only a noetic one. Thus, as was true with Schleiermacher, God's redemptive work in Christ is not to be under-stood as a divine corrective for a creation that, without the fall, would not have needed it; rather, the covenantal relation it reveals is to be understood as the goal toward which humanity was directed all along. In fact, for Barth it was the basis for creation in the first place.

Content Similarities: On Interpreting Evil

In their understanding of evil, especially natural evil, Schleiermacher and Barth display remarkably similar logic in what they say, and a ready illustration of this appears in their respective interpretations of death.[19] Both theologians view death as in itself a natural part of life. They do not suppose that human beings lost their "natural" immortality

---

19. See *Gl*, §59, postscript; §76.2,3 (cf. §72); and *KD*, §47.3,5.

through divine intervention, as a punishment for original sin. Human nature was *created* mortal; it was not subjected to mortality after its creation. Hence, it has not undergone any essential change in connection with the fall.

However, the fall can be represented as producing a change or, more to the point, a derangement in the human *perception* of death. Under the sway of sin, human beings may indeed interpret death as a divine punishment or as something alien to their nature, and therefore as something to be feared. But this perception, as real as it may feel, is properly understood as only a subjective, and not an objective, reality. Through Christ, one gains the proper perception, which makes it possible to banish one's fear of death and to embrace life as one should.[20]

Not surprisingly, Schleiermacher and Barth use much the same logic when describing the other "natural" evils that confront humanity. Indeed, the former's understanding of such evil, and perhaps social evil as well, appears to correspond quite closely to Barth's description of the "shadow side" of Creation. That is, natural evils do not represent the incursion of some alien or unnatural power, but rather the natural—one could even say necessary—"contrasts," "harmonies," or "challenges" that God included in Creation to enrich life. Were they not included, the world would be incomplete; were they included from a source other than God, the rule of God would be challenged. Of course, Barth differs considerably from Schleiermacher by speaking not only in terms of the "shadow side" of existence but also in terms of "nothingness," that is, radical evil, which is in no way natural and is indeed a supreme affront and challenge to the honor and glory of God.[21] But this does not detract from the similarity that does in fact exist between them in this other respect.

Content Similarities: The Divine Purpose

How one explains natural evil says as much about the integrity of God as it does about the integrity of the natural order,[22] namely, the divine purpose behind creation. By focusing on Christ as the key to human

---

20. See pp. 114–15 and pp. 160–61.
21. See pp. 103ff.
22. See pp. 75–77, 81–82, 96ff., 110ff., 121–25, 150–51, and 181–84.

nature and history, Schleiermacher and Barth are also able to make certain affirmations about God and God's intention in creation, because they see at the heart of human nature a particular feeling for, or relation with, God—a feeling or relation that should be construed not as only first coming into existence in order to "correct" what Adam and Eve corrupted, but as the ideal or archetype upon which all humanity is ultimately patterned. Here again, Schleiermacher and Barth adopt and adapt the lead of Calvin in asserting there can be no knowledge of God or self in isolation, but only in relation—a relation defined preeminently in christological terms. If one carries this logic further, one may also conclude that humanity need not suppose there was an initial divine action (in creation) followed by subsequent divine reactions (the punishment of death, along with the other curses associated with the fall, as well as the later gift of redemption). The natural order can be understood as constant because the divine being and activity is understood as constant, at least when both are viewed from the outset through a christological lens. This is certainly a plus for theology's relation to modernity, because it echoes the latter's assumption of the constancy of the natural causal nexus.

But this does not mean that Schleiermacher and Barth derive their positions from some modern, external norm, even if they are compatible with such outside viewpoints. Rather, both develop their positions out of a view held by Calvinistic tradition, namely, a supralapsarian understanding of the one eternal decree. Only now this view does not refer simply to the notion of eternal election, but to the whole expanse of God's creative, providential, and redemptive rule.[23] Theirs is no process God, altering or improvising the divine purposes as history unfolds. Rather, theirs is a traditional God, undergirding and governing history on the basis of his own eternal and constant being and will.

Moreover, as both Schleiermacher and Barth make abundantly clear, this being and will is one of grace and love. Barth asserts this divine character from the outset of his doctrine, and repeats it over and over. Schleiermacher, by contrast, asserts it primarily by making it the very climax of his entire system. This is why, as he noted to Lücke,

---

23. Cf. Richard R. Niebuhr, *Schleiermacher on Christ and Religion* (New York: Charles Scribner's Sons, 1964), 248–58.

he decided finally not to reverse the order of the First and Second Parts of his *Glaubenslehre*, because the climax of that work had to be his doctrines of the divine love and wisdom.[24] This means that, to the Christian, the divine "acts" of creation, preservation, and redemption must not be thought of as distinct works, but as *one* act motivated by, and realizing, the divine love.

With this observation, the final piece falls into place, revealing to us that for Schleiermacher as well as Barth, a christological orientation pervades not only *how* they say what they say in their respective doctrines of Creation but also *what* they say. It suggests as well that, for all their respect for the insights of the modern age and their efforts to produce theologies compatible with those insights, the primary impulse behind their dogmatic labors is still the desire to be true to, and accurately represent, the faith they have received. While differences still exist between their respective methods and their respective doctrines of Creation, Barth and Schleiermacher's christological orientation toward creation brings them far closer together in their theologies than apart.

---

24. See pp. 20–21.

APPENDIX A

Examining Richard R. Niebuhr
on Schleiermacher

———ᶜᵐᵐᵐ———

Richard R. Niebuhr's book, *Schleiermacher on Christ and Religion*, is one of the standard works on the "father of modern theology." In it, Niebuhr covers a wide range of issues in Schleiermacher interpretation, including the relation of Christ and Creation. At first reading, this segment appears to say or support many of the things I have asserted. But digging a bit deeper, particularly into a long half-paragraph found on pages 246–47, his various points and distinctions appear a bit ambiguous. As a result, it becomes possible to read him in one of two ways. The first, which may actually be the most common way of explaining Schleiermacher, would contradict one of the key points of my thesis; the second, which seems to exercise less sway among scholars, would support my position. Thus, while I could certainly justify an appendix on Niebuhr's position for no other reason than clarifying the thought of a key Schleiermacher scholar, I am also obviously interested in enlisting him as an ally for my interpretation rather having him as an opponent for the more common one.

The problem lies in the way he describes—or fails to describe more carefully—on the one hand, the *actual religious consciousness* arising in conjunction with Creation (the sense of absolute dependence, which Niebuhr apparently indicates with the term "creation-faith") and Christ

223

(the sense of redemption), and, on the other, the *doctrines* based on those consciousnesses. In my reading of Schleiermacher, one may speak of the actual religious consciousness of Christ as determining and to that extent presupposing one's actual consciousness of Creation. One may also speak of the doctrine of Creation as the logical presupposition of the doctrine of Christ, even as the latter also informs and to a degree determines the content of the former. But one ought *not* to speak of an actual consciousness of Creation or of a "creation-faith" as the presupposition of one's actual consciousness of Christ, because in such a case the term "presupposition" can only refer to a temporal and autonomous precedence, the possibility of which Schleiermacher excludes. The universal sense of absolute dependence never exists independently in actual experience; it is always conjoined with some historical religious consciousness that modifies it, to a greater or lesser degree, in particular ways. For example, in actual experience, one may have a Christian "creation-faith," an Islamic "creation-faith," or perhaps a polytheistic "creation-faith," but never a generic or neutral "creation-faith," because the feeling of absolute dependence is an abstraction derived from specific religious consciousnesses arising in specific communions.

How does all of this compare with Niebuhr's description? He begins with an assertion that seems straightforward enough: "Schleiermacher did not go the length of maintaining that the *doctrine* of creation depends on the *doctrine* of Christ. To reason in that fashion would be to lapse into the rationalistic Christianity that Schleiermacher repudiated."[1] If by the word "depend" in this statement he means that Schleiermacher did not *deduce* one doctrine (as a theoretical construct) from another, like a corollary from an axiom, then I may agree with Niebuhr. In this respect, Schleiermacher was empirical, not rationalistic; he grounded his theology on a historical consciousness, not a theoretical "first principle."

Yet does this mean the Christian understanding of Creation depends *in no way* upon the Christian understanding of Christ? Hardly. Niebuhr continues immediately with the observation that Schleiermacher "did perceive that the religious consciousness expressed by the first article

1. Richard R. Niebuhr, *Schleiermacher on Christ and Religion* (New York: Charles Scribner's Sons, 1964), 246.

of the Apostles' Creed is a consciousness decisively molded by the redemption wrought by Jesus of Nazareth."[2] So, according to Niebuhr, there is *some* sort of dependence of the Christian understanding of Creation upon the Christian understanding of Christ. Niebuhr summarizes Schleiermacher's view by saying that "he realized that the matter of the doctrine of creation does not stand in a simple external relation to the matter of the doctrine of the redeemer and redemption. *Creation-faith is and is not the presupposition of the doctrine of redemption.*[3] I certainly agree with the first part of this statement, insofar as it points to the integral relation of the two doctrines and excludes conceiving of Schleiermacher's system as, for instance, a patchwork of a "natural theology" attached to a Christology. But the second part of this statement I find misleading, and not because Niebuhr uses the apparently vacillating phrase "is and is not." Rather, I am concerned with his use of the term "creation-faith" employed in juxtaposition with the phrase "doctrine of redemption," for it makes creation-faith sound all too much like some actual, fundamental experience, capable of existing on its own not only in relation to a *doctrine* of redemption but in relation to the *basal consciousness* of redemption.

Does Niebuhr intend this implication? Probably not. Yet there is enough ambiguity in these terms and in the way he relates "form" and "matter" to lead one to think of "creation-faith" as a discrete, rather than abstracted, consciousness. Consider the way he explicates how this creation-faith is and is not the presupposition of the doctrine of redemption:

> It is the presupposition of [the doctrine of?] redemption, because it is the feeling of being absolutely dependent . . . that the redeemer *reforms* and *informs*. It is not the presupposition of [the doctrine of?] redemption, because it is much more [?] than that; genuine [actual?] creation-faith is dependent on the redemption wrought by Christ, because the feeling of absolute dependence is fully [?] formed only in and through the agency of Christ, the Spirit and the church. Hence, the conception of God as creator and governor is a conception that is more appropriately descriptive of a *fully formed* Christian religious consciousness than

---

2. Ibid.
3. Ibid.; emphasis mine.

of a *minimally developed* religious consciousness. For the doctrine of creation is the religious expression of the person who has come, by virtue of the redeemer, to a *full* acknowledgment of and consent to the omnipotent power of God in himself and in the world.[4]

As the parenthetical insertions and emphases in the above citation suggest, Niebuhr's description could be much more precise. While his earlier comments (pp. 230–31) make a different impression, here he leaves himself open to the charge of postulating the existence of a universal consciousness of creation that is essentially or materially the same in all actual religions. By speaking of the redeemer "reforming" and "informing" creation-faith, by speaking of certain aspects of creation-faith as only first being "fully formed" in the consciousness of Christians rather than the "minimally developed" consciousness of other religions, even by speaking of "genuine" creation-faith and defining it in what amounts to quantitative or developmental terms, Niebuhr inadvertently implies that creation-faith has a prior and autonomous existence to, and is essentially constant under the formative influence of, each particular historical communion.

In other words, by expressing his position in the terms he does, Niebuhr leaves himself open to the interpretation that the *same content* of creation-faith is actually present in the religious consciousness of all, even if the "specifying" consciousness of "less developed" religions cannot make all its various aspects clear. Read in this way, Niebuhr seems to promote a variation of the long-standing misinterpretation of Schleiermacher, that is, that he made the feeling of absolute dependence the real heart of his project and the discernment of a universal "natural religion" his ultimate goal. To be sure, in this reading a universal natural theology would no longer be attainable, since on the doctrinal level different communions are in fact constrained by their historical origins. But on the level of "consciousness," members of such "less developed" communions could be viewed by Christians as possessing, nascently yet nevertheless entirely, the same feeling of absolute dependence—even if the members of such communions cannot or do not fully articulate it in their theologies.

---

4. Ibid., 246–47; emphasis mine.

Needless to say, such a reading of Schleiermacher is inconsistent with the one presented over the course of this book—and mostly likely with Niebuhr's as well. The weight of evidence indicates that he does not view "creation-faith" as a discrete consciousness essentially unaffected when conjoined with the consciousness of redemption. But regardless of how one interprets him on this point, the result for my interpretation of Schleiermacher's doctrine of Creation is the same: Niebuhr supports my thesis that its *content* is at least in part christologically influenced. On the one hand, if the general consciousness ("creation-faith") and the specific consciousness ("redemption-faith" in the case of Christianity) are related to one another as matter and form, then the more fully and intricately a given specific consciousness is able to form and define that matter, the more extensive *and thus different* will its content be *at the level of doctrine*, even though the content of the original consciousness is not itself altered. On the other hand, if the general consciousness is not just externally formed but internally altered by the specific consciousness, then it goes without saying that the translation of that consciousness to the level of doctrine will result in a theological expression displaying a unique (in this case, christological) content.

APPENDIX B

Too Anthropocentric for
Current Ecological Concerns?

By viewing not only humanity but the rest of the created realm exclusively through a christological lens, Schleiermacher and Barth both tend, in one way or another, to have a very anthropocentric attitude toward nature. In Schleiermacher's thought, this shows up in his assumption that humanity is the "mediator" between the realms of spirit and nature: It is the "representative" of nature to God, and the "mouthpiece" of God to nature, as well as God's agent in shaping and determining nature. In Barth's thought, this shows up in his claim that the covenant between God and humanity is the *reason* for creation. It is, in effect, merely a means to an end. In other words, Schleiermacher and Barth appear to leave little, if any, room in their thinking for the notion that God may have a relation to, or concern for, nature apart from humanity. Given our present-day ecological concerns, this has to be viewed as a serious shortcoming if their approach is to be used as a resource or springboard for current constructive theology.[1] But is it, in

---

1. A number of authors have recently shown interest in this issue, although sometimes only in passing. To give an indication of the range of thought currently evident, consider the following examples: George N. Boyd, "Schleiermacher: On Relating Man and Nature," *Encounter* 36 (Winter 1975): 12–13, 18; Daniel B. Clendenin, "A Conscious Perplexity: Barth's Interpretation of Schleiermacher," *Westminster Theological Journal* 52 (Fall 1990): 289; Gerrish, "Nature and the Theater of Redemption," 135–36; Thomas A. Idinopulos, "The Critical Weakness of Creation in Barth's Theology," *Encounter* 33 (Spring 1972): 167; James A. Nash, *Loving Nature: Ecological Integrity and Christian Responsibility*

fact, a shortcoming that can be accurately ascribed to these two theologians? Or could they, perhaps with some modification, still serve as resources even on this topic?

Barth's position is the easiest to clarify with regard to this issue. While he might seem to be the most obviously anthropocentric, he also recognizes the possible implications of his position and takes steps to exclude at least some of them. He does this in the final book of his doctrine of Creation, in §55, which is entitled "Freedom for Life." In the first subsection of that proposition, entitled "The Reverence for Life," two passages stand out as relevant. After outlining the theological presuppositions upon which he will base his subsequent discussion of ethics, Barth asks: Should this outline include a portrayal of human life in its connection or perhaps even unity with animal and plant life, and thus life in general? He answers with a clear no, but only because his theological *method* precludes any such portrayal. Consequently, he can say no more, one way or the other.

> For one cannot assert that the man addressed by God's Word finds himself spoken to and must recognize himself as a participant in the life of animals and plants or as a participant in an almost universal life-act, however this might be interpreted. He may be of the opinion that this self-understanding should be regarded as the correct one; but he has gotten it on his own from somewhere else, and not the Word of God.... For the Word of God is presented to *man*. In addressing him, it is an event in *his* life. That man lives in the cosmos, that he is a neighbor of the animals and in a wider circumference the plants and their life and all further life-forms, and that his life has many things in common with them, is not denied in this event, but tacitly—and yet only tacitly!—presupposed. But it is in no way evident that the Word is presented to all his neighbors in the cosmos in the same way it is to man. It is not even once evident that there is actually a corresponding event in what we consider to be their life.[2]

Essentially, Barth's position is an agnostic one. One simply cannot know if God relates to the rest of nature in a manner both appropriate

(Nashville: Abingdon Press, 1991), 140, 151; and H. Paul Santmire, *The Travail of Nature: The Ambiguous Ecological Promise of Christian Theology* (Philadelphia: Fortress Press, 1985), 145–55.

2. *KD* III:4, §55.1.

to them and comparable to the way he relates to humanity. There are two reasons why this is so. First, one cannot know for the simple reason that the "object" of that encounter is the God-*man*, and not some other combination of God and creature. Since the God-man not only reveals, but *is himself the revelation*, the apparent lack of an equivalent incarnation itself suggests that such a relation does not exist— although one can never be sure. Second, even if such a relation were to exist, one could not know of it, because Barth's method would not allow it; the "event" or "personal encounter" that is the basis of one's knowledge of faith is by its very nature "nontransferable." In this respect, it is as fully subjective as Schleiermacher's "feeling," for just as one cannot truly experience another's feeling, neither can one experience another's event. And if this is the case among humans, it must be even more so between humans, animals, and plants. Hence, the Christian must remain ignorant as to how, or even if, God and nonhuman species can have a reciprocal relationship.

However, this does not prevent Barth from describing how humans are to regard and treat other species. This description is based on several scriptural passages. The most familiar are, of course, those from the two creation stories (Gen. 1:26, 28; and 2:19), and it appears to be from these that he draws his fundamental point: Humanity is granted lordship, but with that lordship comes responsibility. On what does he base this claim to lordship? Why should we suppose that, of all the species in creation, humankind alone is granted such power and authority? Barth responds by saying that humanity

> is *the* animal creature to whom God reveals, commits, and binds himself
> in the midst of the rest of creation, with whom he makes common cause
> in the course of a particular history which is neither that of an animal nor
> that of a plant, and in whose participation in life he expects a knowing
> and willing recognition of his honor, his mercy and power. Hence the
> *higher* necessity of *his* life! Hence his right to any lordship and command.[3]

That is, humanity is in a unique position compared to other animals, and thus it is granted prerogatives they are not. This being said, however,

---

3. Ibid.

Barth also clearly states that humanity does not own the plants and animals, nor does humanity exercise any natural right or authority over creation. Ultimately, ownership, right, and authority can belong to God alone. However, God delegates these things to humanity, and it may exercise them if, in each moment, it does so with an attitude of reverence, gratitude, praise, and—when the killing of animals is involved—repentance. Indeed, Barth states that the killing of animals is legitimate only as a "*priestly* act of *eschatological* character," citing Romans 8:18ff. as the basis for suggesting that it will occur no more in the new eon.

How should we judge Barth with regard to our current ecological concerns? His attitude on this particular topic would still likely be classified "anthropocentric" by the standard of our present-day sensibilities. Nevertheless, Barth does provide two built-in "checks" and one "open question" that could serve to restrain the less desirable effects of that attitude. The first is the affirmation that God's is the ultimate dominion, while ours is but a delegated and limited one. Thus, we may not simply do with nature what we will, without accountability, but are always answerable to God. The second is the alternate vision and higher ideal presented by the image of the new age. With the eschatological image in mind, one would always be compelled to question any complacent or unself-conscious acceptance of our present natural order and way of doing things. The third is the fact that we can never exclude the possibility that God may indeed relate to and have concern for the natural realm apart from humanity. As a result, we would do well not to be presumptuous in our relations to nature.

How does Schleiermacher's position compare? By its very nature, his method, like Barth's, is too subjective to allow for any claim of an independent "religious" relation of nature to God. Schleiermacher posits the "feeling of absolute dependence" as belonging to humankind alone, although as a composite of body and spirit, we may indeed serve as the representative consciousness of the world and also act as the go-between for the realm of spirit to nature.[4] Yet how might he define these roles more precisely in light of the ecological concerns we are

---

4. See, e.g., *Gl*, §59.

now addressing? *The Christian Faith* does not really help us much on this issue, because when it speaks of the Christian's attitude toward and activity in "the world," it is referring primarily to the contrast between life within the church and life without, and the ideal that the church will one day encompass all of human society. However, one of Schleiermacher's sermons, preached on the text from Job 38:11, gives us some indication of how he thought the Christian should regard and act in the natural realm. To be sure, although it is suggestive, the main point of this sermon was hardly one of ecological concern in our sense of that term; it would be anachronistic to suppose it was so motivated.

Schleiermacher expounds this text on a number of levels: He expands it, uses it analogically, and spiritualizes it, so that God's "restraining power" is seen in human nature, in societal movements and trends, and in the ongoing life of the church as well as in his control over the natural world at creation and through divine preservation. With reference to the natural world, much of what Schleiermacher says sounds quite traditional, although, as one would expect, he does not describe God's restraining power in supernatural terms. Instead, he speaks of God maintaining order by means of the balance of powers between various natural forces. He also makes clear that this order is not always peacefully maintained. Our own rather casual observations, as well as those of more serious naturalists, present us a world showing

> manifold traces, both on the surface and in the depths of the earth, of great and repeated disturbances. The hidden subterraneous fire has cast up vast masses from below, devastating and transforming the face of Nature; the sea, which the Lord seemed to have gathered together and shut up with impassable barriers, has yet often overflowed.[5]

In the face of such occurrences, it may appear that God's providence has actually broken down, that the forces of chaos constrained at creation have in fact broken loose. Yet further reflection, based not on any natural theology, but on maintaining consistency with the fundamental feeling, will make clear the role of such disturbances:

---

5. Friedrich D. E. Schleiermacher, *Selected Sermons of Schleiermacher*, trans. Mary F. Wilson, ed. W. Robertson Nicoll, *The Foreign Biblical Library* (New York: Funk & Wagnalls, n.d.), 214.

> We no longer see in that apparent destruction a revolted power of mere
> Nature, but the governing will of Him who commanded that the waves
> should so far overflow, in order that the just proportions should be
> obtained *for each new step in the order of things.*[6]

Thus, any dualism evident in the balance of natural powers will be
interpreted not as a battle of darkness and chaos versus God's power of
light and stability, but as a dialectic entirely under the governance of
God. At times the usually stable boundaries separating the various
forces of nature will indeed be breeched by one or another of those
forces, but they do so only according to God's will, in order to establish
a new natural equilibrium. In other words, God achieves by such means
a natural *Aufhebung* of the created order, so that "everywhere we see
arise out of the seeming destruction a new and better order of things."[7]

How should Christians respond when they witness such events?
Given Schleiermacher's description, Christians will presumably have
at least three reactions. Perhaps the most immediate will be the sense
that they can but stand in admiration and awe of God's power and
purpose. Another will likely be the personal sense of comfort and reas-
surance which can arise knowing that God is in control, even in the
midst of such upheavals. And the third one might be the thought that
when humans witness and realize these things, they do so not for
themselves alone but for all other creatures as well. They become, in
effect, the Creation's self-awareness. Thus, one could be tempted to
argue that Schleiermacher shows a real appreciation of, and respect
for, the natural world *as it is*, in its own various conditions and tumul-
tuous processes. As such, he might be viewed as a possible resource
and ally for our own ecological concerns.

Yet the proper Christian role is not merely that of passive spectator.
As a Christian, one may certainly appreciate the various ways in which
God furthers the progress of the world, but one is also duty-bound to
assist that advancement. Hence, while the focus in this sermon is
directed primarily at furthering the progress of "rule and order in the
spiritual world" (i.e., in *all* social and interpersonal relations, not just

---

6. Ibid., 216; emphasis mine.
7. Ibid., 215.

in religious matters), Schleiermacher also has some straightforward and very revealing things to say about the Christian's relation to nature. Consider the following:

> And if it is this very Father in heaven who appoints to everything its just limits and appropriate law, and if He has given us of His Spirit, manifestly this cannot but have the effect of leading us also to endeavour *to maintain and restore limits and laws everywhere.* First, in the Kingdom of Nature; for when, in the beginning, the Most High made over the earth, with all that breathes and moves on it, to the first parents of our race, it was His design that man should subdue it, and have dominion over it. *Thus we ourselves are to be the standard of all earthly things; their relation to us is to be brought out in all circumstances, and is to be the true law of their being, and to this we are to direct our efforts.* And if the Lord should again, for the moment, set free the forces of Nature from this law which is ordinarily in operation, so that they overpass the bounds appointed to them, and lay in ruins, more or less of the works of men, then what is the only wise and fitting course? Not, surely, to sit calmly waiting to see what the issue may be; still less to allow ourselves foolishly to be seduced into irregularity and strife, throwing it over on the Lord to restore, as He may please, the old state of things out of the new disorders. No; *all such events should be a new call to us to bring our measure and rule to bear more powerfully on external Nature, to establish more and more the dominion of mind over it, and to impress on it ever more deeply the stamp of that dominion; in short, to subdue it more and more, by every means, under the spiritual power of man, whom the Most High Himself has appointed as its ruler.*[8]

While generalizations are always in some respect inaccurate and therefore hazardous to make, the above citation certainly seems to reflect an industrialist attitude toward nature not uncommon in the nineteenth century. It also clearly suggests that for Schleiermacher, the teleological impulse in Christianity will not manifest itself merely in spiritual ways, that is, in seeking to advance the kingdom of God, but also in concrete ways, that is, through the advancement of human

---

8. Ibid., 226; emphasis mine.

civilization in controlling nature. Nature presents us with myriad opportunities, especially in times of upheaval or disaster. Christians must not shirk these opportunities, either through passivity or fatalism, but must instead embrace them as occasions for impressing even more fully the stamp of *human* dominion upon the natural world. In light of our current ecological concerns, if this is indeed Schleiermacher's attitude, then his thought in this particular regard comes across as far too anthropocentric to be of help, while Barth's position appears to be a more suitable resource.

Selected Bibliography

Primary Sources

Barth, Karl. *Christ and Adam: Man and Humanity in Romans 5.* Translated by T. A. Smail. New York: Harper & Row, 1956.

———. *Dogmatics in Outline.* Translated by G. T. Thomson. 1949. Reprint, New York: Harper & Row, 1959.

———. *The Epistle to the Romans.* Translated by Edwyn C. Hoskyns from the 6th ed. London: Oxford University Press, 1968.

———. *The Faith of the Church.* Edited by Jean-Louis Leuba. Translated by Gabriel Vahanian. New York: Meridian Books, Inc., 1958.

———. *The Humanity of God.* Translated by John Newton Thomas and Thomas Weiser. Richmond, Va.: John Knox Press, 1960.

———. *Kirchliche Dogmatik.* Vol. I, part 1, *Die Lehre von Wort Gottes.* Zurich: EVZ-Verlag, 1964.

———. *Kirchliche Dogmatik.* Vol. III, part 1, *Die Lehre von der Schöpfung.* Zollikon-Zurich: Evangelischer Verlag, 1957.

———. *Kirchliche Dogmatik.* Vol. III, part 2, *Die Lehre von der Schöpfung.* Zollikon-Zurich: Evangelischer Verlag, 1959.

———. *Kirchliche Dogmatik.* Vol. III, part 3, *Die Lehre von der Schöpfung.* Zurich: EVZ-Verlag, 1961.

————. *Kirchliche Dogmatik.* Vol. III, part 4, *Die Lehre von der Schöpfung.* Zollikon-Zurich: Evangelischer Verlag, 1957.

————. *The Knowledge of God and the Service of God according to the Teaching of the Reformation.* Translated by J. L. M. Haire and Ian Henderson. London: Hodder & Stoughton, 1938.

————. *Letters, 1961–1968.* Edited by Jürgen Fangmeier and Hinrich Stoevesandt. Translated and edited by Geoffrey W. Bromiley. Grand Rapids, Mich.: Wm. B. Eerdmans, 1981.

————. *The Theology of Schleiermacher: Lectures at Göttingen, Winter Semester of 1923/24.* Edited by Dietrich Ritschtl. Translated by Geoffrey W. Bromiley. "Concluding Unscientific Postscript," translated by George Hunsinger. Grand Rapids, Mich.: Wm. B. Eerdmans, 1982.

Schleiermacher, Friedrich. *Brief Outline on the Study of Theology.* Translated by Terrence Tice. Atlanta: John Knox Press, 1966.

————. *Christmas Eve: Dialogue on the Incarnation.* Translated by Terrence Tice. Richmond, Va.: John Knox Press, 1967.

————. *Der christliche Glaube nach dem Grundsätzen der evangelischen Kirche im Zusammenhange dargestellt.* Edited by Martin Redeker. 7th ed., based on the 2nd. 2 vols. Berlin: Walter de Gruyter, 1960.

————. *On the "Glaubenslehre": Two Letters to Dr. Lücke.* Translated by James Duke and Francis Fiorenza. American Academy of Religion Texts and Translations Series 3. Chico, Calif.: Scholars Press, 1981.

————. *Selected Sermons of Schleiermacher.* Translated by Mary F. Wilson. Foreign Biblical Library. Edited by W. Robertson Nicoll. New York: Funk & Wagnalls, n.d.

Secondary Sources Cited

Bolich, Gregory G. *Karl Barth and Evangelicalism.* Downers Grove, Ill.: InterVarsity Press, 1980.

Busch, Eberhard. *Karl Barth: His Life from Letters and Autobiographical Texts.* Translated by John Bowden. Philadelphia: Fortress Press, 1976.

Duke, James O., and Robert F. Streetman, eds. *Barth and Schleiermacher: Beyond the Impasse?* Philadelphia: Fortress Press, 1988.

Gerrish, B. A. "Nature and the Theater of Redemption: Schleiermacher on Christian Dogmatics and the Creation Story." *Ex Auditu* 3 (1987): 120–36.

―――. *Tradition and the Modern World: Reformed Theology in the Modern World.* Chicago: University of Chicago Press, 1978.

Gilkey, Langdon. *Naming the Whirlwind: The Renewal of God-Language.* Indianapolis: Bobbs-Merrill, 1969.

Harvey, Van A. *A Handbook of Theological Terms* New York: Macmillan Publishing, 1964.

―――. *The Historian and the Believer.* Philadelphia: Westminster Press, 1966.

Hick, John. *Evil and the God of Love.* London: Fontana Library, 1974.

Louth, Andrew. "Barth and the Problem of Natural Theology." *Downside Review* 87 (July 1969): 268–77.

Niebuhr, Richard R. "Christ, Nature, and Consciousness: Reflections on Schleiermacher in the Light of Barth's Early Criticisms." Pages 23–42 in *Barth and Schleiermacher: Beyond the Impasse?* by James O. Duke and Robert F. Streetman. Philadelphia: Fortress Press, 1988.

―――. *Schleiermacher on Christ and Religion.* New York: Charles Scribner's Sons, 1964.

Ogden, Schubert M. "What Is Theology?" *Journal of Religion* 52 (January 1972). Quoted on page 18 in *Readings in Theology*, edited by Peter C. Hodgson and Robert H. King. Philadelphia: Fortress Press, 1985.

Rahner, Karl and Hebert Vorgrimler. *Dictionary of Theology* 2d ed. New York: Crossroad Publishing, 1981.

Redeker, Martin. *Schleiermacher: Life and Thought.* Translated by John Wallhausser. Philadelphia: Fortress Press, 1973.

Sykes, Stephen. *The Identity of Christianity.* Philadelphia: Fortress Press, 1984.

Tracy, David. *Blessed Rage for Order.* New York: Seabury Press, 1975.

Index

DATE DUE